By Michael Strange

WHO TELLS ME TRUE

Michael Strange

WHO TELLS ME TRUE

by

Michael Strange

"Who tells me true, though
in his tale lie death,
I hear him as he flatter'd"

NEW YORK

CHARLES SCRIBNER'S SONS

1940

For
Leonard, Robin, and Diana

ACKNOWLEDGMENT

The poetry by the author quoted in this volume at the beginnings and the ends of chapters and elsewhere is reprinted here, by special permission of the publishers, from "Resurrecting Life," published by Alfred A. Knopf, "Poems," and "Selected Poems," published by Coward McCann, Inc.

Contents

[xi]

CONTENTS

Illustrations

[xiii]

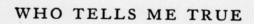

WHO TELLS ME TRUE

ee

Heritage

MAMA was Austrian on her mother's side, Hungarian on her father's—and a picture of Grandpapa, taken in London, looking very dark and debonair and casually balancing a top hat on his crossed knees, was always poised on top of Mama's white desk at Newport near one of my Austrian Grandmother, Ida Rachner von Rauhenstein afterward Madame de Loosey, attired in a meek white dress with hair looped heavily over her ears and holding a spaniel in the crook of her arm.

Apparently this gentle wife had borne my grandfather two daughters who lived, Natalie and Emily, and four who did not—when nearly twenty years later, a seventh girl, my mother, had appeared. "And think of it," Mama said, "when I was only two weeks old, your grandmother, putting her arms up to brush her hair that was so long she could sit upon it, fell dead before her dressing-table mirror." And I would fancy my poor little mother brought up as an only child, making, at only five years old, a voyage across the winter seas with my grandfather, who was to be the Austrian Consul General in New York from 1850 to 1870. Apparently everybody had been dreadfully ill on that trip, even the stewardesses, nor had there been any one to look after a perfectly well hungry little girl. Finally arrived in the glacial cold of a New York winter, she had contracted such a dreadful cold and earache that she was unable to hear her music box play; even when her governess held it directly against her cheek.

At the age of six or seven, my mother had been returned to Vienna to be educated in the house of her sister Natalie, Baroness Kubeck, twenty years her senior—very beautiful it has always been said, and apparently, for her day, too exuberantly romantic.

My mother grew up in the gay, autocratic Vienna of an Emperor still in early middle age, with an Empress at the height of her romantic charm. The Strausses, "père et fils," were tossing off with happy frequency their nostalgic waltzes during her adolescence, and these were played by the younger maestro himself at the balls the year of her début. I was shown a colored daguerreotype of such a pretty dark-haired girl, caught in a pose of genuine bashfulness, dressed in yellow tulle that was attached at the most fantastically awkward places with bunches of violets.

When I saw another extraordinary photograph of the head and shoulders of a blond young man, coolly beautiful as Galahad—a kind of spiritual Robin Hood in a cap with a heron's plume, Prince Henri Liechtenstein, the partner of her first cotillion—it was the first intimation I had that masculine beauty might materialize outside the covers of my *Blue Fairy Book.*

[2]

I loved to hear my mother speak of the excitement she felt when the Empress would arrive at the Spanish Riding School with half of her wonderful hair falling in great waves down her back, of her slenderness, her ultra-royal bearing, her excessive sadness. No one understood why she should always be quite so sad—which made her the more intriguing! And on her arm Mama wore seven gold bangles spelling out her name, Blanche, that she never would and never did take off, because they had been given to her by the Emperor's brother, the Archduke Ludwig Victor, who had made her this present as a child, since he was "attentive" to my Aunt Nancy. "But your aunt was too romantic," my mother would say, at which Papa interpolated, "She behaved like a damned fool." And it appeared that my aunt, married to a distinguished, elderly husband (I always pictured him as the incarnation of Tolstoy's Alexis Karenin) had fallen in love with a handsome Herr Robart, the leading actor at the Burg Theater, and directly crossing the canons of Viennese society in not disposing of the matter by renunciation, or an affair, she had been divorced by her husband, lost the custody of her child, and married the actor to retire to obscurity so far as society went.

However, Herr Robart's picture, in the toga and wreath of Brutus, stood on the white chiffonier in my nursery at Newport and I greatly admired his stalwart figure and the fiercely noble turn of his actor's head.

"Sieben hundert zwanzig Wienstrasse!" All during my childhood the address had a magic sound. Boxes of sweets were sent out from it, a marvellous light pink candy wrapped in paper that was frilled at the edges, a confection of apricot and sugar, tortured into the minute shape of Viennese breads; while from the household at Heitzing, where my

[3]

aunt and her Herr Robart were installed, in a house that rambled about a garden—and was only a stone's throw from the vast parterres of Schoenbrunn—came more sweets and many books in light yellow paper covers, since, as long as she lived, Mama preferred reading in French and German.

Aunt Nancy apparently never regretted having played a fool to the world, although only one intimate remained loyal—Princess Trautmansdorf. I always imagined this lady, God knows why, as enormously stout, squat, freckled, but with kindly eyes. I suppose I felt it must have taken some sort of bourgeois strength to support Aunt Nancy in her frailty.

Aunt Nancy went to the theatre for each performance of her husband's, and when it was time for the curtain to go up, she left his dressing room, and went forth alone into the vast proscenium to take the seat always especially reserved for her; nor do I doubt that she shut out, by the warmth of her love, what must have been the bitter animosity of hundreds of eyes during many a season.

Indeed, she really tested in the wear of daily life the truth of her hazard, that in the very dregs of her spirit romance was uppermost. I did not see her until I was sixteen, many years after her husband's death, when I came for the first time to Vienna with my parents in June. And then she looked like a very old actress, complacently pushing quite a belly in front of her, always dressed in flowing white draperies—reminding me of a passé heroine of Wilkie Collins. But I could see that my father was both amused and appalled at the obviousness of her make-up. And how infuriated he was, when arriving at the Bristol Hotel we discovered that my aunt had engaged the Pierpont Morgan suite for us, since apparently millionaires and Americans were hyphenated in her consciousness. After she had drifted serenely away and my father was ringing for porters to carry our luggage to a small suite under the roof I remember his shouting at Mama, "What in God's name do you expect from a woman who ran up a bill of $20,000 in a shop for cigarette cases?"

Vienna in June, with the trees all thickly out, and such gay cafés crowded with loitering, life-expectant people, and a "Prata" packed with officers who sat their thorough-breds with such ramrod backs, Hussars in black uniforms with gold braid—Dragoons in blue gold-braided coats and red trousers—how irresistible I was sure they would all be, in the unvarying role my fancy gave them.

Unfortunately there were no officers at 720 Wienstrasse and my uncle, Baron Kubeck, turned out to be the living spit of Karenin with his slim narrow-shouldered figure everlastingly buttoned into a frock coat, except when he took us to the opera. He lived only in a wing of his large house, with his daughter, my cousin Blanche, who had returned to live with her father after a disastrous marriage that, it was rumored, hadn't lasted all of one night. Fortunately for Blanche; she was a character, "une originale," and soon after her marital disaster she became not only a fan of Napoleon—whose marble busts of varying periods shone sternly out of the peaceful dusk of her sitting room—but a distinguished journalist as well.

I was, however, hideously bored by the interminable meals and conversations of my relatives, so during them I devoted myself to mental invocations (at which I have always been adept) of enchanting officers who were swooning with love for me, especially dwelling on one very handsome Dragoon officer who frequented the Bristol—luckily always in his uniform—and who, it seemed to me, had changed his seat in the dining room to look me over more at his ease.

At that time the only things that counted with me were the books I read, and possibilities of romance; and I would travel through the gay green miniature mountainous scenery of the Austrian Tyrol, on my first trip to Europe, without lifting my nose from Ainsworth's *Windsor Castle*, causing my mother to cry out in tormented incredulity—for if ever there was a scholarly traveller it was she—"Why Baby, here we are at Innsbruck and you haven't once looked out of the window!" when next day, of my weary tramp through the vast medieval château, I would only recall being attracted by a portrait of L'Aiglon in a white uniform loaded with orders.

After a charming visit, with only one disagreeable interlude—a bilious attack during which I had lain in despair on a sofa a couple of days, attended by my uncle's ancient doctor, who told me, "You have the tragic eyes of Marie Vetsera"—we were seen off at the station in Vienna by my aunt, who seemed at this point to dissolve in tears, for my mother had always been like a daughter to her, and perhaps we were none of us to meet again.

Looking back, I think it was in Aunt Nancy's rambling, tree-shaded, vine-smothered house that I sensed for the first time a congenial atmosphere. People had lived here the kind of life which I did not yet know was the only life I was ever to care for. An artist had lived here, painfully, triumphantly perfecting himself; and the house was full of the trophies of his march, and the tables were loaded with photographs of famous writers, actors and composers. "What strikingly brooding faces all these artists have," I thought, all except the singers, who seemed to me even then to possess a stuffed, dated appearance. I remember pausing by one photograph of an especially flame-struck head. "The Abbe Liszt," said Aunt Nancy, "and you should have seen with what poise your mother played a four-hand piece with him, when she was years younger than you." "The Great Liszt?" I cried. "The Liszt of the Hungarian Rhapsody?" "But yes, but yes!!"

The dear, painted-up old lady! When I met her, she was still going to sit by the grave of her husband on fine days, while she read the poems of DeMusset. How absurd she would seem to much of our diffused, distraught, despairing modernity. But as I grow older, she appears, from the retreats of memory, blessed and distinguished for having known, in her fashion, how to keep alive a life of the heart.

And I felt sadly that one of the last tangible links with her had been sundered when at Newport one afternoon, coming in from a drive with my mother, I heard her cry out, and rushing into her room, saw her standing in front of the bureau drawers which had been thrown violently open, and ransacked, leaving trails of tissue paper and empty boxes all over the place. Mama had been robbed of her slender store of jewelry, and worst of all it seemed to me, of a heavy gold snuff box that bore within it, on the cover, a miniature of the Emperor Maximilian, with a dedication to my grandfather, whose beautiful daughter (my Aunt Nancy) had just been appointed court lady to the Empress Carlotta, and was to go with her to Mexico.

"Gott erhalte—unsern Kaiser": whenever I hear the great hymn of Austria, so noble with genuine tenderness,

I feel wistfully that some part of me lives in exile. All the childhood of my mother, murals through the music in pictures somehow identifiable with it. Her genuine, if naïve, reverence for God and Emperor, her belief that he was about God's business—which must have made a sudden passing of the royal calèche, with its taut postillions, and the digni-fied friendliness of the bowing Emperor so thrilling for a small girl walking the Vienna streets—my mother learn-ing all the details of housekeeping at Leichwitz, her sister's country estate—how to bottle jam, air linen, write out menus, work in the dispensary, visit and comfort the sick; how unreal, it seems, like a Christmas card, or the precepts of "Little Elsie." But to me, from the bull's eye of the maelstrom, when so many obligations have vanished into thin air, and nearly all of us live a life so savage in its crowded haste, so psychopathic in its isolation, so disordered and lost from the solace and primary order of some tradi-tion and faith, how nostalgic with sanity my mother's upbringing seems.

As a growing child she had combed the galleries of Europe, chaperoned by my aunt or a governess, and so gained, by her 'teens, a knowledgeable love of fine painting and sculpture. Of course, what she saw in her wanderings became rooted in her imagination and memory through the cultural atmosphere of her life at home. No wonder she was upset at my passing between the Alps with a book of Stephen Leacock on my knee. But neither of us realized then that with whatever instinctive intelligence I possessed I had already grasped that for me there were no more traditions to be trained in in order really to practise them; that no cul-ture would ever be likely to find its way on living terms into the cut and dried naïveté of the schools I was sent to;

and that there was no time, and increasingly less and less inclination in the feverish, strained lives and occupations that surrounded my parents, for them to be able to go on thinking in the old European way.

After our visit to Vienna, we went to Carlsbad and I think the Carlsbad of 1907 could not have been so different from the Baden-Baden of Turgeniev's *Smoke*. The patients rose at sunrise and went down through the first fresh beams, to the strains of a military band, to drink their stinking Sprudel Water. There was much amiable sauntering and the delicate but concentrated flirtations that go on with a cure when you are shut off from the outside world. However, it was my father who was taking the cure, not I, and I felt that some of my fancies must now materialize when, like the coda in a musical composition by Franz Lehar, the blond-haired dragoon from the Bristol in Vienna appeared at Carlsbad with his father, and still in his uniform. We were introduced by the Austrian Ambassadress to Washington, at that time Baroness Henkel-Müller, and only a few days later I was listening at a keyhole while my astounded father received an offer for my hand from the elder Baron Lazarini. After the Baron had touched upon the fervor of his son's attachment and passed out the word —possibly not agreeable to my father—that the young people would have to live at Krakow until his son's military service had been completed, I remember his asking in a voice which came through the keyhole with an especial resonance, "And what would be your daughter's dot?" To which my father shouted in no less than a second, "Not a damn cent!"

Next morning the young Baron wrote to me with creditable despair and passion, but added that his father had commanded him immediately to rejoin his regiment in Krakow for an indefinite period.

At this miscarriage of life itself I considered writing a play. It was to be a tragedy of disillusion in the manner of Ibsen. The moment seemed propitious, because an old crank of a Norwegian doctor, who visited us, assured my father that the thousands of people who came to Carlsbad for the waters were all dangerously duped, the springs being sheer poison, which did not kill them outright only because of the periodic sanity of their dissipated lives. "Duped in one way or another," I thought grimly and then instead of writing the play, I cast more foolish glances about me that brought matters to a head with a fantastic little racing tout, always in loud checks and with a mustache waxed up for comic opera, Baron Mazini, and a Polish nobleman with tarnlike eyes that were always in shadow beneath the rakish slope of his Homburg hat.

Papa, on learning that the racing Baron had bribed my maid to know when I would walk in the mountains, kicked his hat and cane off a chair at the Hotel Pups at the lunch hour one sunny day, while the Baron contrived to go on sitting at the table, shivering and looking the other way.

And poor Baron Petrini had his German letters, which I couldn't decipher, found and read by Mama. "But what does he say?" I pleaded with her one night, when we had just come up from dinner and were having it out in my bedroom. "That he loves you," she replied, "but regrets that he cannot marry you because he is married already. However, he suggests that you elope with him to Prague." "Prague, the artistic capital of Bohemia!" And visions passed before me of celebrated artists with sable coat collars turned up to their freezing ears, travelling through the middle west on concert tours that were one long red-carpeted path of adulation. "Yes," said Mama, "and he will be waiting to know if you will go with him or not tonight. He will be standing beneath your window from dawn to dusk, waiting for your answer. Why not let him have it now?"—And lifting a pitcher of water from the basin, she poured it straight over the sill.

But even the *kudos* of these swiftly evaporating conquests was taken away from me, when we were dining one night with Baroness Henkel-Müller and I saw my father throw his head back and burst out laughing: "So, that accounts for all this attention to the Baby! You have told every one she's an heiress. But my dear Baroness, I am not the rich Oelrichs! That is my brother and he only married a rich wife!"

At this point life seemed to hold nothing whatever but disappointment plus humiliation.

About two hours' drive from Carlsbad, bolstered up on great rocks that overlooked hundreds of miles of the rich land of Bohemia, stood the medieval castle of Engelhaus. Its castellated turrets majestically snug and miraculously aloof, drew my fancy. It was wonderful to see in broad daylight such an affirmation of one's dreams, and I decided to run away, to escape forever from my parents, and to spend the first night of my freedom alone, among the ramparts of this magnificent retreat which seemed indeed to have been consecrated to the meditations of Parsifal, and the conclave of Arthur's knights.

So one morning, very early, I was off—swinging along

the open road with some food tied up in a napkin, and seven dollars. After many hours of stern marching and delighted loitering—for how wonderful everything was when once you had escaped and did not see it any more in relation to the life you had known, or to who you were, or to what was expected of you, but just in its own right—magic unfolded. Every thought drew me down a universe of thinking. From every human gesture—each shape in the clouds, and quiver of the shining leaves—came qualities, voices that I had never seen or listened to before. When once in sight of the heroic castle I sat down in the shade of a grape arbor beside an inn and quite overcome by the joy of living asked for something to eat and drink.

What was coming to me out of life that I had never known before? The intoxication was almost unendurable. I forgot time was passing, and that I might be overtaken. And I was, by my mother and father in a victoria with a pair of badly whipped-up horses. They knew my love for Engelhaus and the direction that I had taken had been noted by some one when I left. Impressions of me had been confirmed along the way, and there they were, leaning from either side of the victoria, my father blowing and blinking with fury; love, anger and relief struggling together on my mother's face. What would have happened if they had not caught up with me? I am not sure the spell would have faded. . . . I think it might have grown as I walked into it and maybe preserved me so well in its enormous strength that I need never have gone back.

My father was recruited, on the maternal side, from the Mays of Maryland, who apparently all stood well over six feet in their socks, and were debonair tigers in a war or

Chevalier and Madame Charles de Loosey

Grandpapa Oelrichs, with his head on a tired slant

Grandmama Oelrichs

MR. AND MRS. CHARLES MAY OELRICHS: PARENTS OF THE AUTHOR

so;—and as a matter of fact, last year, looking over some patriotic verses for the radio, I came, in "Maryland, My Maryland," upon allusions to the "dashing May," which brought the prowess of this tall, blond family of lovers as well as warriors ("for how much in love Lillie Langtry was with your cousin Fred May," Mama would sigh. "Why he was the love of her life.") out from the myth of my father's dinner table conversation into the background of romantic fact.

My father's father, Henry Oelrichs, emerged from the Oelrichs clan of Bremen, which had dealt for some hundreds of years in the cargoes of ships and eventually became the sole agents for the North German Lloyd in New York. When my grandfather, Henry, sent out to learn and later take charge of the American branch of the business, encountered in Washington the former Miss May of Baltimore, he courted and married her at the moment of her convalescence from the extraordinary death of her first husband, Mr. McCrae. This gentleman, apparently neither willing nor destined to be the victim of Sherman's "March to the Sea," had, a few months before the outbreak of war, wilfully burned up himself, his South Carolina plantation house, and his slaves—fortunately at a moment when his wife with her two small daughters was visiting in Charleston.

My grandparents went to live in New York and a second family was born to them, Hermann, Harry, Charles, Lucy, and Hildegarde; on the word of tradition a lusty, handsome, quarrelsome lot. And of course living in the North, with a mother who came from the South, my father's little boy's life was complicated with the loves and hates of the Civil War. And I heard that when beautiful Aunt Pussie, a daughter of Grandmama's by Mr. McCrae, had fallen in love with Robert Livingston in the Northern Army, there had been domestic fireworks in the fanciful glare of which my aunt had eloped with her handsome lover to sever all connection with her family for years.

And my father would vividly tell of how Lincoln was hated in the North just after his election, and of how he had clung to his mother's hand one sultry afternoon in the midst of a great crowd drawn up in front of the Hotel Astor to watch for the arrival of the President. Mr. Lincoln had appeared alone in an open barouche, and when his carriage came to a standstill, he had slowly stood up and, courteously removing his hat, bowed toward every side of the dense mass of people before, in an unvarying stillness which Papa remembered as terrible, he had gotten out of his barouche and disappeared into the hotel.

After Papa was graduated from St. Paul's School at Concord, he was sent back to his father's country to the college of Braunschweig and there his lovely, manly baritone— that I would hear during the first years of my life floating up to me as I lay musing myself to sleep in the blue nursery on "Oh That We Two Were Maying" and much of Schubert and Brahms—was trained by Franz Abt, the famous singing teacher of the day. But shortly after his return from this German college, love letters were starting off for Miss Blanche de Loosey, Care of Baron Max Kubeck, 720 Wienstrasse, calling on God and Providence to witness his desire to make "his darling girl" a bride the following autumn. My mother coyly returned from Vienna, and after a fairly short courtship at Newport they were married in Aunty Havemeyer's drawing room in New York, by Archbishop Corrigan, in the presence of what might be called the "crème de la crème" of society, and went, after the traditional honeymoon at Niagara, both of them extremely young, roundfaced and almost entirely foreign in temperament, together with Mama's entire trousseau from Girand Sœurs, the ace embroiderer of the world, straight out to Cheyenne, the authentic "hell on wheels" of the day, to take up a stake in the cattle business that Theodore Havemeyer had bought for Papa.

And there my sister, apparently ravishing at once, had been born with only the help of a doctor who smelled of whiskey, stank of tobacco, and even refused to wash his hands before participating in an event probably also supervised by the Reservation Indians who, around supper time I learned, liked to press their noses against the windows and grunt sheepishly for bacon and garbage.

I could fancy that sunset of my sister's birth, with the cowboys riding noisily in from the prairie to swagger at the bars, firing away at the evening star, or a face that had gotten on their nerves, with the nonchalance of youth when it is free to be absolutely drunk with hope.

However, the adventure was a financial catastrophe. Papa's steers were attacked by a strange malady, their horns whitened in thousands along the prairie—that he told me smelt so magnificently when the salmon-pink wild roses were full out—and my parents came back to what might be called the civilization of 1886. But I love to think of that time they had together before they struck Newport and New York, when they possessed their personal rapture in the spaciousness of the West, with all around them a spirit of wildest expectancy.

So a few years before I was born, Papa had quit his Deadwood Coach outfit for the castrating garb of a broker, and had entered into a partnership on the Stock Exchange with E. C. Potter, Mr. Havemeyer's son-in-law; and the business of these two élite young men did not seem to suffer from Ned Potter's having received a rap on the head with a polo mallet just at the start, causing him such a grave concussion that it was rumored that he would never be quite the same again. And our household, set up at Newport and New York, began to follow with *insouciance* at first, the fluctuations of the Wall Street market.

CHAPTER II

Childhood

"*Who is here . . .*
Who has ever been actually present
Since departed the child and all his divine sense of the
true absorption . . .
Since vanished with fatal unnoticed unerring subtlety
The Child . . ."

MY FATHER had at first rented and then Uncle Theodore Havemeyer—guardian angel of the family fortunes, in spite of his harsh whiskers—had bought for us our Newport house at 64 Kay Street, formerly lived in by Bancroft, the historian, whose picture we always left hanging on the library wall—a kind of mascot who should bequeath to us his venerable age and success.

And I loved the dear yellow wooden house in which I lived from babyhood until my marriage, with its old-fashioned gables painted in white, its shaky tower up which I hopefully climbed through thousands of cobwebs on each Hallowe'en of my childhood and girlhood, a candle in one hand, and a mirror in the other—upon which I might but never did—receive the glint of my lover's face.

The blue parlor, the green parlor, and the red dining room where we took lunch with Rosa Bonheur's closely packed violent animals being herded hither and yon in tremendous engravings on either side of us! And there was a cozy library where the chairs suddenly got comfortable, and I could stare up at dozens of pictures lining the walls, to ask my mother, the eternal story-teller, why Mrs. Lorillard Spencer wore a coronet in her hair, like the Goddess Diana, why the plumes in Mrs. Belmont's hat were half as big again as Mr. Belmont. And my mother never failed me, with brilliantly stimulating replies about Mr. Belmont's appearance in armor at the Bradley Martin Ball, and of how the beautiful Mrs. Lorillard Spencer, having had a great sorrow, had gone to nurse in the Philippines. Then she would sigh and put away her sewing to go off and dress for some five o'clock "cotillion" with my father, who at that incredible hour would be all dressed up in a tall hat and frock coat.

For me the word "cotillion" conjured up the greatest promises of delight, and often on a midsummer morning when I crept into my mother's pink bedroom with the sun just gilding the tops of the chestnut trees, I found her room transformed not only into a toy shop with all of her favors, but into an aviary as well; for best of all were the mornings when the bird cages stood about on tables and chairs, covered by towels, and each holding a tiny parakeet or canary.

Our "grounds" as they were called were nothing to write home about, just three-quarters of an acre or so of lawn planted with chestnuts, elms and a few silver birches, intersected by gravel pathways. But endowed with fancy and expectancy, how immense they were!

64 KAY STREET, THE NEWPORT RESIDENCE OF MR. AND MRS. CHARLES MAY OELRICHS

"And I loved the dear yellow wooden house in which I lived from babyhood until my marriage."

THE INTIMATES

Top: My mother in the box seat beside Uncle Theodore Havemeyer, with Papa behind her.

Although I saw them increasingly less and less together, it seemed to me in the years of my first impressions of Newport that my parents led a gay and happy life. Often in the evening, Papa would sing German Lieder in the green parlor, and lying in my small blue and white nursery cot, while gaunt Bessie lit the gas to warm my bottle of milk—which threw off an immemorable odor of consolation—I would make, from my spellbound listening, an enduring memory. And sometimes the slender, fascinating, retroussé-nosed Mrs. Little—rumored of Creole origin—joined my father in singing duets; and there were slight puffs of indignation from Mama when the encores were too enthusiastic.

You could see that the social life of these naïve gay people revolved upon a remarkably small axis; there was the affectionate assurance of intimacy in all their quips and sparkle. And I used to wonder where they got their gaiety from, seeing each other as much as they did. Maybe it was an age when you did not have to be a genius to remain a child; and what easily felt gallantry there was between them! Something really seemed to be going on, kept whipped up, I suppose, by a play between stern codes of morals, excellent manners, and last but not least, to remember now in 1939, the God-given vitality of their natural inclinations.

I loved to watch the start of their coaching parties. My uncles, Willie Jay and Theodore Havemeyer, were always relieving one another as presidents of the coaching club, so that my pretty mother became constantly entitled to the prestige of the box seat. When I heard the tally-ho, I rushed to the gates to watch the four-in-hands come rumbling down Kay Street, dappled by sun and rich summer shade, the lovely high-stepping horses straining their tensely groomed bodies under the flashing harness; and aboard the gay-colored coaches were ladies who really resembled bizarre snowdrifts of lace, taffeta and silk. Their neat ondulayed heads were tightly veiled and bewilderingly hatted, as coquettishly they tilted up miniature sunshades to dilute a little the admiring glances of gentlemen in frock coats and gray tall hats, who seemed always to be wearing the most impeccable boutonnières.

How much laughter there was, and how many hampers of food and champagne were stowed away at the back of the coaches! And when my mother had climbed, with protesting modesty, into her box seat, the grooms ran nimbly obsequious from the horses' heads, and sprang into their places, and in each coach two long silver trumpets were lifted. Then to the most brilliant of fanfares off they started for their country picnic.

My brothers, Harry and Charlie, and my sister Lily were six and eight and ten years older than I was, which gave me the sense of being an only child. So I watched their lives with the detached interest of a commentative stranger, but I was overcome with a furious sense of injustice—and offended privacy—when I saw my brother Harry strolling toward me in a mood of desultory idleness, singling me out to tease.

My elder brother, Charlie, stocky, brown-haired and brown-eyed, was a great sentimentalist and called Mama "Ocean-spray." In fact he worshipped her so (although she paid less attention to him than to any of us, and always related out of conscience pangs, I suspect, how patiently Charlie had endured his dysentery at Cheyenne, when the other two raised the roof) that he ran away from Mr. Edwards' school at Morristown one sunny morning out of nostalgia for her, to appear penniless and gasping at the Hotel Gerlach and look at us all out of such hungrily affectionate eyes! He was immediately sent back; which I felt would never have happened to my younger brother Harry, sullen, blue-eyed, slender and freckled, who could work himself up into the most frightful rages—in fact you were always watching his moods, for you knew he couldn't control them.

But my sister Lily was absolutely lovely from the very first; the slenderness of her waist, her amazingly thick pigtail that waved forth from beneath the smartest taffeta bow, and her slim face with its enchantingly wistful structure, all filled me with dumb admiration. I recall holding my breath with proud pleasure in my crib one night when Lily brought one of her friends into my nursery to show me off; and feeling above all things that I must not let her down, I kept my lashes, the only good point it seemed to to me I had, tightly closed on my cheeks, although I longed to meet her friend and catch at her hand and talk. Occasionally, however, Lily could infuriate me more than any one else on earth, and at such moments I instantly relieved my feelings by rushing to her dressing table drawers and flinging their contents out of the window.

Lily was Papa's favorite, although he loved me and was often obliging about swimming me out to the raft on his back on calm summer days when he wasn't squiring across the Atlantic the beautiful red-haired actress, Miss D—deW. I heard the nurses say she was too cheeky for a "kept woman." "Kept" where? I mused—here she is always at the beach with my father, and the only woman who can look ravishing after a wave hits her. Still at other times I thought Papa looked at me with a distrust that could deepen too swiftly into anger, and sensing his readiness to "take me down" I answered it with as much insolence as I dared.

But I shared with my brother Harry my mother's favor. She was my furious partisan in everything (even when I kicked one of my nurses so hard in the stomach that she threatened a lawsuit) and as a small child, I returned her love with a degree of imaginative apprehension I have never lavished on anything since. For I always felt, especially in the city, that I might lose her, that she might get trampled under so many wheels and heels; and when she was late in coming in to dress for dinner, which was often, I would stop at the window, my face pressed against the pane, staring into the wretchedly illuminated darkness, convinced that what was out there might well do anything to any one. And when I heard her step, and she came in, then in the joy of being released back into life, out of this void, this vacuum of suspense, I would pull off her long fur boa that seemed to be always damp with sleet and to contain a bunch of violets, and wrap it ecstatically round and round myself.

Mama's beaux and Lily's beaux were with us at all hours of the day and evening, and it was extremely difficult for me to judge who belonged to whom. I think it was occasionally rather difficult for them to make up their minds, and I remember that the household air of those days was spiced with an exciting rivalry, seeming to come vividly to a head one night just outside my door, when a duo of infuriated voices about a "Yale Prom" suddenly ceased with a sound of ripping material.

Nor was tensity lacking in the relationship of my parents; and one winter night in New York I listened to what sounded like the breaking up of chairs in Mama's bed-room while an argument bombarded throughout the house about the impropriety of my mother's having followed my father to the "Aryan Ball," a masked ball at which you might even find yourself under a palm with a hairdresser! I heard it shouted out! "A masked ball," I mused! But my sympathy went instantly over to my father who had gone to his enjoyment masked, therefore on purpose not to be himself. What an understandable aim! Then how awful it must have been in the midst of such enchantment to hear your name in the world of dreary daylight called out, especially somehow, by your wife.

The Newport ladies of those days were trying hard to emulate their sisters in cosmopolitan Europe, and it would have been thought extremely "bourgeois" for attractive matrons not to have gentlemen about them who were "attentive." So many people came in through the great front door, hammered in square panels of oak, ornamented with a huge brass knocker, by which in my ability to more and more nearly reach I could measure my height each year. And I studied them with that absorption peculiar to children—with that disembodied intensity of childhood when there is no conscious self to interfere and prevent the making of memories, so that time flies traceless as a ghost— when time is still alive and passing slowly because of its great depth.

Surely Mr. Prescott Lawrence was Mama's "bag" since the hair was getting very thin on top of his head, but there was a Mr. Bo Bo Sargent, who wore his hair so beautifully plastered down and a gardenia always in the lapel of his pearl-gray suit, whom they both alluded to as a dumbbell. This seemed wildly unfair to me, when I discovered that he always read the papers to them upside down, so that all the side-splitting things he told us were really coming out of his head.

And of course Lily's friends rampaged all over the house. Bobby Gerry, freckled, lanky and good-naturedly arrogant; sallow-faced Robert Goelet with a kind of humor squinting out of his eyes as well as an uneasy sense of his own importance, and of his unimportance too, I thought, looking him over more closely. And Edith Gray, our neighbor, Lily's confidante, blonde, gray-eyed, white-skinned, like a Maltese kitten and a fox. Her I labelled "Still Waters Run Deep" after overhearing a couple of her sessions with beaux from my secret seat in the chestnut tree.

I particularly fancied my father's intimate, short, dark Oliver Belmont, with his Daniel Webster collar, and slow urbanity, his face rutted with lines,—from the hopes and disillusions of his life as a lover, I suspected. For certainly he must be a romantic man, since his house had the only pipe-organ I had heard in Newport, which when it started booming, sounded to my enchanted ears like angels appearing in thunder. And when it transpired that Mr. Belmont's Indian servant, Azar, slept at night across the threshold of his master's door, a drawn dagger between his teeth, I had material in me for novels and poems for months. And how thrilled I was one morning when I came downstairs for my breakfast to find Mr. Oliver Belmont still in the house (Papa had had a stag dinner the night before—how good those stag dinners used to smell from the top landing of the stairs, their aroma somehow preserved in the heat of the gas-jets); in fact, he was sitting up sound asleep, on a sofa in the blue parlor with, beside him, my father, also oblivious. And a book had fallen to the floor between them which I picked up open at Enoch Arden.

Very soon I began to take a gambler's interest in my lovely sister Lily's flirtations and would sit for hours without stirring, concealed in my favorite secure perch in the chestnut tree, while the unconscious couples spun out their destinies beneath me. Occasionally I became so excited, when it seemed that some false move was thwarting a desirable end that, beside myself, I shouted down sudden advice or warning, to be instantly pulled from my place, and whipped unless I got away.

I was extremely partial to one blond, curly-headed young man whose spectacles intensified the chastely earnest expression of his blue eyes. "He's just the man for Lily," I thought. "He'll be able to take care of her vitality between his good looks and his stuffed-shirtishness."

But apparently the carefree life of "The Intimates" was turning into "Opera Bouffe." Great beauty must find its setting in huge rooms, wilful travel, carriages and diamonds. It was an undisputed fact that Lily was a great beauty and my choice for her was not rich.

Newport was becoming the élite hunting ground for titled bachelors in search of a beautiful wife with a fortune, and many attractive gentlemen were to be seen writing their names down at the Casino as soon as it opened, and having their pictures taken in groups on the porches of fashionable boarding houses for wider circulation. It often happened that not long afterward they would be found making themselves at home in our house, where I suppose, in such unpretentious surroundings, they could relax and forget business.

Great marriages, in which my sister of seventeen was violently interested, were being arranged all around me. May Goelet was to become the Duchess of Roxborough, and looking at her picture on Lily's bureau I thought to myself, "Well, she looks disagreeable enough to be able to take care of herself anywhere, even in England."

But I was sorry about Consuelo Vanderbilt marrying the Duke of Marlborough, for she was exquisitely pretty. Her frailty and height made her look as if she might break in two in an adverse breeze. And then I heard it said that she had wept all night at the conclusion of the settlements between the Duke and her father. What were these settlements that tied people up in them against their will? For what did they barter this mysterious something which they cared for enough to cling to with tears?

I put a few leading questions to my sister, a great friend of Consuelo's, who went around the house in those days with such a determined expression that it made her lips look thinner, to be angrily told that if I went on playing with "street children" I would never get "anywhere" and would end in the gutter as well. Just where was "anywhere"? I mused, and surely she doesn't mean the actual gutter! But how dreadful talking to older people was. Their answers bewildered me so much more than my own questions.

I was, however, used to my sister's hourly doubts about my ever achieving a worldly success, for it was true that I made few friends among the stylish children, the kind who went jogging arrogantly about in "governess carts," their dresses trimmed with Irish lace, their hats floppy with chiffon, while a groom and a maid preserved them, I supposed, from the frolics of adverse chance. I was continually found instead, in the company of boys and girls who had no protection but their wits and did their playing in the street directly in front of their small cottages. And the well-brought-up children returned my disfavor with warm interest; indeed my mother was humiliated and dumbfounded at being thrown a hint or so about keeping me out of their way! I remember it was chiefly against me that I told them evil stories, and as the English nurses said, put "highdears into their 'eads." One day of unforgettable amusement and terror (because I was found out), I accepted a dare to steal into the grounds of our neighbors, the Grays, and mounting a little hill planted with fir trees, that faced the street, and also a small cottage in which lived a very grim old man whom we all detested, I elicited from this bibical personality of sour judgments—as he sat rocking in his shirt sleeves with his whiskers bristling—a real damnation, by dancing for him with my short skirts and my starched little petticoats held up to my chin. What an ecstasy of amusement there was in that dance that drove him in wrath from his porch and unfortunately directly over to our house, to tell my horrified mother.

So when one of these sullenly unwanted "smart" children was asked to spend the afternoon with me, I usually led her to my mother's room, where some little chairs stood about for my especial use, and giving the small guest a book, I took one myself, and went to sit down and read at the other side of the table.

From my earliest childhood I loved reading. Never shall I forget the all-embracing magic a book had for me. First I pored over my gift books, the *Dotty Dimple,* and the *Little Elsie* series, but soon struck by the inane triteness of this venture I was off on my own with Ainsworth, Wilkie Collins, Dickens and Scott, to finally, before I was eight, wind up with the *Arabian Nights,* which I filched from the top shelf of our neighbor's library—and whose many unfamiliar words produced in me a feeling of dangerous warmth.

However, one little girl whom I was encouraged to play with I rather liked myself. She had smooth hair arranged in the manner of "Alice in Wonderland," and a peaceful, rather vacant expression in her eyes, that I soon discovered to be assumed. She was the niece of a friend of my mother's, the Widow Campbell, and lived in a small cottage a few doors away. Nor did she seem greatly to care for her aunt and chaperone, telling me vivid stories of how Mrs. Campbell pinched her two servants in matters of diet!

Now this affected me into listening sharply, for I had lately taken greatly to servants, and would stand on a flagstone outside the kitchen door for half an hour on end, until Bridget, our full-bosomed cook, could spare me a few moments for the exchange of news.

I found servants interesting because in talking with them, and trying to elicit their sudden and sometimes coarse outbursts of laughter, there was a degree of heat, of getting at something, that I missed in the arid politeness and bored evasions of my better-bred elders. It seemed to me that their eyes and a certain way they had of smiling, which I would now characterize as lewd, nearly gave something away, something I was desperately anxious to find out about. And then the summer before at Southampton I had fallen quite madly in love with McDermott, our swaggering handsome Irish coachman, so much in love indeed that, the stable being at the back of the house, as well as my bedroom, as soon as my nurse had put me to bed in the summer twilight I rose up again; and after watching McDermott tilting himself back against the stable door, dressed only in a flannel undershirt and his livery trousers, as he whistled, and mightily polished the harness for its evening appearance, then sometimes it seemed that I must make him know I was there. So stretching out my arms on one occasion, I sang him the love song of the moment, which started off, "O My Dolores, Queen of the Eastern Sea"; and McDermott did not snub me at all, only gazed toward me listening, until, the words giving out, he threw me a kiss,—whereupon I fell back abashed and more than satisfied on my bed.

And here was this Alice-in-Wonderland child telling me that the servants in her aunt's house were starved, although an icebox was kept crammed with food that they were not allowed to touch. "Why that's like Tantalus," I decided grimly, "it must not go on!", and I laid my plans for "The People *vs.* The Widow Campbell," only waiting until she had gone off to drop her cards in silver salvers on that shining afternoon, and until I knew the servants were detained by my friend in another part of the house. Then, going to the icebox I lifted out all the food in boxes or dishes, to throw the whole violently and ruinously down on the grass. And then I ran like the wind!

For hours there was an ominous silence. Then the terrible voice of the Widow Campbell standing on our very threshold was heard ordering my mother to come downstairs and see what "Little Blanche" had done now!

But the widow made a great tactical error, for she lambasted me so unmercifully, she assailed my reputation in the neighborhood with such virulent exaggeration, that Mama, of course, would not take it, and the quarrel had soon dropped me altogether out of it, and was concerned with so furious an altercation on major topics that the two never spoke to one another again as long as they lived.

In fact, when I crawled out from one of the empty stalls in the barn and slid up to the house, Mama had forgotten my existence, and was still spluttering about that "outrageous woman who should have been pushed off her grounds by the police." This quarrel became famous in Newport, for Harry Lehr did a kind of Ruth Draper rendition of it in which he irresistibly imitated, in a high falsetto, the furious back-chat of both ladies, and, of course, I did not need the widow to forbid me her gate and keep me forever from the wretched little girl who had incited me and told!

Very early I began to wonder how it happened that any one got born, and my mother's replies about the work of storks in a lily pond situated below "Crossways," the home of Mrs. Stuyvesant Fish, only strengthened me in my conviction that something was under way so interesting that apparently no one was able to speak of it calmly or clearly. So one day, obsessed by my desire to come to an ultimate conclusion if not about the origin of life, at least about any difference that might have occurred in the species, I rushed across Kay Street to the jolly fat family of the poultry dealers and discovering the baby boy drifting unsteadily about the yard by himself, I sat down, coaxed him onto my knee and was just about to swiftly deprive him of his trousers, when halted by the terrified cry of his mother whom (I recall as my only great acting triumph) I actually persuaded of my innocence, when I convinced her that I was only obliging the baby in a crisis at his own request.

But wonder, when it was hypnotic, magic that is, could lift me breathlessly out of my *cul-de-sac* of sexual suppositions. Once every summer the circus came to Newport, selecting usually a burning morning in July. And when I heard the blare of the steam organ rolling down Kay Street, I would think as I ran to the gate, "Here comes the joy of Juggernaut! Anything can happen!" And as the elephants and camels began to pass in their aloof majesty—rocking on towering seats such glittering ladies and gentlemen, to be followed by scarlet wagons with lions and tigers that leapt at their gilded bars to roar at my open mouth as they passed; to say nothing of the clowns upon whom it was better not to look for fear of attracting their bizarre attention (and how wonderful it had been when one of them, covered in white paint and dressed in his ballooning pepper and salt stripes, had caught my nervous half-glance, and laying his hand on his heart, smiled at me in a weird and memorable way); then, on such mornings I prayed, "Let me go out into all of this without knowing that I go, for here is something I will never have to wake up from as long as I live."

However, entirely untaken, I returned into the house for a cool glass of milk, and what a tragic mistake it was later to visit all this glamor in action! For when, clutching a bag of peanuts, I entered the huge circus tents pegged down in some empty fields in the early afternoon, I could only recoil from the wisecracking clowns, flying trapezists, and animals tortured into naïve tricks. Was this all they could do with the burning kaleidoscope of fancies they had stirred awake in me?

[31]

Catholic children were not allowed to read the Bible, but I loved sitting all alone in my room at dusk. Then lighting the candles before my holy statue of the Virgin in a blue snood and white dress, her feet on the head of a golden serpent beside a Christ who pointed to a huge and bleeding heart that was attached to his white dress, I opened my New Testament to the Gospels, heavily underscoring with an excited pencil those lines where it seemed to me that sense and style had drawn dynamically together.

Yet I found religion, outside its ceremonies, gravely depressing. I was sent for my religious instruction to an incalculably ugly, brown-black wooden structure of a Newport convent, whose mortuary parlors were always filled with the clattering rasp of cars over the ill-laid tracks of Spring Street. "Who made the world?" droned the nun. And longing to say, "I often wonder," I had to repeat "God made the world!" "And who is God?" and so the immense questions would knock at the wilful, sardonic scarcity of my comprehension—and nothing whatever be garnered in but a memory of waste.

But on the way home, if the maid of the moment was sympathetic enough, I persuaded her to stop off at the wharves, and climbing down into any small boat attached to the pier, I waggled a paddle in the water. And as I watched the darkness come over the harbor—the slender tilting masts turning black against the sky, and the water gently lapping around me—then the God-forsaken dreariness of the straggling houses and warehouses along the shore took on the bulk of mystery and majesty. And with the twilight advanced enough—while my attention swam up into the spectacle utterly engrossed—it all might have been anything anywhere, but secretly I always hoped that I had arrived at the mouth of the Bosphorus.

And yet, curiously enough, it was only during the ceremonies of the Church that I could dramatize myself on a grand scale. In church I was able to lose, for a few hours, my obsessive curiosity about love, and could even imagine myself a figure consecrated to some paramount destiny. "Must I drink of the Cup?" I would mutter (with unconscious blasphemy) and tears started to my eyes, especially if the choir took one of those vocal rises that are like a happy disturbance among the angels starting for another cloud— and I kept on kneeling and weeping, when everybody else stood up, till my mother yanked me to my feet.

Tibi, my dearest mother, with what sentiment and charm she prepared the event of my first Communion. I was to make it alone, in quite a lovely old convent on the Bay; alone in a new white dress and a tulle veil, bordered by a wreath of minute white roses, and very early too, and, of course, without my breakfast.

An organ played while I came up the aisle by myself, holding on to my prayerbook and rosary, and feeling for the first time a disembodied importance, and also like crying, probably from exhaustion. For nearly all night it seemed, I had dreamt of an immense Eucharist, spearing all the sky with its chromatic rays. My mother and a few friends knelt on either side of the little chapel, and I saw with satisfaction that they were deeply affected. And afterwards there was a little breakfast, arranged by the Mother Superior, a very happy breakfast—even the lay sisters who served it smiled at me with a kind of warmhearted approval. I had approached the Bridegroom!

I saw my wreath and veil once again after that day, when my brother and I were sorting my mother's things after her death in those large, white closets filled with the neatly folded, pink-ribboned parcels perfumed by sachets. There it was again! so neatly and tenderly laid away—imagine the time to feel events so deeply that one wants to preserve their echo and savor them again and again. Was there ever such a time?

I must have been seven when I became enamored of a pale boy who lived at the other end of Kay Street, Harford Powel. He looked almost deformed in his extreme delicacy and a hunched way he had of carrying his shoulders. He was some years older than I was, and as he paid to my long glances and continual interceptions on the road no attention whatever, I discovered a remarkable truth, to the effect that it was possible to extract much pleasure from imagining the notice he withheld!

One of the finest listeners to my triumphs over Harford was my uncle Harry Oelrichs, my father's brother and my favorite uncle. Uncle Harry had been an invalid for many years and spent all his time either sitting up or lying down in his bed on the ground-floor room of his little house on Cottage Street, attended to by a devoted nurse. Perched on his stomach, which made such a wonderful mound under the sheet, I would speak at great length of my cruelty toward Harford, for which I could never forgive myself, until my support rocked under me, and, coughing with laughter, Uncle Harry would have to be given a drink out of the long glass tube.

But although my uncle looked very handsome and stout, with his black curling hair and beard, in which the moist red lips stood out with a peculiar tenderness, and although his blue eyes seemed always fired with laughter, still I noticed he could not open or close his hands. They remained transfixed in a semi-open posture with dreadful swelling.

"What happened to Uncle Harry? Why can't he move his hands?" I would ask Mama when I got home, to receive the cryptic reply that Uncle Harry had gone around the world on the *Lysistrata* with Mr. Gordon Bennett, and it seemed I must accept the fact that no one could survive, unscathed, a trip around the world on Mr. Bennett's yacht.

But this uncle was one of my few true friends, and I was led into his room one day by my mother, with a great constriction at my heart, to find him lying down and breathing very hard. "Hello, Uncle Harry," I whispered. "Why don't you sit up?" "Baby, Baby," he said in a queer voice, as if he were mumbling out of his dreams, "Get the damned doctors away before they kill me!" "Of course," I told him, "but where are they?" At this point, however, my mother wheeled me abruptly about and pushed me toward the door, although I kept wrenching back my head to meet those eyes that looked after me so avidly!

And next day I was taken back into the little cottage, and saw that the shades in Uncle Harry's room were pulled down; and my mother on his threshold pressed a bunch of flowers into my hand, "to give to your uncle, because you and Charlie were his favorites." And there lay Uncle Harry, absolutely still and very pale, with his eyes shut tight in the midst of the most overpowering scent of flowers, and as we came in, my sister rising from a chair, and seeing my long look of spellbound bewilderment at the figure on the bed, burst into tears.

Trembling, I laid my flowers above the shape of his

crippled hands under the sheet, hoping he would now say something in spite of the grown-up people being there whom I knew he had never really liked. But he remained in his great silence, with such a queer sunken look to his head on the pillow, that suddenly, unable to look any longer at this aloof, yet torturingly exact symbol of all our good times together, I rushed out of his room. Then I saw, wreathing his threshold, a great wisteria vine in fullest azure bloom, giving off the most nostalgic, sweetish, and sickish perfume, I thought, "Why, Uncle Harry smells exactly like his wisteria!" And somehow it was this that made me realize he was dead.

A few months after my uncle's death an extremely agreeable thing happened, for I came down that autumn with a mysterious fever which was extraordinarily enjoyable. A truce was called to every order. I was only entreated to taste concoctions of a fairylike lightness, where I lay wistfully dreaming and dozing at will in Mama's huge double brass bed in her pink and white bedroom with its agreeable smell of matting, and a fine view of the trees out of three windows, while Mama herself would come in with lips that trembled, I noticed, as she opened a box containing a fishpond made of blue cardboard, sent to me by Birdie Vanderbilt: "And that you will be able to play with soon, my darling."

It seemed from the extraordinary silence kept by my family outside the door that I was shortly expected to die, and I considered this eventuality without apprehension or regret. You cannot be afraid of losing what you do not know, have never come to grips with; and probably to the unpierced psyche of a child there is no reality other than the moment. And this moment was fantastically delightful, for I opened my eyes between dreams on a daylight that just threaded through the curtains to languidly count over new toys, all in the role of a much-loved gentle child fading patiently out of life like the heroine in one of my favorite stories, "The Birds' Christmas Carol." It also seemed that if ever I rolled back my lids, I stared straight into the alarmed and permanently embarrassed face of young Doctor Knapp, who was terribly in love with Lily, and endured the wildest ridicule for her pains—Doctor Knapp who could apparently get hair to grow on both sides of his face without his potency being able to carry it across his upper lip.

Not long after, in the middle of one of those delicious nights, in which fever lent such a piquant edge to fancy, I was gently roused for an introduction to my trained nurse, to which I responded with the long look of drowsy spirituality that I felt was incumbent on my role. And I remember how satisfying it was to sense my effect when I heard her exclaim to my mother, "What wonderful eyes she has!" And then, there seemed to pass a moment of strong emotional tension between the two, and I heard the nurse say, "Now you must not give way, Mrs. Oelrichs, we'll have to pull her through." "How wonderful! All that out of a single look!" I thought as I dozed off again.

But a few weeks later, there was hilarious shrieking through the house through which I made out, "The Baby hasn't got typhoid! The Baby hasn't got typhoid!" So that was what they had supposed I had, typhoid fever! My cousin Julia Jay had died of it at eighteen, very painfully I heard, because they had insisted on bathing her in ice water up to the very end, when her wardrobe of such enchanting clothes had all been sent over to my young sister.

Well, whatever I had had, this interval of being let alone with my thoughts and dreams was apparently drawing to a close, and I learned I was to go to Pomfret with my mother and trained nurse to convalesce. "And you got your malaria," said Mama, severity back again in her voice, "from hanging over that sewer on the way to the One Mile Corner." "What sewer?" I cried, knowing perfectly well what she meant. "You don't mean the brook that flows under the big rock where I go to catch tadpoles?" "I do," said Mama, "and what a fool Bessie was to let you play there." "But that brook flows into the big marsh where I go for my violets and bluebells." "You will never go there again," said Mama. What a betrayal of felicity! So I was never again to hear that particular brook gurgle over the stones—what if an unpleasant scum did mar the edges—never again to see the brilliant green of the swamp growing streaked with bluebells in June—nor stand uncertainly poised on tufts of bog watching out for snakes. Apparently you had to pay for a lapse from life with malaria!

And now the flowing taste of jellies—
The moist sweet feathery caress of flowers—
While always near the rhythmic gestures of my mother sew-
*   ing—*
And of the peaceful sound of her work
And of her gentle sigh toward me—
So commiserate—so protecting—
O how sweet and warm and clear for the pavane of dreams
Was my sick room—
And now what pathos in this picture of my mother—
Who suffers more from me still than from any other—
While I have come to pain—through so much else.

CHAPTER III

No More Songs

As yet it was a human world; couples walked arm in arm in the evening, and so when the shadows lengthened and faded on our lawn, and the first star appeared in the pale heaven—and water dripped from the evening watering of the geranium window boxes—while my family were all safely upstairs dressing for their parties, I skimmed along on the inside of our neighbor's hedge and—taking my pace from the loving couples of sailors and maids walking on the other side of it—learnt about love from the proletarian angle.

The tempo was changing. No more songs were sung in the green parlor. More and more victorias dipped into the cobblestone gutters, and scrunched luxuriously up the well-raked gravel to our front door to leave cards on my mother, which, on fortunate afternoons, our adenoidal English butler Henry (hired for the summer months only) would be sober enough to gather onto a silver tray.

And I always climbed from my rope swing to watch this stylish process, for although the ceremony remained the same, it differed perceptibly enough with the grace of each lady. The word, "nouveau riche" began to be flung about, and who *was* he or who *was* she, was being constantly asked. Evidently it was getting necessary to find out who *were* the people of the people one saw. Endless family scenes blew up on this score and I lived in perpetual terror that the doubtful pedigree of some of my friends would find its way into the conversation.

Social ambition began to rear its perennially ludicrous visage on every side; and one morning shortly after breakfast, I found a lady actually crumpled up on the stairs outside Mama's door, weeping bitterly because my good-natured mother had failed to procure for her an invitation to somebody's ball. "How pretty she was," I thought, crouched in the abandonment of her grief, and wearing a lovely morning gown of pink taffeta and lace. I noticed, however, that her forehead, clustered about with blond curls, had that billiard-ball protuberance which I have since grown to mistrust.

I began to take in the fact of "failures" in Wall Street, and some puff of fever seemed to enter the door with my tired good-looking father on Friday evenings when we met him at the Wickford boat either in our smart private hansom drawn by a high-stepper with a bunch of violets behind one ear, or in the Hayward Livery cab of our even mean. And from the moment he stepped wearily into the cab, there would be arguments heightening into disputes, so that riding backwards on a small seat at my parents' feet, I was filled with dejection.

It seemed, after dusk had fallen, that all the poisonous uncertainty of how the bills were to be paid, and whether or not we could afford a town house for the coming winter was lifted into the invisibility of dusk. And often after I had returned from stalking the maids and sailors behind the hedge, I would find them all gathered on the front piazza, placated and at peace, waiting for the victoria or electric brougham to take them on to their parties.

I remember them all so clearly one evening, Mama, Papa, Lily, Harry and Charlie, particularly resplendent with powdered hair, in costumes of the Louis XVI period, waiting to start for my aunt Tessie's "Ball Blanc." Each one held a mask, and I remember my sister put hers up to her eyes, striking me for the first time, I suppose, with that thrilling loveliness of coquetry which must make its promises in secret, and within the bounds of grace.

About this time I had my first whiff of the coming racket; of what the machine could do with a little over-statement in festivity. For one afternoon in midsummer, as I stood on the porch waiting for my pony carriage, I saw a phaeton turn in our gate, driven by a lady in all her seasonal finery, with beside her a man covered with dirt and mud, his head thrown back on the seat, his eyes closed, looking as though he were dead, and realized with horror that it was my brother Harry. Apparently he had been returning with a gay party from lunching at the Clambake Club, with Vinson Walsh driving his new Mercedes, when, taking a corner at too sharp an angle and failing to make it, they had gone straight over a small bridge, overturning the car into a creek!

Vinson Walsh was instantly killed, and his sister, Mrs. Edward McLean of Washington, more or less seriously injured. Nor will I forget the stillness of my father, standing waiting on the porch for the phaeton to draw up, and the gentleness with which he lifted out my brother, to carry him in and lay him on his own bed, while all of us loitered about the darkened rooms until the doctor's visit told us that he was only stunned and suffering from a broken arm.

The country roads and all that lay on either side of them had seemed to belong to me in my pony-cart drives. The looks of the seasons over the fields and gardens, the changes in the air, all were so lavishly registered in me. And then one day, without warning, an inestimable loss —the closing of the countryside from my adventurous drives. For one Mr. Augustus Jay, a jaundiced looking man, was loose on the narrow lanes with an infernally pumping, stinking Mercedes. And my pony Midget simply would not meet this thing, but threw his feet wide apart and his head back, and himself went back and backwards— though I jumped from my seat and pulled him forward by the reins—until we all upset in the ditch.

Thinking back on those years of my childhood, I can understand a little the strain and exhaustion and final indifference that came over my father's spirit regarding life on the Stock Exchange, if there is such a thing. It became increasingly impossible for him to hold to his path in the vast jungle that big business was causing to grow up. This called for a technique that he had not, nor very likely any of his forebears. He had gotten his living, as they had, from the start of a small inheritance and a decent use of ability. He had done well with his partnership on the Exchange —had handled the large accounts of his social associates with wisdom, and retained them for years. But there were deaths. Bankruptcies became more frequent. Incredible appearances and disappearances began to be made through the wheel of fortune; and in a whirligig social structure, in which the basest and smartest crudities began to come naturally to the top, people of my father's caliber faded with some irony of mood from the scene.

The tempo in Wall Street began to resemble that of a roulette wheel—a wheel in which you had to be "on" to a hundred and one gadgets concealed under the table, before you made your bet! And Newport was a three-ringed circus: even as a child I could feel the mounting beats in the pulse of our household. The quiet intimacies, the simple gaieties of my parents and their naïve coterie of friends, were giving way before an influx of millionaires and their wives, who bid for their inclusion in society with a lavish display in everyday living, and Haroun-al-Raschid entertainments.

And in the meantime we lived our increasingly nervous life—always at our home in Newport in the summer, but in the winter in houses we rented anywhere from Gramercy Park to Fifty-fifth Street, or in small family hotels on side streets.

Oh, those cheap hotels to which we resorted on the fluctuations of the market! How dreadful were the rooms when we arrived with our bags in the evening, before Mama had time to order in palms from Wadley and Smythe, and throw charming tea-cloths over the tables and set out the *repoussé* silver tea service.

As soon as I learned to, I sustained these breaches in life by reading, and remember especially one day how dreadful it was to dislocate myself from Ainsworth's *Windsor*

Castle, and the lusty pageantry of Henry VIII's life, filigreed by ghostliness as the great tale is, and descend with
my nurse to the hotel dining room, dusty and close with
the smell of yesterday's beef and lukewarm water, and
only retrieved by occasional glimpses of young Mrs. Dana
Gibson, then at the height of her "Miss America" good
looks.

But from the first I loathed the city, for in all of it there
seemed no one for me to play with, a matter never to be
remedied, on account of Mama's attitude to germs, which
she had fancifully concluded were more prosperous in parks
than in streets. So if ever I was sent out for a meal with
another child, the fraternizing element of a stroll afterwards among the animals was forbidden, and I was walked
along instead on the street side, craning my neck with a
particular nostalgia over the wall at Sixty-fourth Street,
toward the brown castellated window-barred home of the
boa constrictors. How I longed for just a glimpse of the
polar bear which was described to me as having taken his
captivity the worst of all.

Indeed, one of the few pleasant memories I have of the
city in those days was of being taken for the first time to
the Opera, to a matinée of "Lohengrin," with Jean
DeReszke in the title role. I sat in a box with Lucy and
Johnny Dodge, spruced up to the nines, thinking that never
before in all my life had I seen a beauty so magical as that
of Lohengrin who, standing up in the Swan Boat, with his
golden curls and beard—while the light flashed on his
armor and helmet—had slowly, slowly passed down the
lake and forever out of sight of Elsa, who had been enough
of a fool to ask him the one question he warned her he never
wanted to hear.

Whether we dwelt in the city or the country, wherever my mother was, everything gleamed in order, except the totals of the bills she kept in neat stacks tied up with pink ribbon. "What!" my harassed father would shout, "eight thousand dollars owing to Dunstan for dresses to put on your back and Lily's!"

"Where else could we put them?" she replied.

"But you never told me," swore my unfortunate father; and it was true that he never knew how much he was in debt.

But despite this friction, they had many good times still, and interesting friendships. And I especially remember Madame Nordica, one of my mother's intimates, and prima donna of the Metropolitan Opera, looking down my throat one day and telling Mama that I would have "a voice." But this bit of news did not concern me at all, as obviously the real business in life was a successful début and marriage with a rich and handsome man about whom no one could say "Who *was* he?"

And I became conscious as I drove out to leave cards with my mother in the afternoon, that the spacious wooden cottages and villas set in the midst of those beautiful Newport lawns, with their amazing smoothness and royal shade, were giving way to marble palaces, and in many of these footmen stood at the door in knee breeches and powdered hair, to receive our cards, looking, I thought, like props for "Alice in Wonderland."

The talk of "social climbers" waxed warmer, and bits of gossip impressed me disagreeably: One day I heard Papa say, "Well, I don't think you ought to receive her; for after all, she sold her child for a million dollars!"

In solitude I retired to think this out; since the lovely

half-Spanish woman who left cards on my mother in the smartest victoria imaginable—drawn by a single high-stepper that was driven by Bacchus, a celebrity among coachmen, a grotesque exclamation of sheer style, who drove with his knees nearly up to his chin—intrigued me more than any other caller she had!

Indeed it seemed to me Mrs. L's pallor was lit from behind; never had I beheld such a sheen as there was on her black hair, and her big eyes were so dark, so almost foolish with sweetness. Yet she had sold her child for a million dollars! What torture of desire for something else had driven her to make such a bargain? Wasn't it the same thing that had us all in its clutches in different ways?

Maybe there was a quality to shudder about in all this seasonal festivity! And haunted by such thoughts, I took particular pleasure in walking out into the country after supper with my parents, on those rare occasions when they had no engagements for the evening; for as I frisked along in front of them, and looked back to see that they were holding hands, I experienced a strange surge of wellbeing, even at nightfall—my most difficult hour, then and now —since there they were, together and happy, and obviously not thinking of selling me for anything in the world.

However, disquieting sagas continued to drift in. A certain couple arrived in Newport, and after some distress, of course, had with remarkable rapidity achieved the top. The man was tall, handsome, still in early middle age, but prematurely gray, from overwork my father said. His wife, whose contests had no doubt been mostly in dreams spun out over the society news columns from the depths of a comfortable suburban armchair, looked fresh and young enough to be her husband's daughter. Then it happened that after only a few years' enjoyment of their wealth and social prominence Mr. X had a stroke and became paralyzed when, one night, his wife, coming into her husband's sickroom, glitteringly fresh on her way to a dinner party, had gotten some of the mush that he was attempting to lift to his mouth spilt on her frock. "She had to go back and change," said my mother, "and imagine, she was so angry with the poor man that she never even went back to wish him good night."

I was as much depressed by this story as I was by the sight of Mr. Ogden Goelet, a distinguished elderly gentleman, whom I would see walking about on the arm of his nurse, passing through immense iron gates and walking slowly up the drive to his house, a copy of one of the chateaux in Touraine. "Poor Mr. Goelet," I heard, "he's not able to digest anything but hothouse grapes." And again my father said "Goelet has worked himself to death." Then Mr. Goelet became obscurely related in my mind to stories of warning and doom in my book of Greek mythology.

It was all very curious. Things seemed to turn out far from well with these inhabitants of palaces, and yet it was of the air around me that I should go as soon as I could to live in one.

My round-faced cousin, Herman Oelrichs, did live in one, and he was my favorite cousin, for he had a great sense of humor, which I thought he needed, dressed as he always was in ringlets and long-trousered sailor suits, while I, having my hair cut like a boy's, to increase my strength it was said, was generally attired in the most flounced girlish sort of dresses that our German seamstress, with her indelible and somehow appetizing odor of onions and fried potatoes, could devise. And how such a bizarre couple as Herman and myself ever managed to win the children's flower parade one August afternoon in a tiny hansom sown over with goldenrod, will always remain a mystery to me, on what Aunt Tessie would scornfully call "this God's green earth."

It seemed to me that the household at Rosecliff, where Aunt Tessie and Herman lived in a marble imitation of the *Petit Trianon,* surrounded by a wonderful rose garden—at which it is safe to say no one glanced save the gardener—was strongly addicted to Society as a business.

My aunt Tessie, attired in white elbow-length gloves, princess lace dresses, and towering picture hats, seemed always starting for another point, in her victoria or electric brougham. And I fancied she must ever appear out of glittering hallways—from between lanes of potted hydrangea plants in their spectral August bloom, and lackeys in knee breeches and powdered hair—to say nothing of her obsequious buck-toothed English butler Herbert, and that master clown-companion of all social "éliteness," Harry Lehr.

How clearly I see Harry Lehr's husky figure gotten up in a white flannel suit, and a kind of comedy straw hat, remark his mincing step, hear the timbre of his clown's laughter, catch in the piggish glint of his blond-lashed eyes, deprecation, hysterical nonsense, and the deformity of a long sadness. Then he shifted Aunt Tessie's poodles from one arm to another, broke her up with his buffoonery, and intrigued her with news of original figures for the next "cotillion." Was he the last of a great line of jesters, proffering his services to the hollowest pretense of money-royalty in "The Gilded Age"? I would hear from his stepson as we stretched out on the raft at Bailey's Beach, how he stormed through the house at night (while those who were awake shrank further under their bedclothes), the mask off his spirit, which looked out from its frustrations, already a little mad.

But I thought that my aunt, between her outbursts of laughter and a delightfully cool manner she had of swearing, seemed restless and unhappy, and perhaps this was the reason that, as I heard, she flew into such rages when the servants exceeded their weekly allowance of tea. And I learnt that before she had married my uncle she had been Miss Fair, of a famous mining family recruited from the "Forty-niners," and I would repeat to myself, Mackay Flood Fair O'Brien, ignorant as yet of the Ballad Form, and picture the "Forty-niners" to myself, as four gigantic men in sombreros with beards like Buffalo Bill's, striding over the blue dreamlike foothills of the Sierra Nevadas armed with pick axes, cracking off the surface of the earth— to lay bare sheer plains of gold. The result of all this good fortune was that already in our childhood, Aunt Tessie, with her Irish beauty, classic nose and extraordinary humor too, had decided to remain amicably separated from her charming husband with his noticeably high blood pressure. And well do I remember the strain it was to sit at their luncheon table on one of my uncle's rare visits, listening to their pretense at intimacy. Eventually each adopted the other's edge of the continent, he living quietly in San Francisco, she lavishly in Newport and New York.

But at my mother's sister's, at Aunty's (Mrs. Theodore Havemeyer's), just across from Aunt Tessie on Bellevue Avenue, there was an Austrian flavor of sumptuous living, domesticities faithfully served, and a waltz-time aura of romance, mostly contributed by Auntie's five daughters who seemed to me beings of languishing sentiment and glamour.

Aunty never went out into society, but let it drift back to her, dividing her time in a mood of generous sentimentality between her husband, Uncle Theodore—whose bristling white sidewhiskers and playful sternness always frightened me to death—almost a dozen of children, and several dozen grandchildren, while added to the entourage, at the moment when I remember her first, was a dour-looking German composer, author of some piece which endured, I believe, through Aunty's patronage, only until the end of a single performance at the Paris Opéra House.

Aunty floated about gently in her unrestrained stoutness in white chiffon draperies, topped by curious white hats (reminding me of French actresses gardening on the Riviera during their last days), and everything was delicious at her house, even soup in summer. Oh, the divine aroma of creamed barley soup, mixed in with a scent of summer matting in the room where we used to take luncheon, and I felt fiercely toward my father when I heard him say how ridiculous it was for a "woman of Emily's age to go about with her hair dyed black!"

For me Aunty had no age, because she left me no doubt that she still had a life of the heart, for had she not told me one evening at dusk as I walked with her at Mahwah, her country estate in New Jersey—by a pond quite covered with lily pads, and with a deserted cottage in the background—about a young man of her intimate acquaintance who had been found dead at his desk, his pockets stuffed with bits of paper which bore only her name, "Emily"? And

picturing to myself the scenes of desperate entreaty (I
didn't quite understand about what) which must have
preceded the fatal act, I asked her, "But Aunty, when did
this happen?" (she was well over sixty at the time), to be
told with a distant sweetness, "Last year!"

But one evening, visiting Aunty at Mahwah while I
waited about amongst a group of cousins for supper on the
porch I heard my cousin, Marie Tiffany, exclaim, "How
can little Blanche be so wretched-looking when all the rest
of them are so handsome? Why, she looks like the 'Yaller
Kid'!"

Probably at that moment of hurt rage and desolation
was pierced the limbo in which had lain profoundly undis-
turbed the question of my own effect, to which an answer
scarcely replete with assurance was delivered up a few
months later. Then, sent to attend a smart dancing class, I
discovered that whenever the little gentlemen in pumps
and white gloves were directed to take partners for "The
Lancers"—and we were a few boys short—I was invariably
among the couple of little girls who got left. And, as a
blacksmith pursued his trade across the road from the
Newport Casino, striking on his anvil through bars of "The
Blue Danube," I thought with nostalgic desperation,
"Why, that sound is inside me."

But it was true. I resembled a gnome, dank-haired, sallow-faced, with large circles under my eyes, and I dare say
it was because I must submit to an appearance which did not
seem to please any one, and worried my parents, that I
conceived the idea of at least exaggerating it to an interesting point. So a little while after this I bought a pair of
cheap eyeglasses, and blacking my teeth with charcoal, I
contrived, whenever I could, to wear a skirt and jacket

that didn't match; thus, I dare say, experiencing some of the strange elation I was after.

Of course, interspersed with these neurotic experiments in heightening the gloom, would come moments of brilliant prestige. I remember that one afternoon, after performing "Little Bo Peep" in a children's "Tableau Vivant," my mother led me up to a tall pale gentleman with strangely liquid eyes and a dark crest of hair brushed straight up from his rather narrow forehead, who sat on a lawn dotted with marquees from which punch and ice cream were being dispensed, to tell me: "Baby, make a curtsey to the Grand Duke Boris." And the Grand Duke Boris, a cousin of "Nicholas the Last," had taken me on his knee and told me with what appeared a lazy passionate expression, "You were the best, you know—the very best!" So for some time afterwards I often gazed gratefully at his picture framed in silver in the blue parlor. It showed him in a marvellous braided uniform that made him look as fine, I thought, as the leader of the band at the Casino.

But although Aunty herself walked with her slow, gentle dignity through long spaces of calm and tragedy, she was not overcome, but continued to care for spacious rooms, empty of society small-talk, and for cozy gardens with which she was on intimate terms—while each afternoon, through thick and thin, she locked herself away in her music room, to play the four-hand pieces of Bach and Brahms with the favored musician of the moment. Indeed, she stuck to her great composers even with the din of Babel and Babylon beginning to drown out the cloppity-clop of horses' hoofs outside 244 Madison Avenue.

[52]

Looking back, I do not think my aunt was particularly intelligent, and yet, because ingrained in her was a delight in the cultural amenities of life (and although some of these added to her girth, her chef, Perere, being reputed the best "food-tosser" in America), she bore up with dignity and peace until her tranquil end.

Whenever Mama and Aunty felt New York life to be too oppressively alien, Tibi would go to a Viennese luncheon with Aunty in the Antique Room, and there surrounded by men in armor, who later repaired I think to the Oliver Belmont collection—and waited on by Mattie, her major domo, in black satin knee breeches, and a couple of footmen whose shoe buckles reminded me of the Signers of the "Declaration of Independence" in my history book—they talked about their youth in Austria and no doubt sensed, through food, that magically connecting link, a proximity again to their real selves in that old world which their hearts and spirits understood.

Both of them held to their traditions until the end. Chaos was never let in, and their temperaments are precious to me in memory for the incessant order that surrounded them as well as for their unconscious lack of extravagance in all things; and I envy too their steady faith in the doctrines of the church and the spirit behind these, that consoled them in life, and surrounded their death with magnificent and touching ceremonial.

Aunt Tessie, however, my aunt by marriage, was not so fortunate. She had been begotten and brought up in the racket of money-getting; her father had struck gold in Virginia City (named after his wife); and with magical abruptness, existence had reversed from the wary antagonist whom you must throw every morning in order to survive yourself, into a slave servile to the whims of Aladdin.

So Aunt Tessie's extraordinary humor and beauty had been transferred as if by the stroke of a wand to a plan of life, and into the constriction of values and manners with which she was as perilously unfamiliar as an actress who has only glanced once at her role.

Gardens, music, literature were all names to her, not means of sustenance, nor was there any standard abroad in the Newport of those days gradually to correct her ignorance.

Gorgeous toilettes, society—a flux of faces in and out of rooms, on beaches, in casinos—absorbed her. Yet eventually, and because, I think, all the time there had been that sensibility which showed in her beauty, her spirit—delicate enough to have been made unendurably unhappy, because essential harmonies and consolations were lacking—lost its reason. I have heard that during those last years when none of us ever saw her, she would wander, a fragile and still incredibly beautiful person, her raven hair with its deep wave gone snow-white, through the rooms of her immense marble copy of the Villa Trianon, reseating her guests over and over again, pressing them to take just another ice, one more glass of champagne!

CHAPTER IV

Vanity Fair

IT SEEMED that the Rawdon Crawley Vanity Fair atmosphere of incessant money troubles, moving lavalike beneath a spurious surface of contagious gaiety that pervaded our house, had its culmination in the marriage of my sister, July twenty-fourth, 1902, not to any of the crowd of boys who had frequented the house, although some of these I had gathered were good enough "matches," Bobby Gerry, Robert Goelet, Alfred Vanderbilt, etc.—but to a millionaire out of the west, Peter Martin, a black-haired, blue-eyed fellow of Irish origin, who, although not good-looking, was filled with the charm of a nature that could live without ennui, entirely for amusement.

The morning of my sister's wedding, I woke to the horror of having to find out whether it was raining or not, for if the vast marquee erected on the grounds for the hundreds of guests could not hold them dry and happy for the wedding breakfast, what then? And without opening my eyes, I listened for the even hushed sound of rain on the leaves, for its patter on the tin roof, when, relieved to ecstasy, I opened my eyes on a cloudy morning.

Without dressing, I crept downstairs by myself. All the work had been finished the night before, the way it is on Christmas Eve, and there were the so-familiar rooms, garnished with cleanliness, solemn with flowers. Everything seemed to be holding its breath importantly for this good-by to Lily—the grandfather clock in the hall that my father wound up every night, the exquisite Dresden figures on the mantel in the blue parlor that Mama would never have any one wash but herself. I could see that everything was prepared and waiting, and I think I must have sensed then that change is a kind of sacrament.

And soon the calèche and victoria from my aunt's stables were at the door, the horses pawing the gravel in the weak sunlight, and shaking the white favors behind their ears. The coachman was smiling, everybody was smiling, while my father looked very handsome and irritable as he paced up and down waiting for Lily; and I, who was to be her maid of honor, waited with him at the foot of the stairs, in my chiffon and lace dress, topped by an absurd picture hat lined with chiffon and bearing a huge white plume that weighed down the hat too far over one eye. There I stood, brushed and combed within an inch of my life, clutching a huge basket of jasmine, and I felt that to have so much apprehension, gaiety, and sadness inside of me at one time was more than any one should be called upon to endure.

And then we heard the rustle of my sister's huge court train, being held up and turned by the maids as she started down the stairs. She looked unforgettably beautiful as she came toward us, with that striking quality that beauty has

—can only have—when it has forgotten its own existence. She came toward us, very tall and slim and fair, in her princess lace wedding dress, in her tulle and orange blossoms, carrying a huge spray of white flowers on her arm, and looking as if she did not, and never would, see any of us, and was only a part of distant things as miraculously lovely as her own image appeared to our eyes.

The crowd at St. Joseph's Church pressed their faces against the windows of the carriages and actually murmured and called out good wishes to my sister as she stepped out. Her marriage, the marriage of a famous beauty and Newport belle to a millionaire, was keeping the pageantry of a Newport season up to the mark.

A dark church with its blaze of candles at the far end, and many people dressed in their best held in by ropes of white ribbon and spears of nosegays, all turning expectant faces vibrating with memories and hopes, toward the slow file of the wedding procession advancing to the strains of "Lohengrin," tides of emotion meeting in an atmosphere of ancient ceremony—the Church may have failed in many ways, I think it has, but I have seen too that its ceremonies can be superbly worthy accompaniments to the deepest events of life.

The wedding breakfast could not have been more gay. Harry Lehr threw out from his distinguished, piggish, theatrical, effeminate personality a fine performance. The hoarse laughter of "Mamie" Fish was never still. She had the elements of a true comedienne, her harsh gaiety had the bitter overtone of a grotesque disillusionment with herself and every one else. One knew as one looked at and listened to her, that she sensed well the triviality in which she drowned her time, and that her brash mirth concealed an ever more exasperated cry at the impotence of the kind of life that went on around her.

The menus, music and the Bacchanalian spirits of the guests were all over my head and there were no other children present. Posing for photographs, seated at my sister's feet and still clutching the basket of jasmine, was a nightmare! But finally the rice had been thrown at the dashing figures of the bride and groom, who disappeared into another equipage from my aunt's stables, an elegant coupé this time. Mama had gone upstairs to cry, the party had dispersed, the bridesmaid cousins, Dora Havemeyer, Moppie Jay and Isabel May, had all been driven off by their beaux. And when, after wandering off somewhere to think it over by myself, I returned a good many hours later, really needing some one to talk to by that time, I found they had all gone off to another party at the Clambake Club, while rumors were afloat that Papa and Charlie, having plunged off the rocks around the Club, were racing each other out to sea.

And now my sister had gone, and not with either of the mates I had chosen for her—one for steadiness, and one for glamour—of whom I must go back and speak.

A few years previously, at the time of my sister's début, when I was about eight years old, we were living in a very luxurious, charming house, for us, Number 35 Madison Square. The drawing rooms were always filled with people, as was the gas-lit dining room with its tapestry-back chairs. And in a high-ceiled room hung with yellow damask I fell in love with a dark canvas upon which could dimly be seen the figure of a young man in a frock coat with high lights on the tops of his patent leather shoes. His wonderful eyes followed me all over the room as I purposely walked from side to side in order to draw his uncanny glance after me.

At Number 35, I had a large gray-blue nursery to myself, with a coal fireplace in it, and on winter nights, as the arc of light faded on the ceiling, I would spin for myself the most consuming of romances, in which I always played the principal part. But this portrait in the library must have been psychic preparation, for as a matter of fact, I was just about to fall in love for the first, and I often think for the last, time in my life.

The object of my sensuous precocity was a beau of my sister's, Lawrence Perrin of Baltimore, a young man of extraordinary beauty, dark-haired, olive-skinned, with amazingly piercing eyes. But despite the ascetic drawing of his face, he was strong, and, it turned out, he could be violent! I saw with pleasure that my sister seemed to favor his advances. Meeting them one winter day together on Madison Avenue, returning from Mass at that terrifying Father Doucy's (who would stop his sermon to call out by name anyone who came in late—"Lily Oelrichs—is 11:30 the best you can do for Our Lord, Jesus Christ? Must the Blessed Saviour Himself put up with your laziness and irreverence?"), my sister clad in a tight-fitting tailor-made jacket and skirt of pale gray, with a toque of plum-colored velvet perched on her brown-blond hair, while Lawrence ranged beside her, eerily dark in a black coat with an astrakhan collar, it seemed to me that these two were figures of superhuman loveliness, and made for one another. I did not want Lawrence for myself; I was philosophical about that. A child's love may have the philosophy of age in it and perhaps the disingenuous purity of wisdom belongs to both ends of life. If only she made Lawrence happy, all would be well. But I noticed she didn't. There were continual quarrels and it occasionally seemed that Lawrence was being ejected from the house to return and beat on the front door after midnight, holding furious altercations with Papa in a dressing gown, while snow flew in the doorway, and I crouched on the top of the stairs. What could Lily be thinking about! And then I discovered—it was of some one else—of the man she afterward married.

One afternoon when this treacherous pair were out together, and a sympathetic maid had let the deceived Lawrence in against orders, I found him stretched out full length, oblivious to form, on a narrow sofa in our drawing room. Taking in all his elegance and beauty and despair in one infatuated glance, I rushed over to him, and kneeling down, made the most unselfish declaration of my life: "Lawrence, I love you! If you want me, you can have me as soon as I grow up. If you don't, I will help you get any one else you want. Only give up Lily! She is false to you."

At this point Lawrence naturally came to his senses and sprang to his feet. "I know where they are," I told him, "and I'll take you there." Just how I got past my nurse I don't remember, but dishevelled with excitement we arrived at Durland's Riding Academy just as my sister, holding her side-saddle habit and crop in one hand, and wearing a black tricorne, was dismounting, accompanied by Peter Martin, Irish-featured and mild.

"There she is," I pointed, shrieking, "and that's Peter Martin. Kill him!" Perfectly furious, my sister grasped me by the back of my coat collar while Peter smiled in an uncertain manner; and then by virtue of my outburst, every one laughed, and Lawrence and I went back to our hansom cab tightly holding hands.

He was mine now, I had only to grow up. And my mother always remembered with horror that when he came to call on her, even a year later, and long after my sister's marriage, that on hearing his voice in the hall, I rushed to the stairs and precipitated myself down them, risking my neck really, if he had not caught me in his arms at the foot.

However, behind that taut beauty and those amazing eyes, so strange and a little crossed in their regard, was madness! And not long afterward Lawrence walked to the White House with some arrogant conviction pounding in his brain that called upon him to try and shoot President Taft, and was, as a natural consequence, locked up in an asylum.

And then one afternoon, some months after that event, I was sitting in my nursery at Newport, when I saw a man turn in our gate on the run. He wore a Panama hat and a good-looking suit, but he was unshaven and wore no collar or tie—and I knew, with such a terrible pounding of my heart, that it was Lawrence. He had escaped from the asylum and I heard him repeating in the hall, "Where is Babe? Where is she? I must see her!" And my mother answered in a voice so even and quiet and unlike hers: "She is away, Lawrence, visiting some friends." And then, apparently, Mama had had the presence of mind to get him back somehow into the hands of his keepers.

But that winter in the gray bedroom at Number 35 Madison Avenue, I was becoming intractable with fancies and more unhealthy-looking every day. Also Miss Parkhurst, my teacher, stout, gray-haired, with an Alexandria fringe and, it seemed to me, a most disagreeable odor about her of ink-stained rulers and the worn wood of schoolroom desks, told Mama that I really ought to be sent to school and have the society of other children. I didn't know exactly what other children were. My brothers and sisters were so much older than I was. Anyway, I didn't care one way or the other, since I was less and less drawn to Miss Parkhurst who, I had found out, considered the frost-bitten severity of her nose a classic point.

So Mr. Rosa, a very stylish gentleman, with sideburns and a heavy watch chain, whose ambition to die in Rome was eventually gratified, persuaded my mother to allow me to attend his classes. I heard with relief that these only lasted a couple of hours and that there were no more than eight girls to a class. So to the Rosa classes I went, overlooking leisurely Forty-second Street and Bryant Park, where, in fidelity to Mr. Rosa's mortuary ambitions, the walls were hung with pictures of ruined temples and fragments of columns. Our teachers were the Misses Leonora and Helen Tomes, two slender, sallow-faced, sensitive and charming women. They always wore black taffeta blouses and the neatest of grosgrain belts, woolen skirts with a train, and long gold watch chains that swung with swift dignity as they walked about the room carrying wooden wands pointed at the ends with which to rap us on the back for posture or inattention. And they called us with *éclat* Miss Oelrichs, Miss Webb, Miss Alexandre, Miss Greene, etc.

Of their three or four years' struggle to teach me something, I recall only the look of Spain and France, and Italy (the boot) on colored maps I made, and the dense ennui I experienced with the story of Robinson Crusoe. How dreadful that he should have discovered a man "Friday," who went on contriving ways to keep this bore alive.

But I had one original experience at school, for soon

after my arrival I was not just teased, as at home by my brothers and sister, but for the first time openly laughed at. And I can still feel the blood of mortification in my cheeks as I sat on a chair for the first recess, with my schoolmates ringed uproariously about me, crying out between fits of laughter—"Look at her head! Look at her feet!"

CHAPTER V

"The Most Exquisite Phase"

Adolescence—
The most exquisite phase
Reminiscent of a slender blanchèd blur
Leaning against trees that are dim as shadows,
And yearning skyward awake
Over serpentine reflections
In brooks during dawn. . . .
Adolescence
Reminiscent of furled garments
Blowing back against the rush
Of imperious limbs—
And again reminiscent of bacchanal-swerving,
Bending, flashing, abruptly away
From the thieving of innumerable garlands. . . .
Adolescence
Tanned with the glittering stain of sunlight,
Stained with those crimson juices of sun-ripened berries,
Eager, restless, confused!

Dazzling as sea-foam and attenuate naturally
From the pensive lure of brooding dreams—
I salute, I exalt your beauty,
O Adolescence—
The most exquisite phase.

ADOLESCENCE had arrived. To watch people across a dinner table so absorbedly that every vestige of yourself vanished and your mouth might be hanging wide open was no longer possible, no longer enough.

How were those eyes floating above the pink-shaded lights reacting to you became a question, and with that query so much of the æsthetic, passionate intensity of childhood passed, together with that humility of unexpectant reverie which gives to children's faces their young-prince look of flowerlike nobility.

Now in adolescence came furtive self-consciousness, and an agony as to whether you were pleasing or not, bumping your moods up and down at a tempo to discombobulate utterly those intervals of long straight staring that had returned such immemorable richness.

By this time I had emerged from the gnome, and become rather good-looking in a lusty manner, though I resembled my father so much that all his friends called me "Charlie, Junior." And what a dreadful delight there was now in walking past the "reading room" on my way to play tennis, where all the gentlemen sat in rows, their long drinks beside them, desultorily taking in the morning life of Bellevue Avenue, their Panama hats tilted back on their heads, their feet often stretched up on a chair. All of which I took in in a sidelong glance, "for a lady never looks into a club," said Mama.

Adolescence at 22 East Fifty-fifth Street was not very exquisite. The clatter of Madison Avenue street cars permeated the front rooms while the back ones overlooked the usual row of yards, and this anchorage, where we remained four years, represented only a moderate state of well-being since the family "till" had lately been subjected to a "panic."

The principal bogey in the house at that moment was Theodore Roosevelt, the trust-busting President, whose noble interference in business my father, with the professional's ire for the amateur, pronounced to be an outrage; which was O.K. by me, as I did not care in the least for Mr. Roosevelt's photograph, representing a sturdy, spectacled gentleman whose orgiastic grin, framed by an enormous mustache, spread out under eyes which I thought peculiarly humorless.

The New York of these days had not dreamed of its transition into "The Metropolis." No hint of what was to come had brushed the inhabitants. Only a few stinking little motor cars puffed about. The electric broughams and victorias did not seem menacing, while they showed pretty women off remarkably well.

Hansom cabs still ranged about looking for fares, and you were likely to come across some enchanting actress like Ethel Barrymore ravishingly tilted forward in one, to have her go by at a pace that released the whole picture of slender beauty, grace and charm of costume. You saw people in those days. A walk fed you with real contacts, and what an original kind of nostalgia there is now in memory, because it bridges so much more than a difference in the age.

All the gentlemen from the Union Club, anchored next

to the Cathedral, knew the pretty school girls by sight, and the pretty school girls knew them; while the principal actors of the season, and other celebrities, were also very quickly spotted by us as we sauntered up Fifth Avenue after school, three or four abreast.

"Here comes Charlie Cherry," some one would whisper excitedly, to throw a striking attitude, which might arrest the matinée idol's merry dark glance for an instant.

The "Mills Twins" (now Mrs. Phipps and Lady Granard) passed in their open landau, looking so insolently smart in their velvets and furs, their hats teed up precariously on enormous pompadours, that they did not need to be pretty. "They are like the sisters of Cinderella," I would think, "opulent but doomed!" And it seemed to me that driving in an open carriage gave you a wonderful chance to project yourself on the public. If only we had one, I would think wretchedly; and even on my way to the "bloc," to take my examination for the Brearley School, most of the horror was retrieved by driving there one muggy October afternoon in Aunt Tessie's open victoria, attired in a mauve tailor-made, and a straw hat set at a rakish angle. For no matter what might happen in the Brearley fortress I had at least achieved the plaudits of the crowd.

During my adolescence, *Town Topics*, the Society scandal sheet, played an enormous part in every one's life. Climbing matrons were driven to despair by its jibes; indiscreet young married couples went in terror of its insinuations; hardy financiers whose pile concealed a more than ordinary toll of ruined persons hastened to try to buy off the editor; and as a child and young girl I knew every one of the principal reporters by sight, and with sardonic amusement would watch them sitting behind the dowagers, (especially behind old Mrs. Kernochan whom we called, with that genius for veracity that children have, "The Sitting Bull,") taking notes of her gossip which, starting out as it always did on a strong note of vituperation, could be very likely printed straight off the reel.

One gay August morning, during an International Tennis Tournament, I noticed Mr. R., one of the prime reporters, dangling near me in his pale gray suit and cap, where I stood before a jeweler's window with Jack Rutherford, betting on the results of the matches—a gold bangle it was, to a leather cigarette case. I went on, stating my part of the bargain (for at my age I feared no evil from any pen) and forgot the incident, when a week or so later, my father stormed into the house from the Reading Room, that natural harbor of stiff drinks, crying out that my virginity had been called in question in the public print, my reputation ruined, and my chance of marrying any decent young man annihilated.

He flourished in his hand a copy of the dread sheet, with its black and white cover of two pretty ladies in leg-of-mutton sleeves whispering to one another! "What does this mean, Miss?" he shouted, as I read in one of my finest spasms of family fear a long paragraph about a young girl who the blind could see was myself, that had already been found testing her powers of extortion before a jeweler's window upon a green youth. "If I knew who wrote that," thundered my father, "I would kill him." "Well, I can tell you just who it was," I said, "and his name and address as well." "Why, how on earth would you know about such a person?" cried Papa, naïvely exposing his estrangement from the sophisticated resources of my way of life.

And off he darted in a livery stable cab to return hours later, smiling in a crestfallen way. "I saw the wretched little creature; I shook him like a rat! He admitted the article, but said he hadn't meant anything by it. He crawled on his knees before me and I hadn't the heart to beat him up. He has promised never to say another derogatory word about you in his filthy sheet in which I told him I preferred you not to be mentioned."

However, Mr. R., going now in fear of his life, and also meeting the solid contempt of my gaze each time I spied his pale gray suit on the vivid Casino lawns, proceeded to try to reinstate himself in our family's confidence by building me up in a series of astounding articles in which Blanche Oelrichs, "the precocious racketeer" gave way to "a girl so in advance of all other girls in good looks, that not since the days of Ava Willing (Mrs. John Jacob Astor) had anything been seen to touch her, etc., etc."

It was said that my entrance at Freebody Park, a vaudeville show changing its bill once a week, and to which even girls who were not "out" were allowed to go, had caused a sensation. It was all very pretty, but knowing the facts I was spared any inflation of ego. However, these paragraphs of forensic praise were cut out and pasted into a scrap book by my mother, and did me a great deal of good with the boys, who were, during the advent of these publications, quite pleased to be seen around with me.

Looking back on my adolescence, my preoccupation with boys seems excessive, and yet outside the fact that I was not lacking in temperament, there had always existed the invariable dictum that the only career for a woman was marriage, and that it was natural for her to think of it continually until she achieved it. It did not seem important for her to know about any other thing than how to draw to her side a young gentleman with money. Nor was it necessary for her to learn to become anything except the person that such a young man would select.

I began to realize that money had a way of sliding toward money and that rich people wanted their sons to marry rich girls. This was brought home to me particularly in my friendship with the Herbert boys, Michael and Sidney. They were to me the absolutely fascinating nephews of Mrs. Ogden Goelet and Mrs. Cornelius Vanderbilt, and during their holidays in Newport, they drove about in a plum-colored jaunting car of Aunty Grace, and happy were the days when it anchored in front of our black gatepost.

Michael and Sidney were Eton boys and had a nonchalant humor and self-confidence entirely lacking even in the football captains of Groton and St. Marks, whom I now numbered among my timid beaux. How conversationally gauche and stricken these victorious athletes were in comparison with the lissome, marvellously groomed Herberts! Why I had all and a little more than I could do to keep up with them!

There were parties at Aunty Grace's, and Aunty May's, and wandering about the royally clipped and smooth parterres of Mrs. Goelet's great garden, Michael and Sidney would propose to me by turn, in the starlight, and next day scratch with a pin on the walls of our dingy summer house —which Mama had had transported from Aunty Havemeyer's grounds because Papa had proposed to her in it— "Blanche Herbert."

And yet I knew very well that over and beyond our being all children, marriage with penniless Blanche Oelrichs would never have been permitted to Michael and Sidney by any of their strong clan.

However, these boys decanted the nostalgia of real charm into my young life. They blew over my eager ardent mind the first fumes of sophistication, of that quizzical complaisance between a long grappling with the indisputable demands of nature, and the requirements of outer form, that, synchronizing over stretches of time, have produced civilization. Michael's face was the most purely aristocratic face I have ever seen, the kindliness, weariness, integrity were all there, in that almost too exquisite refinement—in which one could sense the apotheosis and end of a chain.

However, though there was no shadow of dowry in my background, the year before I came "out" I was proposed to by a very rich young man. His family, in the last twenty-five years, have achieved the "social top," wherever that may be. But at the time of his proposal, he was somewhat in need of that nebulous absurdity I was thought to possess: "social position," so he proposed in the lounge room of his steam yacht, both amusing and alarming me by bolting the door for action first! After expressing his desires, he cried out: "And my father says he will give me an extra million if you accept," at which moment I discovered my worldly education also had borne no fruit, for scanning his profile, I immediately forbade him the liberties of a fiancé, although discretion not being dead, I told him that he could write me while I was in Europe, if he wanted to.

In fact, it was one of these letters to Paris, mentioning again the extra million, that sent my sister into paroxysms of disapproval. "Don't you realize how dreadfully difficult things are for Papa, and what on earth do you expect?" But I knew that I expected thrill and rapture to go with this great acceptance on which was to pivot all my life. Let the Damoclean sword of poverty—of "not being able to keep up," of "a pretty girl must marry money," of "you are so helpless, what can you do?" "You have no idea how fearful it is to be without money!"—let the gibbering go on. Thrill and rapture must go with the acceptance of this tie of ties.

CHAPTER VI

The Golden Mask

THE MORE unattractive the houses we lived in, in New York, the more pertinent to life was the theatre, yet I don't suppose at first I was any more in love with it than most romantic girls of fourteen. I was thrilled when the "foots" went up, and the golden masks on either side of the stage showed their eternally sardonic black gashes of eye and mouth. I lived through the play with the actors, and when the curtain went down, felt chaotically forsaken and had to be born back again into the commonplaceness of my own existence, for dynamically commonplace it was getting, now that my mother's and father's youth seemed to have come to an end with Lily's marriage, and they no longer had her friends to flirt with. Indeed, so much bickering went on, that often I had to turn on the taps in the bathroom to drown it out, and then staying at home so much, they were more critical than formerly.

"How well do you know a gentleman, Miss," said Papa, poking his head into the parlor one late afternoon, "when you don't trouble to rise from the piano stool to bid him good-by! And furthermore, what right has a child of your age to receive a man who already has one broken engagement to his discredit?"

But the theatre: the theatre was Nirvana from the stuffy apartments in New York, and from the autumnal atmosphere of 64 Kay Street, where, around October, voices would be raised in argument as to whether or not we could afford a town house.

To the Opera House at Newport in the fall and early winter season, came travelling stock companies, some with real merit, and I looked forward to the change of bill with immense excitement, for at the end of even an act, it seemed that the mantle of the players had fallen upon me; surely I thought, as I looked at myself in the pier-glasses of the lobby, this is not my pallor, it's Nazimova's, why she's given me a face!

And during the entr'actes, inebriate with borrowed glamour, I would let something of the expectancy I felt toward life appear in the glances I cast upon strolling gentlemen and boys.

And, of course, I fell madly in love with certain actors: Mansfield, in "Old Heidelberg," what a sinister charm his glass eye gave him! Shea in "Doctor Jekyll and Mr. Hyde" —years later Jack told me what a magnificent actor Shea really was—and then in a lighter mood there was Donald Brian in "The Merry Widow"; I remember going to a matinée of it once with my mother, and having her turn to me in the darkened theatre filled with the romantic sensuosity of Lehar's gay music, to say, "How wonderful to be seeing this at sixteen!"

I wanted nothing from actresses, however, not even

their autographs; and it was only with a contemptuous amusement that I accompanied one of my schoolmates, lovely Dorothy Hayden, backstage one Saturday matinée to a rendezvous with Maxine Elliott, then at the height of her Junoesque charm. Outside the star's dressing-room door I kicked my heels, wondering what on earth could be the good of going in to see an actress. Only people who could give you feelings interested me, and I decided one must become brave enough to commit anything just for the chance of feeling something. But an actress? What was the use! Nothing could happen! And going home I underscored in Oscar Wilde's *Dorian Gray*; "I had a passion for sensations, etc." And with what a fine fury my father, coming across these markings later, flourished the book above his head while he cried out with infinite scorn: "Miss, what does this mean?—YOU HAVE A PASSION FOR SENSATIONS!"

But that day, waiting outside Maxine Elliott's dressing room, my friend came out to tell me that in the kindness of her heart she had asked Miss Elliott if she might bring me in also. "But I don't want to go in," I said; "I much prefer not seeing her, really."

It was my "passion for sensations," however, that had led me into achieving the Brearley School. A very innocent embrace pulled the trick—necking had not been invented. I had gone to stay with my schoolfellow, V. A., and one evening on the porch of their family's summer home at Staten Island, I was removed for good and all "from the outside looking in."

It happened rather in the manner of Turgeniev, in June, after dinner on the porch. I had been left alone on the piazza with V's attractive brother, who could look at pretty girls with a very ecstasy of appreciation from under his long lashes, and in a darkness scented by the powerful wistfulness of syringa—to which was added the drama of transatlantic liners coming up the bay—their bands playing—H (we were fortunately close together on a sofa) had turned to me in this night gone already strange with premonitory feeling, taken hold of my hand—held it hard—when for the first time I sensed that current of unity, which in some tradition of understatement we call Life. And for the first time knew that my reaction to this rarity would never be fear, but only gratitude, which came upon me a few moments later with my tears.

So now, with new currents stinging my circulation, why should I eat more than half of what my mother put on my plate? Surely your lovers preferred you thin; and was I never to learn anything outside the "Rosa Classes"? For I was tired to nausea of reacting to the idiosyncrasies of my nine schoolfellows! their toilettes and mentalities, and lately whenever dainty Alice Kortright, tossing back her corkscrew curls, started off on Robinson Crusoe—lit on Robinson Crusoe one might say, like a dismayed butterfly— I could have screamed! And again for some months Miss Webb, whose placid stomach bulged so uninvitingly over her eternal white sash (that I always thought must be attached to her very navel by the gorgeous pearl pin she affected), had, when anything went wrong in the class, taken to raising her arm and informing Miss Tomes (in secrecy a few moments later) that the spilt ink or missing penwiper could undoubtedly be laid at the door of "Miss Oelrichs."

"I want to know something!" I cried out to my mother (no longer stupefied with overeating), "I want to leave the Rosa Classes!"

"Why, I thought you were quite popular now," said my mother. "Popular?" I retorted! "Why the girls fight for my arm in Bryant Park, but I want an education. I want to go to the Brearley." And finally, between their more pressing arguments, my parents assented.

It was unfortunate for this enterprise that I had already become engrossed in the "Russian Nihilists" whose pictures I had lately been studying in the Sunday Supplements, as they moved forward with difficulty it seemed, a dark chain of men and women, across dismal steppes of Siberian snow. What had made them so indifferent to all the agreeable sensations of Life; must some men be guided by a Light so distant that practically no one else saw it? Had life no flavor, no meaning, unless they could precipitate upon mankind that "Better Life" foretold by the Prophets?

And the story of Buddha fascinated me; that a great prince should have become so obsessed by the problem of suffering humanity, that he could tiptoe off from his wife and new-born son while they still slept in the pale light of dawn, and, hanging his jewelled orders on his charger's neck, strike out through his own gate to be, as Wells described him, "just a lonely man walking toward Benares." It all seemed to me most extraordinary.

For, by what amazing secret steps had his spirit approached such a unique crisis; surely he must have felt that out of his loneliness would come a peace and a power to help the suffering that so obsessed him.

At first all went well at the Brearley. The principal, Mr. Crosswell, figuratively patted me on the back for being the only girl who had ever written him herself to request entrance, and yet my reverence for this school was undermined from the start by discovering that I must spend the same amount of time with subjects loathed, as with those loved.

English and History, which I adored, only for three 15-minute periods a week. Really more time spent on Latin than English! Latin a dead language—what would you need it for but to read inscriptions on tombs, which did not seem an occupation I would ever covet! And English meant poetry in which I was already wildly interested! And why in God's name did I need any Botany? To look at a flower was more than enough, and how, with my flighty attention rushed and mazed, in all these 15-minute periods, changing at the clang of a bell, would anything at all penetrate into that remote recess with its narrow gate— my Mind!

I need not have posed the conundrum. After the first few months of becoming submission, practically nothing did— which was amply visible one morning, when I sent in my Algebra paper with nothing written on it but my name and the date.

A few days later I stood before the great headmistress herself, rage electrifying her topknot of red hair and deepening the dusk of her strawberry skin, while she shouted, "No girl in the Brearley School has ever sent me in such a paper! Are you trying to be impudent, or do you know nothing?"

"Nothing, Miss Eaton, absolutely nothing about Algebra," I told her, and an alarm bell was rung to conduct

me to the principal. Of course, I had been too frightened
to confide that owing to my weakness in Algebra, my seat
was always in the second row in the classroom, so that Anna
Street, my gallant supporter, had been able to do all my
sums for me, leaving me in merciful ignorance of a loathed
subject.

Also, I might have added that our "Math" teacher, the
beautiful, if sallow Miss Arnold, who wore her hair in a
Psyche knot, and resembled Iphigenia bound and delivered up for slaughter, had seemed to entertain, from the
first, an aversion to finding out exactly where I stood;
Miss Arnold, who really taught her class with an ennui
so tragic that it was communicated to me, expressly, I used
to think, in the form of a vapor that I might be kept in
merciful ignorance of a detested study.

However, after a good cry on Mr. Crosswell's shoulder,
and a reminder on his part that a Class 4 girl who had
taken a prize in essay writing, over the "tops" in Class 8,
should not be mortally worsted by mathematics, it was
contrived that Miss Arnold and I should face each other
in some bitter hours of private tuition and supernatural
boredom that came of course to nothing.

But in my second year at the Brearley, interest in the
Russian Nihilists crept up on me, to my catastrophic undo-
ing. For pictures of a tense circle of men sitting around a
table in a cellar beneath a lamp, which could be instantly
shadowed—looking with their crude faces and bulging
foreheads, I thought, rather like those waxen groups of
money forgers in the chamber of horrors at the Eden
Musee as they drew lots for who should throw the bomb—
caused me to wonder if it wouldn't be a good idea to intro-
duce some of this dynamic "planning" into the Brearley.

After all, I had increasingly nothing to fall back on there but a sense of malnutrition, of a dozen things shoved into my mouth that the "time periods" fiendishly extracted again, before I could taste, let alone chew.

So I became the president of a club bent upon minor forms of destruction, and in each other's houses in true Russian fashion, the one drawing the ace of spades from the pack was prepared to ignite the fuse. Of course what we did was preposterous—false calls for fire drills, caps placed neatly under the teachers' feet so that mild explosions followed them wherever they went, or a little of Papa's Irish whiskey insinuated into our "Math" teacher's tomato soup at recess—and yet the madly excited laughter we had from our crimes was a pearl beyond price. But one day, after carelessly outlining a plan through the lavatory shutter, to one of my waiting henchmen, and undeterred by her coughs, I emerged to find a teacher frigidly washing her hands and my friend fled.

Nothing was said then, but my desk was almost instantly searched, incriminating evidence discovered, and after a second emotional scene with Mr. Crosswell, whose charming kindliness could not help me this time, a letter was dispatched to my mother exhorting her to find another school for me in the autumn.

I left without regret, and with something rather hardboiled in my attitude, that came, I think, from sensing that, incredibly as I had behaved, still and withal I also had been somewhat duped in this contact.

For to me, Miss Dunn, our stout little English teacher, was the only one who had given me something directly from what she amounted to herself; Miss Dunn, with her dark hair so neatly parted in the center over such a demure whimsical face. She lifted our stodgy, unformed spirits up on the grace of her own wings, and brought us through the blitheness of her humor and wisdom into the circle of the great poets; and listening to their mighty English spoken so keenly through her mobile lips, one avenue of knowledge at least was given the stamp of allure. And never could Miss Dunn have been so towering an exception if the contrasts to her were not as arid as I believe they were.

Naturally the Brearley, a sedate and distinguished school with points to get to, and standards to maintain, could hardly have cut their curriculum to fit the slow powers of absorption of a lazy dreamy girl. But I as honestly believe that the dryness, the unliving quality of most of our teachers not only toward us, but especially toward what they taught, makes it possible to say that when a girl does fail in such a school the fault is not altogether hers.

What tired atoms they seemed; how conscientiously burdened with theories derived from conferences and books! Never did they come to you with a wise and robust Self, with the exception of Miss Dunn, who really was able to magnetize and therefore to teach.

I think it worth noting here, as I speak of what passed for my education, that although I was left in no doubt that marriage with a rich gentleman was my "Alpha and Omega"—in other words that Society and Domesticity, if I were fortunate, would encircle me forever—and I remember once at Bailey's Beach years later, how brutally I pulled a topknot of curls from my mother's head, in a sudden tempest of despairing grief at such prospects—still not the slightest effort was made to make me understand what either state was about. In distinct contrast to my mother's education during which the bottling of quinces, perfuming of household linen, creating attractive menus for all weathers, and attending to the complaints of the people who served you, had become second nature. "If only you had been given a chance," Jack used to say, "and been brought up on Staten Island by a nigger valet like I was; why my father used to forget about all of us for months at a time!"

So then, never having had Jack's ineffable opportunities, I came to realize how as she grew older, my mother's sense and vitality were marred by her hectic environment. After all, her upbringing had been that of every one around her, but mine emerged from a household like other households around ours, in which nerves, haste and mortal insecurity, while keeping up a front, knocked the face of time into a chaotic mask behind which it was difficult to make out what the realities were. And then she loved me so very dearly, why should I have to do any more than the rich girls with whom I mostly consorted?

CHAPTER VII

Expelled Again

A FEW months after my expulsion from Brearley I heard with some irony that I was to go where Lily had passed two admirable years. She had been a Child of Mary with a Blue Ribbon royally slanted on her black uniform almost at once.

The first morning after my arrival at Manhattanville Convent, a dreary structure of brownstone standing in the midst of a park especially designed, I thought, for the shackled pacing of madmen, I saw by the streaks of dawn in my room a nun who, touching her taper to my gas murmured: "Jesus, Mary and Joseph." "Why, what the hell!" I shouted incredulously—a silence freighted with a ton of bricks and eternal damnation—"why, Blanche, were you not told the responses?" she then inquired, with that stony patience of the religious, and after another arid pause I muttered back "I give you my heart and my soul," ready to sob with shock and melancholy, which was not dispelled by hearing, a few moments later, that hieratic solemn ageless sound of prayer in unison going on directly outside my door. "Ave Maria gratia plena Dominus tecum," a long line of girls, clad in black, with black veils over their heads, were chanting, as slipping in amongst them we walked through gray halls with huge brown folding doors, past statuary of the bleakest white (sentimentalizing the grand to the point of nausea), toward the Great Mystery of the Mass, and such a rotten breakfast!

Meals have always been important to me, and it was at the Convent repasts that I first noticed girls who had mashes, dreamily drawing each other's eyes across the detestable soup while a Nun read aloud from modern Catholic literature—fortunately uncomprehensibly—upon a raised dais at the end of the room.

Now this state I have always left to strictly take care of itself, but on that day I remember how it all offended my taste, and emphasized my isolation, for certainly you couldn't tell any girl who was enough of a fool to waste such a glance on one of her own kind, about how Donald Brian affected you when he did the Merry Widow waltz.

No one, however, got a mash on me. The only emotional response I elicited being one of rage, when a coffee-skinned Cuban caught me on a stair landing one night, to hiss in my ear: "I breaka your face"; which she did not do, only because of my superior brutality.

Nor did I ever become a "Child of Mary." Indeed, I was expelled at the end of three months for participation in a midnight supper of chocolate creams and *foi gras* sandwiches which had lain secreted in my underclothes since my mother's visit some days before. Never shall I forget the apparition of a nun attired for the night, who caught me as I came back along the hall exuberantly giggling, her drained face and turbaned head so like the "Death Mask of Marat" after his murder in the bathtub. This crisis, having taken place in the room of a girl already suspect, culminated in a morning message to my mother to call for me immediately.

She came next day in a hansom cab, and driving back through lamp-lit Central Park in the early evening, I told her there were only two things I would never forget about the Convent. Mother Burnett, our Mother Superior, who, after a tragic love affair had, on the advice of the actress, Mary Anderson, espoused Roman Catholicism and who looked in her nun's habit, with her piercing eyes and beautiful, emaciated features, like one of the twelfth-century Gothic-Madonnas—one of those "chefs-d'œuvre" of a great period—when Faith was still young and agony a genuine part of it.

How wonderful to let your grief turn you into a Work of Art, I would muse as I gazed at her agonized, haggard beauty while she knelt in prayer during evening vespers— the only lovely moment of the day; for then the hideous stained-glass window behind the altar had the sapphire of nightfall to retrieve it—the floor smelt of wax and was flooded with light from the taper that each nun carried. Another day was done; and ever I marvelled by what incomprehensible turnings of mind and heart, inconceivable twistings of a single blow, anyone could have come to sacrifice freedom under changing skies for this grotesque imprisonment.

If only instead she had gone to Egypt by herself with a good maid, and sitting alone, mysterious and lovely on the terrace of Shepheard's Hotel—which I understood recruited guests from all four corners of the earth—then surely some one else would have come up the steps towards her with outstretched hands. And again I had a certain contempt for anyone, who, young and beautiful, retires from the arena of life after a single bat on the head.

Nor would I fail to remember the parched face of "The Bride of Christ," who knelt on a *prie-Dieu* all night outside our dormitory door, her eyes glassily raised and fixed upon planes that lifted her surely into perpetual ecstasy, since no maniacally frequent trips of mine to the toilet could dislodge one iota of that transfixed regard. It was the expression one sometimes sees on the faces of the dead, tranquil, amused; and it was worth cold feet to have been touched by its strange dream.

By the most fortunate chance for me—for to this period I owe what little education I have—it was discovered that a cough I had been barking into every one's face for a week at the Convent was really whooping cough, so that isolation was *de rigueur*.

Miss Eleanora Tomes (from the Rosa classes) was now engaged to take on this first and last lap. But outside the restrictions of the classroom, all the whalebone vanished from her bodice, she was relaxed, charming, amenable at last to my own ideas on education.

She gave me to read a *Life of the Painters* and I could go to the Metropolitan and look up works by the Masters I was studying about, or stand for half an hour if I wanted, in front of a Botticelli, until those extra large wild flowers in the grass beneath the feet of "Prima Vera" became real enough for picking, and the guards cried out "closing time!"

I studied architecture from books, but checked with models at the Museum. She directed my reading, telling me: "Read Poe if you want to, but all of Poe then, and nothing else for months until you have finished, and then write me something about him." And I did.

How glorious it was to study like that! The waxen icy figures of Poe's dark majesty of thought and style got really under my skin. I felt the wild beauty of his uncompromising pilgrimage. It seemed to me a picture in black and white with lightning always in the sky. And I was so touched by his integrity toward his gifts that would never allow him to praise what was unworthy, or to be used in any manner except at his genuine best, and literally when not to do so would have lifted himself, and the ailing young wife whom he idolized, from the bitterest poverty.

I thought him the moon's own son, veiling and disposing his elliptical sardonic rays on a half-frightened gang of poseurs, the New York Literati! How terrified they must have been to have their effusions come under his scrutiny! He was one of the few writers whose personality penetrated so sharply through his work that it seemed to me the man himself appeared with all his magnetism intact through his writing, in the way a great actor does through his role.

But there was one study which I neglected to my lasting regret, and that was music. For years I had been picking out both hands of various operas and popular tunes, while making some feint of studying the piano, when one day Professor Klein, my well-known teacher, with his dark and rather distraught head, informed my mother that I undoubtedly possessed talent, and should be made to practice, and later on take Harmony, Composition and Orchestration, since he was convinced I would ripen into a composer if properly disciplined. But how much easier it was to complain of headache than face a page of music which I could play by ear anyway if I tried, so Professor Klein's desires for my discipline remained unrewarded, and he stopped wasting his time alongside my laziness.

And what a jackass I felt years later, when, coming into the Empire Theatre for a rehearsal of "Clair de Lune," Frank Tours, the leader of the orchestra, handed me his baton, feeling of course that since he was playing a complicated music score, a melange of compositions—by Debussy, Faurè, and myself—I must thoroughly understand the technical side of music; and of course there was no use telling him that I had composed these ballets and dances at the piano, memorized them, and had them taken down by a real musician.

August morning—the bees hum over the window boxes, cool green in the shadow of the awning, and the green outside reflects in the silver of the breakfast table, always polished up to the nines, which is set for all of us except Tibi, who is served on a tray bristling with silver and cheerful china in her bedroom.

There is a big tea cup at Papa's place, and how immaculately, if heavily, he comes in, in his light suit with the pearl pin in his tie, his thinning hair beautifully slicked back, giving off an odor of toilet water, as his handkerchief does of cologne. But in spite of his tan, his face is sallow, a slight paunch commences its deteriorating down-dragging motion beneath his belt. His eyes are worried and blinking (a lawsuit is under way with Aunt Tessie!) as, adjusting his pince-nez, he props a newspaper against the teapot and commences to read absorbedly and eat without zest.

Charlie enters in a kind of heavily agitated flash, his athlete's chest thrown out, looking bewildered, a step ahead of himself, as if he suddenly realized that he had kept on running after the finishing tape was broken. He eats in a fever and finishes by throwing his knife and fork together with a crash that makes Papa look up at him in cool animosity. "It's a wonder they landed on his plate," I think to myself, as Harry the Teaser saunters in, freckled, good-looking, and, lowering his gangling length into a chair, exposes toward breakfast and everything to do with it a rake's sullen distaste.

To what end am I placed amongst these people? What on earth have I in common with any of them, I think, fixing my eyes on a silver platter pyramided with cherries that seem to be magically reflecting the garden green along their polished surfaces. Why do I live in a constricted intimacy under the authority of strangers? Because only my mother knows me, it is only her I love, and can it be good for people in whom I detect such temperament to eat large breakfasts on a burning morning? Ah, but supposing they were dead, beyond any pleasure in breakfast, laid out in their coffins in that peculiar waxen stiff alienation of death; and then a lump, which would never have gathered for strangers, rose in my throat.

The family tie—how irritated, even crazed I was by its pull, subconsciously sensing then, I dare say, that all through my life rotations of pity and fury, close relatives of love, would cause division in my heart and aims.

But soon the electric Victoria would come scrunching up on the blazing gravel, the chauffeur might even slyly whisper as I got in dressed for tennis, "Good morning, Glory!" and free of the hot and heart-breaking little house with all its restless irritation, and overtone of worse to come. The tennis balls would be happily clicking on my bat, flying through the blue air, accompanied by a wonderful sense of acting if my bold strokes arrested charming ladies into watching me as they strolled along in elaborate dresses accompanied by gentlemen wearing the right hatbands. For now I was good at tennis and had lately come off the courts, purple in the face after winning the Girls' Singles. Indeed as Striker, the famous professional of those days, told me, "You have a hard stroke, Miss Oelrichs. If you can learn to keep it up and use your head a little more you will get there every time."

An oasis, that gradually disappeared as a mirage, was a bequest a few months previously to my father, of half a million dollars from my epicurean uncle, Herman Oelrichs, who had lately calmly died of heart failure returning from his Carlsbad cure, on one of the North German Lloyd vessels where he always good humoredly quaffed his tankard at the captain's right.

If this legacy had materialized, it would have largely altered the course of my father's life, saved him, I believe, from the haunting pathos of his death.

For Downtown was getting too much for him. His character, proud to the point of arrogance, was utterly unable to adapt itself to the new degree of scheming—fawning, intensive alertness—ever ready to relax into brutal indifference, and the at all times genial ability to look the other way when some one was being choked off, which the new day required.

"No man ever made over a million dollars honestly," he would say, and I would hear him speak with an hilarity under which I detected outraged pain of the doings of some of the railroad kings who, with their wives, were now bearing down heavily on Newport's obsequious response.

Why, I wondered when his decency revolted so, to the point of lethargy and inanition to what was going on, did our lives continue in tacit co-operation with all the non-sense? Charlie was to be pressed into the turmoil and go shouting from Monday to Friday down to the Exchange where Papa had lost his wondrous singing voice, and the more jacked up the key of expenditure by persons whom my father now designated as actual bandits, the more necessary it seemed not to dive anywhere in order to escape them, but to breast the maelstrom in its own terms, by snaring a super one from whom the inferno would take orders.

However, my aunt Tessie, possessing several millions as did her sister, Mrs. W. K. Vanderbilt (Papa adored good-looking little Willie, years younger than himself, and any homecoming from a jaunt with Willie was always a signal for flying plates), did not relish her late husband's disposition of his money, added to which the laws of California, where my uncle drew up his will, decreed that you cannot exclude your wife. So naturally with her right smart feeling about money, Aunt Tessie was not prepared to pass up what she had a legal right to, and after some flying mud had been gathered up for public consumption in the dailies, Papa was advised by his lawyer and brother-in-law William Jay, to compromise for half the amount. Of course, Uncle Herman had never dreamed that his wife would want the money; he was probably no better judge than my father of people unlike himself.

And after this incident, my father, with the devil-may-care attitude of incurable bitterness—for in his inertia there was no peace—proceeded to live mostly on his capital and Charlie was told he was to go into harness right away. Poor Charlie, I would think, what right has Papa to expect him "to take it," especially when he always looked at my brother so irritably that I felt he could not possibly understand him?

Indeed, this half a legacy had an ill effect on my father. It released him from the immediate pressure of having to work in order that we might eat, and yet because he was already so impregnated with the feverish values surrounding him, it never occurred to him that we should be able to live on the income of his principal. So that our existence continued in the sour distress of essential maladjustment and danger.

How I longed to get away sometimes from all the contradictory nonsense, and a pang is preserved through the years, of hanging over the stair-landing one night, with the hall gas and the parlor oil lamps beating up their inferno of heat into my face, as I listened to my parents discussing whether or not I should be allowed to visit a school friend in Ilseboro. Oh! how badly I wanted to go! And it seemed at one moment I should be able to, when the "who-was-she" element came in. Apparently they only knew by name the brother of my schoolfellow's mother, and, of course, that was not enough, so I was not to get away after all! And what dismal pain I suffered as I stood there, and that sensation of injustice so horribly enraging to youth which senses, at any rate, its trapped helplessness.

"I am engaged to be married to Marjorie Turnbull," Charlie announced to Papa one lowering morning, and when the answer to whether she had any money or not was nearly in the negative, my father went up in smoke. Charlie was just out of college, and what any one's prospects were was becoming an increasingly obscure subject, only to be disposed of apparently in surges of irritated warning. "You'll only regret your marriage once, and that will be always!" Papa shouted, adding to this *coup de grâce* a suggestion that Charlie go around the world for a year to those places I had watched my brother thumb so endearingly on the maps—at his, Papa's expense.

It was a generous offer, but my brother, being a romantic in the Austrian manner, would not take it up. After all, this dictum was against every precept of his upbringing. A girl married money, but a gentleman supported his wife whether he could or not, and Charlie was much too naïve to join me in my eerie intuition that beneath much that you were told ran a secondary motive of exact contradiction.

My "sister-in-law to be" was a beautiful girl of Acropolean proportions about whom no one could ask "Who was she?" because she was of the very best. Her skin had a strange white transparent look, as if the last snow before spring had melted beneath it; and she had quantities of richly golden hair (from the mint of heroic days, I thought), while her eyes had that kind of placid, naked largeness in her face one saw in the mosaics of the Byzantine Madonnas. And in the depths of her heart she was a true Madonna, for in her love for her child was her only real life.

Marjorie's attitude toward what she supposed to be the glamour of Newport life filled me with a sort of hunchback's distorted pity. She was so like a little girl rushing toward the lights of her birthday cake. And I thought if only she knew what was beneath it all, of cheapening and hardening, and if you were nice enough, misery, on account of whatever it is inside of you that will not turn to stone.

On Good Friday, near the date of my brother's wedding, I had just come home from the Three Hours' devotion with my mother. We were seated in the dreary brown library of our Fifty-fifth Street house that missed no clatter of the Madison Avenue cars, eating from trays an Austrian luncheon of cold salmon and pickled onions. It was oppressively hot, and my golden-haired, pale-faced sister-in-law was meekly weakly with us; and as she and my mother talked of Marjorie's approaching marriage, it seemed that every sentence was warped with apprehension about money. Oh, I thought, with a sudden vertigo of absolute despair, is there no peace anywhere? No time at which to expect the exchanges of life to grow sacred and sweet with wisdom and dignity? Is there nothing on which we can count in our American life except harassment?

Of course I saw something of girls whose lives had more security than mine, whose families, although very rich and living in Newport, were conspicuous by their avoidance of the society rush. The fathers sailed "fifteen-footers" with their sons in the afternoon instead of drinking in the Reading Room; the mothers seemed to be always placidly sitting at home, which impressed me for only a short time, since, although these children were kept apart from the wicked blaze of fashion, I noticed when lunching with them that this had been replaced by a domestic torpor of staggering density.

To take a meal with them was to look dulness squarely in the eye—oh, the barbaric insularity of their clannish dialogue, their oafish jokes and silences! I would regard them from under smouldering lids, furious that, having left an atmosphere favorable to the consideration of whether or not the cotillion favors at Mrs. Fish's next ball were to be of silver or gold, I had not at once discovered people interested in telling me something further about my old friends, "The Russian Nihilists."

In the spring after my brother's wedding, we went abroad. I had felt the decks listing under me in my dreams for years, and couldn't sleep properly for months before sailing.

On my first May morning in Paris I walked out on the balcony at the Hotel Magellan, and saw the sun shining upon avenues lined with trees just coming into full leaf. A woman walked by in black, carrying a basket of long loaves, and strangest of all sights, two workmen in blue jeans sat on a bench turned affably sideways to one another, smoking and talking.

Paris was miraculous to me. The great open spaces of architectural planning lay on my mind like a balm after the concussional desiccated metropolis—New York—and here the din of life was subservient to men, not a roar, already swelling in New York, drowning, vilifying the spectacle of their doings, disrupting the design of their thoughts. And the Champs Élysées with the *marroniers* full out, and so many gay, frilled, beribboned *nounous,* clasping waxen dolls like infants to their enormous breasts— calling out shrill instructions to their slim-armed, slim-legged charges; whose fantastically lovely groupings and dartings about among the rich shade of the trees, and the guignols, seemed already a painting in movement. And best of all were the gentlemen in box coats driving mettlesome horses down that magnificent Avenue, who occasionally sidled toward the curb where I walked to look me over with gallant interest.

My sister lived in a lovely house on the Rive Gauche, 18 Rue Vanneau, in a continuous whirl of engagements. Her beauty had matured and brightened, and she was in those days savoring to the full the rare prestige of being young, very rich, and extraordinarily beautiful. Indeed, her beauty had become so striking in the glow of appreciation and success that when she took us to the theatre with her in the evening, I have seen practically every head in the lobby turn as she passed. I remember one little Frenchman in a bowler hat climbing excitedly onto a chair so as to miss nothing of "la grande beauté Americaine."

Peter complacently enjoyed his wife's success. Endless funds seemed to pour in from San Francisco. Their week-days were filled with lunch parties and dinner parties or meetings at the race track. And over week-ends they went to stay at the great country estates of their new friends, the Duke and Duchess de Luynes at Dampierre, the Duke and Duchess de Noailles. Apparently all was well. But I heard my father remonstrating with Peter for allowing Lily to stay up all night, for now, when the parties were over, apparently she was still unable to sleep, and they would go off to restaurants in the Bois, where she told me they collided with the deer coming out to drink in the early sunlight as they turned home at last.

And I thought again of Lily's terrific vitality. What would it do to her if it were never channeled, only spent! And yet nothing was expected of her except what she did so well. Of course, she might have artificially imposed on herself a few hobbies, some interest in charity, etc., but she would not have been her humorous—and I often think from the first—her despairing self, if these would have done her any good.

Was my sister happy? I could not tell! She seemed never really to listen to what was being said—especially when my father reproved her—but only to be humming a brave little song to herself and still looking at some distant thing.

My father spent a great deal of time at the Travellers' Club and Mama was at her beloved museums from morning until night. An intimation that Paris was the capital of pleasure and love was occasionally brought home to me by explosive scenes between my parents that were apt to continue until six A.M., when other guests in the hotel pounded savagely on the doors for quiet, or occasionally came in person to remonstrate.

And I sat in dim churches of forestial immensity, the light faltering down to me through immense triangular wheels of the rose-stained glass windows—saw showers of candles at the feet of Images lost in the darkness—peered through majestic grilles rearing up in front of me, dignifying again with removal, the Altar with its superb sanctuary of gold—concealing the Golden Cup in which lay the Lonely Wafer of Eternal Life! And at such moments I thought the Church did a great deal of good without having to make sense, because it purified the aspirations. And soon we were on our way to visit my aunt Nancy in Vienna.

Adolescence was ending. Soon after my eighteenth birthday I was to make my début. That would mean being grown up all of a sudden, evening parties, décolleté dresses and, above all, the official acknowledgment that I was now quite ready for suggestions concerning my great romance.

eee

Début and Engagement

ONE OCTOBER, with the maples throwing lemon-yellow shadows on the dark wet roads, it became apparent, in spite of the usual arguments as to whether a town house could be afforded to bring "the Baby out in," that I was going to come out anyway in an apartment at 925 Park Avenue.

So a month later in a dove-colored princess dress with a train, and a purple cartwheel of a hat, trimmed with huge startled bows that were upheld by wire, I started "pouring" at the "coming-out" teas of contemporary débutantes, and a few weeks later stood at last hatless at my own, to receive a stream of my mother's friends in our pink and gray drawing room.

In the summer before my début, I had attracted a few absorbing gentleman friends, some of whom were old enough to be my father. The ex-love of a famous actress ("How dare you call up my Baby," Mama would tell this one on the telephone, "a dissipated, elderly man like your-self"), a poetic cripple who looked up at me with a tender, beseeching whimsicality which I found irresistible; and a multimillionaire, with already one suicide to his account. Mama's greeting to him was usually "When you came to the house to see my elder daughter that was one thing, but the Baby!!!" And another young man who looked Mexican, Spanish, criminally voluptuous, but was in reality the kindest, gentlest fellow on earth, and I felt there was a challenging cachet in having him about, since he usually was "attentive" only to the cream of the married beauties. Cyril Hatch had, however, on account of his extreme charm (sensed by both my parents) been absolutely forbidden to see the "Baby."

That summer before my début, Papa worried himself into typhoid fever after the Stock Exchange panic of 1907. So Mama went to New York to nurse him, leaving me chaperoned by one of the dearest souls that ever lived, Miss Lillian Palmieri, whose heydey had been in the 70's. Yet age could not frustrate the grace of her slender poise on this earth and her blue eyes carried the innocent wistfulness of a girl who is going to meet her lover again next summer.

Miss Palmieri was amused rather than apprehensive at the attention paid me by my odd assortment of beaux, so during the six weeks of her chaperonage life and emotion drew perceptibly nearer. Between dates I would listen to, and never forget, her piano playing. I was leaning one day across the lower half of our heavy front door listening to "Miss Pam" playing the Funeral March of Chopin. I was gazing off to the end of our lawn, to where the elms stopped, and across the road the meadows began—their long grasses tipped with fog—that Newport fog bringing in with it the density of the ocean—when suddenly thoughts, feelings, never to be forgotten, came over me— and inarticulately I felt that if it were not for the music— the secrecies of my heart could never be lit up and trans- ported into meanings which need not contrive to find words —that without this music I could never so resign myself to sadnesses yet unknown.

One beau of that summer was near enough to my age to be seriously thought of, and he was a *prima* aristocrat; that is, in American terms. His family had been estab- lished in the same hardware or banking business for nearly a century. Indeed, an atmosphere of stifling respec- tability surrounded his progenitors, yet he himself was a gay blade who, having lingered for some years overtime at the Paris Beaux-Arts studying architecture, had stuff in him to give them grounds for severe apprehension. So this was perhaps why he was able to bring life nearer to me than any of the others. Then in his case I knew there would be no opposition to my marrying him, no question of "who was he!" However, although I spent many pleasant hours in his company that summer, he never got nearer propos- ing than to ask me how much I thought I could dress on a year,—which question, not subservient to more romantic ones, offended my taste and permanently cooled my ardour.

I enjoyed my début immensely. It was wonderful to fool my father by continuing my friendship with the "Mex- ican voluptuary" in the houses of my friends (and now reinforced by more interesting emotions), I waited with disinterested good humor for the proposal of W. I. But this eventuality was never looked for again after a visit I paid his family mansion for a dance his cousins were giving.

For next morning, coming on his white-haired mother playing solitaire in a mob-cap treated with mauve ribbons, in a house so still you were free to marvel at the incessant orchestrations of the clocks, suddenly I remembered Nietzsche's advice: "Live dangerously!" Then rushing to the telephone I contacted the "Mexican voluptuary," inviting him to meet me at the Savoy in an hour, where, through the most hellish betrayal of fate, we were discovered by Papa and treated the casual hotel loungers to a brilliant scene!

The balls in New York were all right, but I thought them less dramatic than in Newport, where you were likely to come across some distraught beauty in the dressing room lamenting a diamond bracelet that she just lost in a "bunker," or perhaps somewhere along the beach. And I remember the parties at 1 West Fifty-seventh Street, Mrs. Cornelius Vanderbilt's, especially, for their ornate dullness from which I would return to my glary blue bedroom, past rattling milk carts to find tall glasses of milk waiting to be consumed or emptied in the bathroom. For darling Tibi treated me on this "Cresta Run" toward social success, and a brilliant marriage, like an athlete whose condition must be sustained.

Tibi was unhappy that winter, but I was too absorbed with my own life and in any case not experienced enough to have understood her unhappiness, but it was already true that long years of nerves, strained to the breaking point, together with an environment of unutterable falsification of values, had done their work, alienating the external lives of my parents, although their hearts were to remain absolutely faithful toward one another until the end. "Faites jamais les reproches, s'ils ont merite, ils sont inutiles!" But my mother, with all her extravagance of temperament and perennial childishness, could never have accepted the cool wisdom of Madame de Sévigné, so reproaches were made, both merited and useless.

My engagement to Leonard Thomas came about like this. In that January of my début, the doctor announced that Tibi's plaster-white pallor, turning now to an ivory-yellow, was really pernicious anæmia. So it was decided she must sail at once for Paris to visit her sister, Mrs. Theodore Havemeyer, and take the injections of a famous doctor.

And in January we embarked, I feeling at one moment rather tragic about missing so many parties, and the next knowing Paris would be irresistible. As a proxy for the Prince Charming, to find whom I instantly ranged the decks, a short, elderly gentleman approached, and speaking of his great friendship for my father, invited me to lunch with him in the Ritz Restaurant. And as Mr. Frederick Prince, crafty-eyed, gray-complexioned, and with a monocle imperturbably anchored in his eye—even in the roughest weather—spoke to me of his polo ponies at Myopia, his hunters at Pau, his apartments in London and Paris, true to the main issue, I began to wonder what it would be like to be "an old man's darling"; from which charmless reverie I was rudely shaken as we debarked at Cherbourg by the appearance of a wife whom he had never once mentioned.

Mrs. Prince came languidly toward the gang-plank, heavily swathed in veils, and followed by a maid hung with cages of parrots. She had about her, I decided, that focusing kind of anonymity, belonging usually only to great

actresses, when this lady, looking impishly up at me from
beneath a hat that might have belonged to Whistler's "best
girl," told me that her son, who had also never been
alluded to, would call upon me the following day.

The cry of boys selling newspapers. All the nostalgic
personality of different European cities comes to me in that
shrill, somehow fateful sound—the things that have been
—the passing of time—the faintness of hope—because it
is dusk again, and I am a stranger wherever it happens to
be. I hear all of it in the newsboys' cry (maybe because
they only get going at twilight, always my difficult
hour).

So now in the early evening, in our lofty, high-ceiled
apartment at the Hotel Beausite (the rooms of which I saw
last year torn open like a doll's house by Communist
bombs) "La Patrie, La Patrie," went shrilling through the
twilight noises of Paris, and Aunty, her hair still dyed the
deepest black, her good-natured, charming face a sort of
strawberry patch of cosmetics and powder, trailed costly
chiffons about the vast salon, while obsequious salesmen
tried, and usually succeeded, in getting her horribly into
debt, over Gobelin tapestries, in spite of the constant jeal-
ous attendance of the musician of the moment—his unpub-
lished *opus* thick in the crook of his arm. How exceedingly
bad mannered and single-tracked these greasy-haired
geniuses were, I reflected! How I loathed their austere
brows, their obsession with themselves, and the gleam in
their eyes when they got anywhere near Aunty.

Almost immediately Mr. Prince, the conjurer, did pass
up an extremely handsome son, with the jauntiest blond

mustache, such gay good looks and laughing poise, and we fell in love over the first bouquet he handed me. Then just as it seemed to me quite certain we must be engaged, one day I walked under a ladder, and got home to find a farewell letter. Apparently Fred's father was sending him indefinitely out of Paris to conclude his studies in an obscure German university. But "he loved me and would come back for me some day."

On this I went off into a major depression, one of those sensorially agreeable conditions of grief, when you know that the "blow" did not matter really, because life is playing all around you, drawing nearer and nearer, so that this little setback is nothing at all, a mere sidestep in the mazes of a dance circling closer and closer.

Of course it was "Penniless Blanche Oelrichs" over again, and the theory of: "To him that hath shall be given."

Between her parties and her recovery in sleep, my beautiful sister would blow in to the Beausite, giving me boxes of bewitching hats, and advising me to accept the millionaire! But when she saw her advice was useless, she suddenly veered to the possibility of my becoming Lady Anglesey. God knows why! as I knew the Marquis only from his reproduction in newspapers, and didn't think he was a particular friend of hers. However, one night I was told to appear, looking my best, for the Marquis himself was expected.

Attired in a cerise dress trimmed with gold lace, and a Llack picture hat loaded with plumes, I went forward in Aunty's landeau to embrace my opportunity to become the Marchioness of Anglesey. And I remember how my heart quaked with excitement as the carriage dipped into the gutter and we passed under the "porte cochère," scrunching up on the gravel to the glass front doors that were flung open by a couple of footmen.

From the far end of the room my tall sister rose, and whispering to me that the Marquis had gotten stuck somewhere in his motor—I remember she spoke to me for some reason in French—she further informed me that I would sit next to Len Thomas instead: "one of our most popular and intelligent diplomats in Europe," whom she supposed I would not care for in the least.

Len Thomas, tall, slender, blue-eyed and fair-skinned, with a neat, well-groomed head and humorous mouth— an American to whom years of sympathetic living in Europe had given a cosmopolitan stamp—was charming to me, and soon teasing me about my sister's desire to have me appear to her new friends, as a European "jeune fille," fresh from the cloister, and in rosily terrified ignorance of life, desiring only to become the chastely reliable partner of a proper "partie."

Books arrived next day, his first present, the exquisite stories of Lafcadio Hearn: books! instead of flowers and candy! I was agreeably impressed; and now Mr. Thomas persuaded Tibi to let me take drives in his Panhard, chaperoned by Katie, whom we always dropped at the nearest confectionery. We would spin through Paris and its environs, sometimes even skirting the great forests of Marly and Fontainebleau, and I thought that these woods, sparsely etched in snow, looked more like canvases of the Franco-Prussian War as seen by the painter Detaille, than they did like themselves.

A few weeks later, one night in a box at the Opéra Comique, with lights from the set of Madame Butterfly flooding into our faces, and the sentimental music soaring up in surges of pathos, I felt that I was falling in love at last, and with a gentleman who had strangely enough never mentioned romance.

On the tail of this psychical innuendo, Lily arrived looking mysteriously disturbed and went into conference with Mama. I learned from behind the keyhole that "The Baby" must see no more of Mr. Thomas. "I never knew it when I introduced him to her," my sister exclaimed, "but now the woman is threatening to throw vitriol in The Baby's face when she walks in the Bois!" By this time on my knees, and glued to my post, I learned that the charming Mr. Thomas, the life of the Embassy at Rome and Madrid, had been for some time involved in a picturesque affair during which so many Roman candles had gone up that he had decided to retire from public life for a spell. So Len Thomas was someone I must not see—I had sensed it from the first! Otherwise he never would have been so attractive.

And now my friend, officially forbidden the door, met me at every conceivable point of my walks with Katie, and so soon as we had safely stowed her, off we flew in Len's Panhard; and our romance developed at ninety miles per hour.

April first, with spring ahead of time as it always is in Paris. A taxi stands before the brown door of the Hotel Vendôme and Len sits in it groomed in an immaculate fashion that for some reason always stands out, awaiting his rendezvous, blue eyes sparkling with amusement and excitement; for he has paid up, he is free, and he can tell a dark-haired slender young woman in the ankle length, tailor-made of the period, with a mushroom hat poised over an enormous pompadour, that he loves and wishes to marry her.

How memories crowd back of that time, and when I look back it appears that from the first, the love and tenderness with which Len dowered me resulted in all sorts of new awarenesses. That, for example, I had never noticed the beauty of outdoors until the spring of our engagement, when suddenly, driving in his open motor in the park, I felt how wonderful it was to exchange the streets for panoramas of earth and trees and flower beds, under the low yellow light of a wonderful sunset. I remember feeling the change to that freshness like a pang.

On an appropriate evening in May, at 925 Park Avenue, Len asked Papa for my hand in marriage. From my usual place behind the door I remarked that, although my father was affable, still it did not seem he was representing me in a fair light, when I heard him say, "Well, of course, Thomas, she's far too young to consider marriage now [I was eighteen]. Besides, she knows absolutely nothing and is extremely thoughtless as well! Why, she drops her pocket handkerchief every time she gets up without noticing it."

"Come on and hear—Come on and hear—It's Alexander's Ragtime Band!" A gay gaunt impish-faced little fellow, who I am told worked in a Greek restaurant, wrote, or rather heard, and probably picked it out with one hand, and maybe after a Sunday jaunt to Coney Island. At any rate, the joyful banality of his aria crashed the country. The "Bunny Hugs" went for it in a big way, and at my engagement, which was announced that August (in spite of Papa's warning anent my imbecility) during a dinner dance at the Clambake Club, it drove couples around the room in a perfect frenzy. Indeed every one was riotously gay, while Harry Lehr, still the jester of our family festivals, on this occasion proposed a great many invigorating toasts.

Years afterward, at a recital in Providence, I was to see myself at that party again through the eyes of one of the audience, who came up to me after I had done my "stuff" and said: "I will never forget you that night, Blanche Oelrichs, for you seemed so happy. I was standing in the crowd outside the window looking in, and I remember you were dressed in a white net dress embroidered with pink roses, and wore a beautiful sapphire ring with a diamond on either side of it on your engagement finger."

So on January 26, at 925 Park Avenue, Papa took me on his arm through an isle of white ribbons, through packed drawing rooms, toward an innovated altar beautifully decked with flowers, while a small organ played the Wedding March from "Lohengrin." And Lily's little son "Baba"—very cunning in his Eton suit and top hat clutched in the crook of his arm—carried one end of my court train, with minute Kathleen Vanderbilt, in a ballerina crescent of chiffon and lace, holding up the other.

CHAPTER IX

Just Before "Over There"

NEWPORT just before the Great War—Newport just before "Over There":—"Over There, Over There, Over There"—with its terrible pounding rhythm of burdened marching men.

Newport before the *Titanic* disaster that came as if some great stage manager planned that there should be a minor warning, a flash of horror—a mammoth ship sinking in a few minutes at night, with men and instruments that had just played "God Save the King" (how superb), and passengers hurtling down a deck that stood on end in the air, to be dropped like sprawling marionettes into the April chill of the water—and for the most part engulfed—before the real show, before what might with no exaggeration be called the most withering ride yet on record of the Four Horsemen.

Newport was brilliant that summer. I see it all through continuous sunlight and laughing gatherings of people at

Bailey's Beach with its brown belt of seaweed that concentrated a veritable stench of the ocean. And on the Casino lawns dotted with hatbands of the most exclusive clubs, and ravishing *dames du monde,* with chiffon parosols, mushrooming over enormous hats and pompadours.

Engraved invitations poured in on a young, good-looking couple, who were also fairly rich. Even when we sat down to dinner in our well-appointed red dining room, more requests for our company would be handed us on a silver salver by my good-looking footman, who later stole a copy of *The Picture of Dorian Gray,* nearly breaking up a valuable set of Oscar Wilde, if some sixth sense, merging his ascetic profile and Wilde's effusions, had not led me in a straight line to his bedroom to recover it.

"My dear, have you heard the young Archduke Franz Josef is coming to stay with Mrs. Goelet? There will be a huge ball with an old-fashioned cotillion." With whom should I dance it? I wondered.

"My dear, I hear Prince Troubetzkoy is painting your portrait." And he was, on the porch of our villa where I lay anchored in a Madame Récamier posture, dressed in white chiffon and lace, over rose-silk. Dear, huge, handsome, naïve, basso-voiced, Russian Pierre, afterwards to become one of my best friends. I would pose for him for hours at a time, listening to the bells of electric broughams and victorias and shaken harness of high steppers going by on Bellevue Avenue on the other side of the hedge, and also to the most enchanting things he told me about myself. But I was still untouched—apart from it all—in the dream of my childhood.

"He hasn't gotten you at all," said Len on the comple-

tion of the portrait, and I remember he traced my face with
his finger, stopping at the corners of my mouth: "Only
Leonardo could have painted you there—I think if I were
blind I could always see that," comes back to me that marvellous tribute to the child who had no real idea what he
was talking about.

In those last years before the Great War, Newport was
at its apex. The ballrooms still had an appearance of distinction, for they were graced by real beauty. Mrs. John
Jacob Astor, with her white hair and dark eyes, fresh skin
and slim lines, so accentuated at wrist and ankles, I remember the extraordinary lovely lines of her instep and foot:
sculped and isolated in a lit-up cabinet, it might have passed
for an extreme sample of breeding. Mrs. Robert Goelet and
Mrs. Craig Biddle, the "Whelan twins," so tall and slim,
their tiny heads crowned with dark wavy hair, their long-
lashed, blue-green eyes under winglike brows in such white
pointed faces. How beautifully they stood and moved! with
their evening dresses caught up under their breasts, wearing
fresh gardenias in their hair, their slim throats encircled by
necklaces of emeralds and sapphire, they were in their
long-limbed slenderness—dead ringers for what the imagination conjures up of the Empress Josephine at the time
Napoleon loved her so passionately.

The ballrooms had great cachet; and the gardens were
wonderful with the moonlight picking out marble steps,
and richly dramatic planting, while a waltz played in the
distance. That extraordinary pre-war gaiety of Newport!
In retrospect it is really quite dramatic, for it seems to me
that in those years, an age related in many ways to the ones
preceding it—Victoria and Pontius Pilate surely ripened

"The Balkan Royalty"

POST-WAR REUNION

"Len" with our boys Leonard and Robin Thomas

under tempos more similar to one another than ours to Victoria's—was wiped out, and superseded by what the Prophet in Revelation might well call "A new Heaven and a new Earth."

Hostesses were deliriously tossed between Hell and Heaven at the advent of royalty. The scramble was cruel. Football was dainty in comparison. The Archduke Franz Josef did arrive that first summer after my marriage. I remember the excitement in the air drifting in over my flowered window boxes from the direction of Bellevue Avenue, when I was told where I lay marooned, watching a sunset—My God! for I had some sort of indisposition and could not go to the ball—that Mrs. Goelet had just driven by with the Archduke, "young and pale and dark, with that fateful Hapsburg look," in her open calèche.

And the following summer nervous prostration was distributed en masse, ecstasies of suspense occasionally breaking for relief into hysteria—for the Grand Duke Alexander, the brother-in-law of the Tzar of Russia, was expected. Nicholas II! "Nicholas the Last" as I heard him called some years later by our "Intourist" guide when we passed, on our way into Leningrad, the private car in which the Emperor had signed his abdication, marooned in an open field.

I was presented to the Grand Duke at a dinner party given by beautiful Ava Astor, where I remember all the ladies lined up directly afterwards in the ballroom for their introductions. And I experienced a species of self-loathing for catching the mass nervousness before the Grand Duke entered. He was well over six feet, slim, dark, the acme of distinguished charm, with his delicate face, pointed black beard and Tartar slanted eyes. And this Grand Duke and

I became great friends. His drinking was a miracle of speed, his point of view genuinely romantic, and he had the penchant which I have noticed mostly in very rich people and royalties, for all sorts of spiritual quackery. However, he was both picturesque and disarming about the action of the "good and evil spirits," although one evening, years later, when we were having supper alone in Paris, he gave me quite a turn when, rising, he suddenly took a piece of white chalk from his pocket and drew a circle around my chair "to keep off adverse influences."

What is it that seeps out of idleness and privilege, defrauding the circulation of its real purpose to survive, compete, excel, and taints common sense until it perishes in hysteria, or in the complexes—as they are sometimes called today—of those who can afford to pay for them?

Around this time I was fantastically spoiled by every one, and feeling one day that Mrs. X, a dowager of great social importance, had nevertheless bowed to me with insufficient enthusiasm in front of the Casino, I actually wrote this lady a note that, while it reproved her for her bad manners, also commented unfavorably upon her nerve in sending in an acceptance to my next ball. When instead of getting as repartee two black eyes and a round of gunshot, her husband actually appeared on our lawn, spluttering apologies and exuding loyalty from every pore. While again of this vintage, I asked a friend of mine quite seriously as we stood before one of my latest photographs, dripping in all my jewels, "Don't you think I look like a Balkan royalty?"

"Why, my dear Blanche, don't you pose after dinner parties with scarves, in the manner of Lady Hamilton?"

said charming Mrs. Ogden Goelet. "You look rather like her, you know. And you should do something with that dramatic quality of yours." And I was greatly in demand for society tableaux in which, despite the promise I seemed to hold out, I was not "so hot." But I covered the scale from Lady Hamilton to the Empress Josephine, crown, train and all, surrounded by obsequious statesmen. Then one night I ran across the stage at the Beaux-Arts Ball shooting silver arrows into the wings as the Goddess Diana —to finally wind up before a startled audience as the Goddess of Liberty, into the costume and posture of whom I had, at the last moment, managed to inject a little punch.

Of course the life we led was futile, and without roots, nor were we using the capacities of any normal person. And yet all the same, I was learning immensely from Len, not because he laboriously taught me, but for the reason that I lived in the warmth of his appreciation for beautiful things.

I would see him walk swiftly over and pick up a lovely original faunlike head of the great Greek Period which we owned, with the same necessitous urge that made him reach for a glass of water. Then the subtlety of line that is seen by the master who is supremely alive himself—and so can report and arrest with all its rhythm intact the transition of living moods—would enter also into me as I stared along with him at the strange impervious face.

His love for Leonardo da Vinci became mine, and when I saw that mystic smiling, that almost sly amusement of the life and death wisdom looking from Leonardo's work, I would think how wonderful it is to live with great things, for their magic penetrates and lifts back veil after veil of

[115]

one's own consciousness. Something that is buried otherwise comes to life in you as you brood over great things.

And often before we went upstairs to dress for dinner in the darkening twilight, Len would play scraps from the Fifth and Ninth Symphonies of Beethoven, telling me as he struck the opening bars of the Fifth: "Could there be a finer motif for fate than that?"

"Why are American women so much better looking than their husbands and beaux?" was often the subject of my ruminations. Then one night, having heard of the arrival of the English polo players, we went to a dance at Phyllis Brooks' and I saw, standing just inside the arch of the ballroom, his arms folded on his breast, a man of extraordinary beauty, whose eyes, beneath a grand brow, seemed to be fixed in dreaming contempt upon the scene before him. "Why, it's Byron! Only taller and better looking," I thought, feeling that in a few seconds I would wake up at home in bed. However, a few minutes later, sitting out a dance with Lord Rocksavage on the balcony, I found that the spirit belied that flying head and amazing form, ambling along at the usual gait.

Yet the present Lord Cholmondely remains my first experience—Laurence Perrin excepted—of that haunting stamp of great beauty that brands memory, thrills open the distant vistas of imagination, brings one closer to one's self —enlarging, disturbing.

I went down often to the little house on Kay Street to see my parents, but it seemed that life was growing increasingly difficult for them. Papa had left off even visiting the eternal mob scene of the Stock Exchange and given his seat to Charlie, who must now provide my parents and his own wife and child with some income, which, in the savagery of competition well started in those days, was quite an infernal task for one of Charlie's temperament and equipment. Then on week-ends, when my brother appeared from the city, confused with the weight of his responsibilities, strung up to breaking point from the see-saw emotion of life on the Exchange, he would have less rest even than my father had had; for the tempo about him was faster, and beneath the social life that surrounded his young family were quicksands in which many of the standards of conduct presiding in other days uttered little bubbles and went down.

To watch the life of many families gave one the sense of a fuse travelling at a fine speed beneath some impossible fabric. For now in Newport the young married couples, who in my mother's and father's time had been exchanging a gallantry that was really chivalry and not likely to be dangerous to domestic happiness, were superseded by a set a good deal more in earnest over their forms of enjoyment. The *mariage à troix* began to be seen and accepted and every pretty woman had her beau—her serious beau—and defied the breath of scandal with amusing nonchalance, often leaving her electric brougham or runabout in the open road for all to see, near Paradise, or Hanging Rock, a spacious chain of virgin woods designed by Providence to get lost in with the right person.

My sister's life was a switchback of gaiety between Paris, London and New York. It had become impossible for her to sleep in country or city before five A. M. but now as I listened to her laughter, I thought "This is not light-hearted any more, this is more like delirium!" And it was only about two years later that, at a great ball in my sister's

house in Paris, given in honor of the young Duchess Antoinette of Mecklenburg-Schwerin, that Peter, in the midst
of banks of spring flowers, orchestra music and dancing
couples suddenly lost his mind and had to be led to his
room and put to bed. After this stroke of horror, until
his death, the following year, he was cared for like a little
child, receiving from my sister during those tragic months,
every devotion.

A little over a year after our marriage, on a blue-and-
gold morning in May, when you know that the apple trees
must be blindingly radiant regiments in the meadows, and
on the hillsides, my son was born at 9 East 81st Street.
And oh! the delicious calm of waking up, of coming back
to life after victory, miraculously well, beautifully slim
again, and even hungry for lunch, while I listened languidly to the May processions singing through the streets
on their way to Central Park. And then my son was
brought in on the crook of the nurse's arm, his tiny congested face, plume of hair, and minute hands with their
scattered waving, as touching as a sudden pang of heartbreak.

Of course, I had had the usual qualms as to whether I
would live or not, and driving through the Park with Len
in my plum-colored Victoria and pair, a month or so before
the baby was born, I wondered, as I noticed at twilight the
barren limbs of the trees growing hazed with buds, should
I ever see them in full leaf?

The first night I came downstairs after the baby's arrival, Len celebrated by having our good friend, Armand
Vecsey, the leader of the Ritz Orchestra, come up with a
dozen or so of his men to play for us, while along with Tibi

"LA GRANDE BEAUTÉ AMERICAINE"

Mrs. Peter Martin, afterwards the Duchess of Mecklenburg-Schwerin.

The Author When She Was Mrs. Leonard Thomas

"I was learning immensely from Len, not because he laboriously taught me, but for the reason that I lived in the warmth of his affection for beautiful things."

we drank champagne and enjoyed the orchestra to ourselves in the manner of the King of Bavaria.

But where was life—life itself—the struggle, the progression, the terrifying devastation of real ambitions or emotions? Life was agreeably ornate as a fairy tale, but a fairy tale was only wonderful by contrast with what you had had to go through to win the "forever after." And when had I jumped through any hoops of flame? Indeed there seemed to be a conspiracy about not to let me find any.

My boy was given into the hands of my cousin "Moppie" Iselin's "Nannie" who kept my inexperience and everlasting questions at bay with a firm hand, while the more professional mothers congratulated me on having such a wonderful nurse. "It would mean everything to the baby, etc., etc." And the baby's cheeks did look stout and pink, and gold came into the rings of his hair, curled in the English manner, while it grew more and more of a conceded fact that I could be of no possible use in the nursery. But where indeed was life? My Hungarian chef sent such delicious food to the table that I began to get a double chin. More portraits were painted that didn't·please Len. Our summer house contained a dining room so enormous that dozens of my friends were apt to drop in every afternoon and dance to improvised piano playing until it was time to dress for their dinner parties. My son slept cozily upstairs on a screened-in porch, insensible to the separation that his nurse maintained between us. A yellow and black Rolls-Royce waited to take me any place I wanted to go. Apparently I had everything on earth. Undoubtedly, as Mrs. Cooper Hewitt once said, "It was obvious to me from the first, my dear Blanche, that you were riding for a fall."

[119]

eee

Votes for Women

LEONARD had his first birthday in London, and I remember the look of that one candle throwing its soft light on his rosy excitement, with Helen Mackay, the first writer friend I had ever had, keeping me company. Indeed I was so anxious to see as much of Helen as I could that one evening, destined for a dinner party, I got into my brocade and jewels at four-thirty in order to be with her from tea time until the very last moment. How astounded she had been when she came upon me all dressed up like a circus queen in the afternoon sunlight, but years afterwards she told me that my comical eagerness had touched her.

London smelled like a room with a high ceiling which had been closed for a long time, and all the young Englishmen we had entertained in New York called on us immediately and were delighted to dine with us again.

A certain lady suggested that she take on my social career, to be arrogantly rebuffed—and I attended my first ball at Lady Herbert's (Michael and Sidney's mother) at Carlton House Terrace.

It was the quietest ball I had ever been to. Princess Dora Rudini, Princess Vittoria Colonna, Lady Diana Manners, the Duchess of Sutherland, all the great beauties in full regalia, sat about in high tapestry-backed chairs, over which leant in frigid devotion famous statesmen whom I recognized from their photographs.

And I recall thinking how attractive Mr. Balfour must have been as a young man, for there was about him that residue of boyishness often to be noticed in Englishmen.

The Prince of Wales was the guest of honor and very shyly he entered the room looking slim and blond, and with a kind of slant to his walk that suggested three-quarters of him would have preferred to be going the other way. But what stonily unreceptive eyes he had—from snubbing surges of loyalty I supposed.

Suffrage . . . votes for women! The militant martyrs of Women's Suffrage were throwing their stark fighting shadows upon that complacent conspiracy of Silence which is so much of England, and at a great charity ball I looked down from my box to see a woman in a tailored suit with a wild, rather noble face, dash in amongst the glittering crowd, to shout some indecipherable words before she was picked up shrieking and kicking in the arms of a Bobbie. Then, to my horror, the women at the entertainment closed in about her, brutally beating the struggling figure with their fans. A few days later, right in front of the Royal Box at the horse show, up sprang a woman to shriek straight into the mild face of George V, who in his gray top-hat, pepper-and-salt frock coat, Russian beard, violet boutonnière and all, gazed benevolently down at her—"Votes for

women! Votes for women!" No doubt she added something
rude at the end which accounted for the extreme brutality
with which she was caught up. Every one was so shocked, so
horrified, so against this one, who was out to get more of
the right of way for humanity's march against stagnance
of heart, retrogression.

And once again the old question turned over in the hazy
reaches of my mind, as to what it could be in the human
heart of splendor or unbalance which would put a cause
beyond all the comfort, pleasure and security of life.

Votes for women. The revolt had for me at first a sort
of scarecrow quality, ludicrous, sinister, pitiful. But surely
something dreadful must have been going on for a long
time to so unsex and madden these women! What had
baited them into all this? And then came the terrible epi-
sode of the woman who flung herself under the hoofs of the
Derby winner to be trampled to death, and as this woman's
funeral passed along the streets of London through crowds
that were respectful at last, I began to believe too, as many
another must have, watching the solemn cortège, that
anything you felt was true enough to die for, when not
a personal issue, was probably right and would come to
pass.

Then my Tibi fell for the Cause. That is, she lent the
green parlor at 64 Kay Street to "The Bengal Tiger"
(Mrs. Oliver Belmont) and to Mrs. Belmont's co-workers,
the militant suffragettes, and on a close afternoon the following summer, it was packed with society dames, fresh
from their lunches of eight courses, who controlled their
skepticism about suffrage, and the speaker Miss Alice Paul,

since the young woman was sponsored by Mrs. O. H. P. Belmont.

Miss Paul, her thin shoulders rising over us in a most unbecoming blouse, held forth with that taut unsexed projection of the fanatic (sometimes so curiously unappealing perhaps because it never holds the crowds' reaction as important as the message, is not part enough of the magnetism that ought to exist between crowd and speaker).

However, after examining the issue steadily for a few moments at the instance of Mrs. Belmont, I seemed of a sudden magically aware that suffrage was necessary, inevitable, without a true argument to be made against it, except by frumps, fools and knaves. So, throwing my hat into the ring, I was at once joyfully accepted, and exploited.

The papers carried headlines describing my alignment with the cause, not omitting Helleu's remarks on my looks; while my sisters in battle, to judge by the kind of jobs they gave me, took me for an engaging mixture of impulsive dumbbell and houri.

Some months after my alignment with the Cause, it was discovered that Mrs. Carrie Chapman Catt, the virtual leader of the party, would not be strong enough to carry the Suffrage standard at the head of the procession from Washington Square to 59th Street (in the last parade that took place before the vote was granted), so the honor fell upon me, the papers declaring that I had been chosen for this task from amongst hundreds of "American Junos."

The great day arrived, and I learned that President Wilson would review us from the grandstand at 42nd Street. Also my father received an anonymous communication which suggested that I might receive physical chastisement before I ever got there. It was a brilliant day in early autumn and the sidewalks of a completely empty Fifth Avenue were lined with tremendous crowds, as, dressed all in white and seated beside the Chief of Police in his clanging car, I was whisked down to Washington Square. There I could see regiment after regiment of women dressed in white, massed behind the Arch, and packed on every side street. Off we started, the band sounding with startling excitement in the canyon streets, and a terrible wind flapping my standard (which had to have its pole shortened at 34th Street by an obliging policeman).

My gentlemen friends leaned out of the window of the old Knickerbocker Club at 31st Street and Fifth Avenue, loudly cheering me as I came along with a great pounding in my heart, immensely exhilarated by the band, the dense closeness of the crowd, and whatever it was I was walking for. Indeed, I was so nearly carried away in some dream of exaltation that I had to be sharply reminded by a poke in the ribs that I had arrived at 42nd Street and must now halt the procession to salute the President! And there he was, a smile on his strangely carven face, lifting and waving his top-hat at us from the center of a packed grandstand.

But it was not until much later, when, my part done, I had come back to watch the procession from the Hotel St. Regis—it was only then, as the afternoon waned and darkened into night, while the white regiments came on and on, that I felt for the first time really the spirit of the cause for which I had walked—the claim of that long, long procession to win its point. The patient walking into the night of so many hundreds of thousands of women, the insistence, the belief of a new day in itself, in the midst of unbelief, the inevitability of a new day, expressing just before victory so long a term of suffering. The dignity and significance of those endless lines of white marchers under the street lamps was most touching! And I was proud to the point of tears at having walked with them.

eee

A Well-loved Visitor Appears with the War

ONE MORNING in England during the early summer of 1914, as my maid ran a brush through my hair on the balcony of our apartment that overlooked rows of the trim back gardens of Felixstowe—a watering place to which we had come for little Len—it was a sparkling morning after a night of rain—I heard for the first time in all my life, and yet without surprise, words that formed into a poem, which, writing down as quickly as I could, appeared later in my first book under the title of "The Youth and His Soul."

> "It is morning,
> The early star-sprinkled morning;
> Everything drinks and bathes;
> The down-flying shadows of birds
> Are dimly visible on the faces of brooks
> And upon the green shimmer of the trees.
> I am moved with a sweet expectation,
> A strange half-smiling restlessness" . . .

It was a strange hour for the muse to have made me her joyous first visit, for much of the happiness, complacency, illusion of the world was about to be overspread by the dark form of eclipse. The Archducal Pair had been assassinated at Sarajevo, and from the incomprehensible entanglement of European politics came rumors of war, which no one took seriously, but went on making their plans for summer amusement, while I walked a great deal by myself along the edge of the North Sea to return with my pockets bulging with poems.

"The echo of iron! the blasting of rock!
It breeds up a rhythm of vast syncopations,
A sound of the merging of hundreds of nations,
It's the noise of a forge, the forge of the world—"

But the German army started to march through an astounded Belgium towards France. Apparently the young Duchess of Luxembourg had gone out in her motor alone to see if she couldn't stop them, or at least get some idea of what it was all about, and M. Sazonov, the Russian Prime Minister, was asking the half-blind Lord Grey, with his strange owl-face—was evidently imploring him—to declare immediately England's position on the violation of Belgian neutrality. But apparently all Lord Grey could say, according to newspaper headlines, was: "England's hands are tied—" For God's sake, tied by what! "Why is England stalling? She won't be able to for long." This was everyone's reaction, and then with the Germans already given a good head start, war was declared one evening in London. The sky, apparently where it had been, had in reality fallen. Everyone in the streets started yelling and hurrahing; groups with their hands on each other's shoulders went romping down Piccadilly, while taxicabs thrown open at the back were already crammed with young officers, sitting on the hood, on the seats, in each other's laps, on the floors, already off to the front.

And, standing in the early evening amongst a great crowd milling before the iron gates of Buckingham Palace, we saw the King, quite distantly, step out on a balcony to deafening cheers when, holding up his hand for a silence that fell so instantly, deeply, swiftly, that it might have been incorporated with everlasting doom, his Majesty read the declaration of war. I remember there was a moment's pause, and then the wildest cheers—hats thrown into the air, strangers wringing one another by the hand—and you would have thought that jubilant news had just come to London.

But later, after dark, we heard the marching feet of the first troops to leave for France going down Piccadilly, and I went and stood at the curb to watch them. Beside many of the men walked their women, looking delicate and hollow-eyed under the street lamps, but how frantically in earnest! And now the singing was lower, less jubilant. Some regiments even passed entirely in silence.

Next day I went down to Felixstowe and was stopped before my cottage by a sentry's challenge and a lowered bayonet. Apparently our maid, turning on her lights to get undressed as usual in her room under the eaves, had been accused of signalling to the German Navy in the North Sea, and I was told at any rate the house must be vacated immediately, for guns were to be mounted at once in the windows facing the ocean. Feeling unreal and also excited, as if I had come to life in a masterpiece of Agatha Christie,

I got my family out of the house and up to London through the channelward surge of troop trains.

"The great cloud darkened the land" and ran up the most terrific debt in human agony, with less advantage to any one than history has yet recorded, or I think and hope, will ever record again. And when only a few years ago I motored down to Verdun by myself and saw in the chill twilight of March that single battlefield, the heaved-up barrenness of those terrible miles—with acre after acre of white crosses—then it seemed to me certain that to justify any such a scale of murdered youth, destiny would stand the whole world on its ear until every ounce of the old brain—that could hatch such an atrocity—should be shaken out of it, in order that this perished youth might be some-what vindicated, by the only balanced reprisal—a new world.

The following winter I was dreadfully ill with that wonderful dispensation of great illness—virtual uncon-sciousness—and came gradually back to life on a milk diet, in rooms loaded with flowers. Then one afternoon in April, just after I had been staring at my hydrangea window boxes and reading *Marius, the Epicurean*—drifting in those lovely, unreal classic panoramas of Pater—abruptly I felt that heaviness and subterranean pain, as if some one were stabbing you through a velvet dress, and also as if a great disc of lead must pass out through the tiny aperture of your heart. And next morning the most beautiful blond-haired, blue-eyed, dimpled baby was born, with a skin that looked, in its frail pallor, as if he had lain for a long while in the snow.

But that summer after Robin's birth there was a strange subtle difference beneath all I said, did, and felt. I needed to be a great deal alone in order to savor the kernel of things hitherto unknown, and out of my musing appeared in a kind of magic lightning, words that brought every appearance on the earth's rim—each inquiry of my mind, and feeling of my body it would seem—into a kind of thrilling permanence which seemed miraculous.

I began to dislike the incessant dalliance of the days with what? Distraction from what? And meals took on a length that was maddening. I was not so much critical as impatient with everybody; and well do I remember one evening—on account of a sort of ringing of the bell of fantastic absurdity. I was sitting alone on Bailey's Beach, watching the twilight catch the sea up into invisibility, through which came the muted sound of waves falling on the beach. I was overcome by arresting, translating that moment, when there suddenly appeared, arm in arm out of the dusk in considerable stateliness, Mr. and Mrs. Perry Belmont. "Why Blanche," they cried out, as they nearly tripped over my shadow, "what are you doing? Writing a love letter?" And as I smiled snakily back at them, I appreciated abruptly how impossible it was ever going to be to say to any one in my former background, "I am writing poetry."

The war went on. Fearful headlines, describing the holocaust, were flashed each morning into our consciousness. Feeling against the Germans ran riot and had also the smug and oily unreality of all such mass hysterias—an official opportunity, I used to think, to get the mildewed festering of other resentments off one's chest in this highly

approved bacchanal of hate! Not that I particularly liked
the Germans! The Prussian Secretary of the German Embassy who, so far, had afforded me my principal opportunity for gauging the nation, I had long found detestable.
Indeed, young Mr. Von Lersner, with pig eyes sunken in
his fat cheeks, and a most unnecessarily aggressive tiny
mustache, had made himself unpopular with me by reply-
ing one night, when I called him down lightly for having
come in very late to a dinner party at Mrs. Stuyvesant
Fish's: "How dare she be angry with me! She ought to be
delighted that I come at all!" And he had added something
more about "kicking Mrs. Fish downstairs" in case he
heard of the matter further.

His chief, the German Ambassador, Count Von Bern-
storff, a Bavarian, was a delightful man and a very different customer, with just the right smattering of charm and
inoffensiveness needed for the Ambassadors of those days.
However, drawn into the terrific conflict of the war, he became what he was, in reality, the courteous ghost of a by-
gone age.

Paul Helleu came to New York that second winter of the
war, and gave me my deathless press appendage (that will
probably head my obituary notice if I have one) "The Most
Beautiful Woman in America."

Helleu was a tall, slim Frenchman with a close cropped
head of hair and square beard. Emaciated and dark, a
twisted sort of agony on his whimsical features, he resembled one of the Apostles of El Greco. And in our dark
green damask library, he would sit for hours, his copper
plate before him, pencil raised, interrogating stare, when
there would be a sudden fury of line-making, during which

he often paused to swear loudly and cry out: "What have you in your head? Every line is crooked! Your smile is crooked! 'Tout était à travers.' What is there in that damnable head of yours?" he would rave on, occasionally rapping it fiercely as he spoke: "Genius?" "But of course," I always answered him, absolutely delighted. Then when the drawings were done, he either tore them up or threw them on their faces on the floor to cry out: "No good! I must start again!"

One night he called me up on the telephone, asking me like a jubilant child, "Have you seen the evening papers? I have given you a wonderful boost in the press. I have said that you were the most beautiful woman in America!" We both laughed, and I told him, "I know why you said that: it's because you're fond of me and we are great friends." "Of course, of course, but I really do like your face the best of all—but then there would have been no story in that."

There was a kind of tragic frustration about Helleu! If only he had not succeeded so early with facile shadows of his real ability. After he had returned to France, I did not see him for many years, and then one gray afternoon in March, just thirteen years after those winter days of our first friendship, when I had rushed out into the Avenue du Bois for air, I ran into Helleu walking in the damp twilight. "You have not changed," he told me. "Nothing has changed but your eyes; and they are terrible with suffering." He was also feeling muted and tragic, having just come from making a sketch from death of his old friend Marcel Proust. "I want to show it to you. It is one of the best things I have ever done, and I must draw you again."

And I did see this sketch of Proust and it was marvellous! and it showed once more what Helleu had surrendered of himself to remain *"à la mode."* And he did make another drawing of me, writing this time on the top "Michael Strange, it is thirteen years since I made the others, and this is bad, but if only you will come back I will do better," and I said good-by to my faithful old friend, in the twilight of his life and of my life with Jack.

But under all that happened now ran the dreadful oppressive sense of what was going on in Europe, proving how psychically impossible isolation is in modern times. And I lost many of my handsome English friends. They passed off after astonished acceptance of their terrible agonies, into that unreal confusing sadness which those who still live have the nerve to call glory!

Also America was having a fine case of president-hatred. How dare President Wilson keep us out of the war any longer? And particularly the civilians were dying to get our swaggering tall young Americans "over there" to bayonet the Boche. But then, how could any one expect "that Schoolmaster to get out of his swivel chair and lead us over the top!" Mr. Wilson seemed to be on the point of impeachment for mildness. And Len was longing to get into the war, not for the excitement or to "bayonet the Boche," but because the courage and chivalry of his spirit longed to be enlisted in a crusade against aggression.

My lovely sister, after Peter Martin's death, had married the Duke of Mecklenburg-Schwerin, the first cousin of my friend, the Grand Duke Alexander. Although this pair had somewhat the same brow, what was behind it was

[133]

altogether dissimilar. I did not care much for my brother-in-law, nor was my esteem increased when I heard that he was in the habit of smashing his orderly in the face on the slightest provocation. However, Borwin, in San Francisco with my sister, now insisted upon getting back to his regiment. So they came on to New York and Lily dressed him up as a stoker, smuggled him on board somehow, and saw him off, herself dressed in an old jacket and skirt, a handkerchief over her head. But I could see she was restless and unhappy now beyond words, and it seemed that her mind and heart dwelt in a haze of illusions, principal amongst them being the belief that from the war, the Emperor of Germany would emerge victorious.

One day, going into the Ritz for lunch, the Ritz still an "intime rendezvous" for a fairly small coterie of friends —the great amorphous mob scene that flows through every hotel now still unknown—we heard rumors that the *Lusitania* had been sunk, and every one felt that this tragic insult would now jolt the Professor at Washington out of his intellectual vaporings into action. And one heard Mrs. Alfred Vanderbilt had left her lunch table and gone in a panic to her room. (Alfred was on the *Lusitania*.)

Then later on the terrible catastrophe was confirmed, and stories of heroism and self-sacrifice came through with a long list of the dead. Apparently Alfred Vanderbilt had absolutely refused to get into the place assigned him in the lifeboat. Did he wish to give it up to some one else, or was he glad that fate had taken out of his hands the predicament of living—that daily, self-made fabrication of occupations and pleasures, that dreary, desperate difficulty of touching reality at any point, which has wearied so many of the very rich into forms of unconsciousness a good deal less clean than death?

And not much later we were at war, and had our own influx of khaki into the streets, with Len using all his considerable influence now to get sent to the front in France as liaison officer. And then his appointment was confirmed, and his mother and I were seeing him off on that dismal plank of asphalt reared with hideous inconsequence into the air, the North Philadelphia Station.

His mother and I were very silent on that drive, no matter what effort he made over us; I knew her beautiful courage was tested in that moment as much as it had ever been. As for me, I had been taught very little self-control but I knew I had then to try to live up to both of them.

But whenever I look back to that time I do not see the grim station overlooking crazy acres of advertisements and glum houses. I see Len in the hall of his family's old house at 23rd and Spruce, standing near the grandfather clock, ruddy, gay, and very natty in his uniform, catching up the boys in their Kate Greenaway linen suits, and telling them farewell in such an exuberant spirit that they yelled and screamed with delight, feeling that some first-rate news had just been handed out.

O once beloved, this grief—
That I have hammered so pitilessly in
Through the tender white skin of your temples—
It will haunt me forever—
And as a child moaning out in the snow
After my retreating steps—
And as the dim sound of hands listlessly falling apart—
Exhausted from pleading—toward my averted eyes.

[135]

CHAPTER XII

Playwright

I was about twenty-two when I had my first friendship with an actor, and then it all came through what might have been called, by an optimist, my writing. At that time I was going through the beginnings of self-education in plays. In every other way Len was my mentor. And in my charming gray-white bedroom with its cherry taffeta curtains I had put up a little bookcase with four or five shelves that were gradually filling up with new and absorbing friends.

That my life with these bookshelves was strictly in private; that I never heard any one mention the names beginning to obsess me, did not seem to matter at all.

Ibsen and Bjornstjerne Bjornson were haunting me. I had just thrown off James Barrie by writing, in quaint emulation of his *Admirable Crichton*, a piece entitled "A Malady of Dreams" and now the Nordic Masters were being gotten off my chest in a couple of grim tragedies.

The last, a curtain raiser called "Heard at Night" happened to get read somehow by Viola Allen (whose picture in the tights and corsets of Viola, in "Twelfth Night," had long been pasted into a place of honor in my scrapbook); and, miraculously, Miss Allen signified she would act in my play! And I spoke to her on the telephone, my throat closing with excitement. Was this the beginning of great things? Possibly she was a little old to play a faithless young wife, being well over fifty at the time, but as during her entire scene she lay in bed, dying, in a dim lit room, only coming out of her haze once at the very end of her grim confessions, she would be marvellous, I thought, and what prestige for me!

Miss Allen was my first experience of the inability of theatre people to let out a good strong yes or no. She would not give up the play, nor could I by any maneuverings of tact or irritable directness discover when, if ever, she meant to do it, nor would she fling me the play and tell me to go to the devil, and learn something about writing before I bothered her again. Then like other green authors, I began to know the domestic habits, relationships, hopes, and fears of my star, until the play got shoved altogether out of our interminable conversations.

And then unaccountably I was in Mrs. Minnie Maddern Fiske's dressing room at the theatre after her performance, and Mrs. Fiske was fascinating me by her mannerisms and her whimsy, and her aroma of greater things, of which the whimsical mannerisms only hinted; but I felt her, for all of her excessive humor and personality, rather a stuffed airtight sort of person; and to me not so great an actress as her wonderful niece Emily Stevens, with whom she never seemed on the best of terms.

A little later I was telephoned at Newport to be informed

[137]

that Arnold Daly thought well of my play, and wanted to
see me in New York about it; so on an August morning, at
nine o'clock, a tactless hour to visit an actor, I walked into
his apartment at 14 East 60th Street. Mr. Daly, in his
dressing gown, and holding a razor in his hand, his face
half covered with soap, ushered me across his threshold
with a theatrical flourish. He was very Irish-looking, going
bald, and I thought to myself: "Now don't let him see that
you're not a Bohemian. Let him dress, undress or shave in
front of you if he wants without batting an eye!"

Later we had a charming breakfast together at the Plaza.
I was complimented on my play which was, practically
speaking, no good at all, when Mr. Daly suddenly asked,
"Do you go back to Newport today?"

"This afternoon, I guess."

"How would you like me to come with you? Don't you
think we could plan for the play a good deal better at Newport than in this heat?"

My husband was nonplussed at my arrival with Daly,
dressed in loud checks and in a very jovial mood. (Later
they became intimate friends.) He received him charmingly but an ace French aviator and exquisite gentleman,
also our guest at the time, remarked audibly after the first
meal we all took together, during which Arnold had told
a dashing story about Prince Orloff and his white Russian
wolf-hound: "Blanche! What a person! *il n'est pas de
votre métier.*" He'll be surprised about "my metier" later
on, I thought with a bilious rush of vanity to the heart.

And then Arnold, Rabelaisian and fearless, was taken
along to a dinner party at Mrs. Cornelius Vanderbilt's
where he unfortunately recognized one of the gentlemen
guests as having frequented, on the same night as himself,

and a few weeks previously, what my cousin Henry May calls a *maison de passe*. Encouraged by the joviality of fine wines, and that sumptuous decor rich people draw about themselves, which does seem, with its display of grapes, bosoms, glittering gold services, and constantly replenished beakers, to indicate Bacchanal rather than bridge, Arnold twitted this guest across the table on some incident of the evening, which made the nature of their enjoyment obvious, to pull down upon us one of the finest silences I have ever lived through.

Arnold and I bathed, and sauntered on the cliffs. He began to call me L'Aiglon for some reason, and the play disappeared for the second and final time. But Arnold Daly was my first contact with the theatre. He showed me something of how the interpretative artist thinks and works, and as our friendship continued I was amused to see how close to the surface were his laughter and his tears. I discovered too that he could turn in an instant from idling and dissipating, and work like the devil. I had never seen any one keep such rigid laws for art's sake, and I was eagerly touched.

Arnold was past his prime when I met him. And the qualities of character and talent, that had lifted him up from the position of office boy in Frohman's office to an outstanding position in the American theatre, were becoming tragically jostled and wearied in the demoralization of delay, in the fearsome dependence on a perfectly incredible, and hitherto undemanded, degree of luck, that went to make a production in the days that were upon him, the days that would do him in and silence that marvellous voice of his, in which was distilled so touchingly the talented essence of his heart.

"L'Aiglon, L'Aiglon," I can hear him say, when after Herculean efforts he had landed a script and a backer (he whose only business, and whose only knowledge it was to act), "the play's all right if only we can get a new third act out of the author." And off he would rush with the author to Atlantic City; where in their shirtsleeves, hermetically sealed in an airtight room, blowing smoke in each other's faces and solemnly drinking milk, they would conjure up a third act! Of course to no purpose whatever.

CHAPTER XIII

I Become Michael Strange

B UT WRITING poetry was pure delight, for you
didn't have to follow up the completion of a poem
with any fearsome trail of efforts and contacts, carrying in their wake so much of unreality and wasted time. So
now I sent off to the *North American Review* that poem
written as I walked by the North Sea called "New York
Etched," which to my grand surprise, was accepted. But
practically on the eve of publication, a lady in charge
of poets called up to sourly tell me I must radically change
a couple of lines if I expected to make the number. And I
remember that miraculously buoyed with self-confidence
I astounded her by performing the feat she asked on the
spot, over the telephone. It wasn't, however, till I'd written "Insaroff," strongly modeled on Turgeniev for the
New York Sun's Sunday story page, and saw the career of a
writer stretching with certainty before me, that studying
my signature for a long time beneath the publications, I
wondered if "Blanche M. Thomas" was really I.

A few weeks after "Insaroff" appeared Mitchell Kennerley, then an esoteric publisher, sent for me, asking to see some of my poems. (How charming everything was except the theatre! the theatre that one loved, and could find no antidote against like the allure of a human being that you have to find false a thousand times before the cure arrives, and not then through revelation, but out of weariness.) So a few days later I was sitting in Mr. Kennerley's office while he held up a thin selection from the weights received, and told me he was willing to publish me.

I was going to be published! I was going to see a book of mine on sale! And I remember rushing out into the rasping clatter of Madison Avenue in a real haze of happiness. "Shall you sign yourself Blanche M. Thomas?" Mr. Kennerley had asked me, looking doubtful. I went home, lowered the shades and lay down in my darkened room in order not to collapse from the joy of being an accepted author, when suddenly and from nowhere that I can conceivably trace appeared in full the name "Michael Strange."

"It's a good name," said Kennerley, "so good you think you've heard it when you haven't, and we'll have no other associated with the book. You shall remain anonymous and get a fair opinion on your poems."

"A fair opinion," I thought to myself, "What on earth does he mean? Why shouldn't people be fair to me, as myself?"

I think it was Arnold Daly who first brought Sir Herbert Tree to our house, and here was a different sort of theatre artist from these exhibits, dishevelled by worry and hysterical with optimism or pessimism that I had run into so far.

Sir Herbert was a tall, urbane, distinguished gentleman, red-haired and light-lashed, who seemed to have stepped straight out of a bandbox of fashion and the most solid of circumstances. He wore an important air easily, and a certain vagueness that was rather attractive in him, protected the inner maneuverings of an extremely agile mind. I loved to watch the grace of his gestures and the fascinating mobility of his very small mouth. And after hectic conversations with Arnold in which it would appear that if only he could get hold of $600 to keep some play "innately great, mind you, L'Aiglon!" before the public for just another week, —then all the world would know salvation! etc., etc. Sir Herbert would drop in for tea to draw amusedly out of his pocket checks for eighteen or twenty thousand dollars, an endorsement from our millionaires of his Shakespearean season.

And I met his daughter, Iris, who was to become one of my closest friends, Iris, about whom he could be very whimsical in that guttural subtle-toned voice of his. At first I could make nothing of her except that she was extraordinary! She looked very Dutch, with her thick lips and heavily retroussé nose, and the yellow hair that she wore in a bang in front and a small knot behind. Staring imperturbably out of blond-lashed eyes, her round face nearly always carried a stolid sleepy expression of extreme non-committal youth, although it turned out presently that she had already lived through some extravagant hours. However, after the first few weeks of knowing her I was utterly charmed. She was a real gypsy and a true poet, a young François Villon in a skirt, a tousle-headed minstrel, whom one could fancy falling gayly, drunkenly, asleep in the midst of his sweet songs beneath the chair of Sir Launcelot.

One evening after some glasses of absinthe together in my studio, we were walking home along Fifth Avenue through a snow storm—I, to dine in the Gainsborough-hung, arid discretion of one of Fifth Avenue's most chastely Greek palaces—when pausing under a lamppost, I went into a strong monologue about the necessity I now had to bite into something real. "Even if the core should be bitter," I threw in, when Iris, also holding to the lamp-post for support while the flakes fell gently past the light above us, said: "Well, you ought to meet Jack Barrymore! He wouldn't bore you."

"Oh, yes he would," I told her. "I don't care for him on the stage or off it. Why, when I was only fourteen years old, I was lunching with my mother at the Hotel Knicker-bocker, and there he was with his drooping mustache and his dazed eyes, *vis à vis* of an awfully made-up-looking woman, years older than himself and all dressed in black." "Well, you seem to have remembered it pretty well," said Iris. "And he is not a bit like that now. He is absolutely fascinating."

So we went our separate ways, with that particular part of my fate crouching in the wings for another span.

One night I had a telephone call from Iris either in-credibly late or in the small hours of the morning: "Michael, dear," she told me, "I have just been married at a party by Mayor Mitchel."

"Who to, in God's name?"

"To Curtis Moffat." And I was told that Len and I must board a private car that very day, and go out to break the news to Sir Herbert who was on tour in Chicago. "We are holding back all of the publicity," she added, "until you can explain to Daddy how it all happened. He will take it better from you than from any one else."

As I came into Sir Herbert's dressing room he was sitting before his blinding light-lined mirrors nearly made up for his most terrifying role, Svengali in DuMaurier's "Trilby."

I cast my bolts directly only because I did not know what else to do; and there fell a silence while I glared defensively into the mirror at the menacing face of the hypnotic Jew who stared back at himself; when (after a pause, bringing eternity nearer) Sir Herbert asked softly, "Has he got any money?" Brushing from me a full knowledge of Curtis' distinguished, but straitened circumstances, and standing up to the malignant Svengali who now towered over me in his skin-tight fitting black frock coat, and fearfully wagging Polish curls, I brought out: "Well, he's got a very rich uncle."

There was more silence, and then, as Sir Herbert leaned toward the mirror to delicately retouch the makeup along his mouth, he uttered a slow guttural musical "Ahhh," and somehow, in that small ejaculation, it seemed to me there was compressed all the fateful disillusionment of parents with their children, all the resignation of wisdom that can never be articulate enough to prevent the dangerous stupidities of those they love.

There is something very disarming and touching about the backs of people for whom you have an affection, especially when you watch them go through a ceremony in an empty church. Iris, in a white suit too large for her, either bought on the spot or borrowed, a large floppy hat hiding all but the lower end of her golden page's head, and slim Curtis in a navy blue suit, holding himself proudly, whimsically attentive to the matter in hand, made a couple significant with their own rarity, and that rather terrible youthfulness of artists, which, one senses, is somehow doomed never really to grow up, nor be able perhaps, successfully to cope with ceremonies, or obligations to God or man.

The wedding breakfast was a huge success; browsing contentedly about, I was drinking a few healths, delighted that it had all come off so well, when a well known Chicago journalist approached me and said, "We have a full page about you in our paper Sunday! You are discovered, Michael Strange!"

I turned aside, rather frightened to hear this, but mostly because of Kennerley's apprehension. For weeks he had been forwarding me kindly reviews. Some even praised the poems, the work it was said "of a young man finding himself with splendor." For the most part they were innocuous. Nowhere were there signs of cruelty or disparagement.

However, on Sunday appeared a full page in the press with photographs and that quotation of Helleu's about my looks, my old friend being termed in this bit a society drypointist; and I given such a fine introduction of a poet to his public as "Society Leader Takes Up Poetry."

And then I noticed a little something else. Mr. Lublin giving me a splendid review in *Town and Country*, in fact likening my poems to those of John Donne—a greater compliment than I knew, as I had not read Donne at the time—evidently felt that to square himself with the vestry-man of literature against a charge of madness, he must start off by announcing: "We consider ourselves especially fortunate and accidentally fitted to give a really honest opinion about Michael Strange's Miscellaneous Poems, since we believe we were the only person on a magazine or newspaper who didn't know that Mrs. Leonard M. Thomas was Michael Strange."

"Accidentally fitted . . . really honest opinion." So, I thought, whatever I do is going to be seen first of all through the fact that it is glaringly apparent I don't have to do anything. Money—that was it—the obsession about money taking one nightmare form or another, interlarding every breath of American air, holding up the mirror of distortion close to me and to every one else. Whatever public I got was bound to consider my work superfluous at least at first, and the real artists whom I so wanted to draw close to, would be naturally put off me.

But it was not until a couple of years later, after my second book *Poems* had been out a few months, that at lunch one day, in our lovely Italian villa (belonging to Mrs. de Kay at East Hampton), my butler, Charles, who had the elongated pallid distinction of a Gainsborough gentleman, put down a newspaper clipping beside my plate. "I thought this would interest you, Madam," he told me. And I read, my first wonderful review that had been committed to paper by a gentleman who, I found out many years afterwards, had taken the book down desultorily from a shelf in a newspaper office, and read it without the remotest knowledge of who Michael Strange was.

And said this first real friend to my poetry of his anonymous author: "These are not showcase poems, where the origin and manufacture of the display are labelled. You cannot read them quickly. They touch you remotely at first as with nightmare fingers. You go back to study them, to concentrate on them, to marry them. Like some of the productions of Poe, Francis Thompson, Blake, Nietzsche and Mallarmé, they show a different face on each visit. Some rhyme, some do not—it makes little difference. They are all the records of lawless moods—lawless in the sense of not being conventional; law-abiding in the way that a comet is or the whorls and horlas of the Fourth Dimension." And then he, Benjamin de Casseres, paid me the most precious tribute I could have received, for after quoting several excerpts he ended with this one from "Vision" and the following remarks.

"And now its pre-sublimal presence approaching me
Is like the shuddering of wingéd descent
Over grails irradiant
And now piercing me like some arch-angel's blade
Its glance stiffens my lashes into a staring obeisance
Until what I feel! Until what I feel!
Surpasses the white burning of a million lamps
Across fields of lilies—"

"Not Whitman, or even Gertrude Stein, as the 'I'm from Missouri' critics will say; but straight from the most marvellous of all beings who wrote our tongue, William Blake."

Dear Len read the notice very slowly, with conflicting emotions, I could see, and very understandable they were. Apprehension was stirring at his intuitive glimpse of great sadness to come, through this restless poet who had not been to the slightest degree visible in the girl he married.

However, life still lacked so much that it continued to

be fascinating, and everywhere I looked for the face that should be marked with the solutions of my happiness or grief. Certain faces attracted me so greatly that I would stand absolutely bemused before them while the person was engaging me in what they had supposed was a conversation.

Every mental and emotional implication of this face would register on my attentive yearning with such potency, indeed I was able, and liable to be so charmed, that in a way the present was blotted out even while it was marking me indelibly. And poems came out of me at such a rate that my maid started to put a pad and pencil under my pillow at night.

How light at first but tenacious and enduring are the strokes of preparation which Destiny gives the design, before a human soul can stand at all revealed to itself in its loneliness—richness—in all the confusion of its intimations.

Ramon Reyntiens was a young Belgian poet with all the requirements for romance that might have been asked for by Dumas fils. He was young and beautiful, with that carven ascetic beauty which makes one see in its thinned nobility the hand of the Angel of Death. It seemed to be quite natural for him to have tuberculosis, while the only work he had ever done outside of writing and reciting poetry, had been filling a secretaryship to one of the great European Cardinals. And then his voice was the first peerless speaking voice I had ever heard. It seemed to vibrate with an off the earth freshness. It expressed the survival of some mortal ordeal. It had the sort of thing in it which seems to me implicit in the phrase "Lest ye be born again," but perhaps he was only a very good-looking young man who knew he had not long to live. At any rate I absorbed from listening to him a good deal better than I could have from any teacher, how a voice can be used, and a spell woven, when a man is able to understand, from the vantage of some uniquely tragic point, the glory or the wisdom of the word he speaks.

Ramon came into the circle of my naïve hunger like the bodily presence of my fancy. He could do for me what I had been doing for every one else—dramatize me to myself, look down the vista of my possibilities for a change!

I can see us now in my library, while the twilight grew in the room, and the impressive beauty of his young face stood out disembodied from time, touching my dream, persuading it to life.

> *Your words a breeze*
> *Blowing up from the turquoise heaving*
> *Of oriental seas. . . .*
> *Your words a fairyland of forests*
> *Humming with the music*
> *Of unique birds . . .*
> *Your sense fantastic for reading*
> *As the dew's hieroglyphs*
> *Over night-purple roses . . .*
> *Yet, what matters your sense*
> *Who possess such soul—*
> *Whose words are tender! deep!*
> *As are those reflections of twilight*
> *In a well of springs.*

CHAPTER XIV

Stormy Weather

My life flowing out into new channels—
O I feel the farewell jar of the old wharves
Against the sides of this newly launching boat—
O the shock of these listing giving wharves thumping my
*   heart*
As well as the lithe gleaming flanks
Of this vigorous eager ship of mine—
Faces deeply familiar dimming there on the shore—
Never mind I both fear—desire—
They shall become eternally polished—distinct—ar-
*   rested—*
In that shattering glare of memory—

A FEW months before we had gone into the war, I met John Barrymore just when I was looking my worst, having scarcely finished nursing little Leonard through a tonsillitis operation.

I came into the smoke-filled room where the "Theatre

Guild Group" were entertaining after Andreyev's "Life of Man" (a heavy bit of Russian confusion) and noticed first, standing in the doorway, handsome Edward Sheldon, dark-haired and noble looking with such a rosily polished skin, as if he had just come in from skating! A few moments later Phil Moeller, a Theatre Guild director, who I always thought resembled the bust of some great musician, asked me if he might present Mr. Barrymore who wished to meet me. "So he wishes to meet me?" I thought, and remembered having seen him a few days previously, bending over a case at Cartier's, while I had been ushered past him with great aplomb, straight into the sanctum of Mr. Cartier himself.—And no wonder, having come to trade in a diamond tiara (a duplicate of the one worn by the Tsarina on informal occasions) for only a single strand of pearls.

And it came back to me, that passing Mr. Barrymore I had been not only conscious of the beauty of his profile, but sensed how well able he was to look to one side of it without seeming to move his head. But here he was bowing and smiling, looking very slim and nervously poetic, with greyish greenish hazel eyes of immense fascination, because they seemed to mirror back oneself in flattering mischievous terms.

He looked elfin and forsaken, an intriguing combination! but very highly strung too. His walk, slanted, oblique, seemed to say that his clothes irked his skin; but what a metamorphosis from the dazed individual I had seen at the Hotel Knickerbocker!

At the time I met Jack he was living with Edward Sheldon in a small apartment in 54th Street, near the University Club, and they seemed a pair of earnest, handsome, exceptional young men, for Jack had changed from the pasty-faced, rather heavy-jowled, mustachioed comedian of the "Fortune Hunter" into the artist who could bring to the characterization of Falder in Galsworthy's "Justice" a superb degree of touching, intelligent acting.

Ned Sheldon had selected "Justice" as the vehicle for Jack's transformation from comedian to tragedian, and what a sensible choice it was. For here was no grandiose costumed blurb of the dark muse, but a modern story of the Little Man, baffled and desperately caught in forces of economic penury, love and the law. It was a disarmingly humble choice and the part was played to perfection. While this Barrymore had taken on a slimness, a fineness, a poetry of head and throat, and seemed to have grown much younger. I did not realize until later that Jack was something of a chameleon, probably a necessary attribute of the actor, and that a portion of the person I met that night was the creation of Sheldon's noble faith in him as an important artist, and of his patient unending efforts to build his friend into a person with sufficient character fully to express and protect his immense gifts. Sheldon was the most protective and wise friend that Jack would ever find, the best friend that any man could have. There was a calmness about the working out of his will, and a dignity about any kind of association with him that had to be lived up to by every one, including Jack. If only Jack had had sufficient ascetic strength to make Sheldon's friendship and his art enough to be had from life, then I believe it is possible that the theatre and the hearts of many thousands of its audiences would still be receiving a sustainedly peerless gift. For to me there is no more noble thing on earth than the love of the comrade who needs from you only that he should see the best in you grow.

[153]

When I first knew Jack all the hypnotic magnetism of success was already reinforcing his natural charm. He had the most astute knowledge of how to handle himself in any situation (his presence of mind with reporters was my despair) and he knew how to conceal this astuteness. Whereas, I could be clearly seen by a one-eyed sailor to have no astuteness whatever, nor certainly any magnetism of success; and none of that stuff of training for a purpose, which added to native intelligence creates a use for the word discipline.

By that spring Jack had come to a few of our parties, a more or less silent, charming, and very decorative guest, and one night I took several friends that included Sir Herbert Tree to see him in DuMaurier's "Peter Ibbetson."

In the role of Peter, Jack really was the radiant lyrical approximation of Romance. And I even thought there was in his beauty a fatal kind of fineness, an unearthliness, which you could not but see through tears, because it was not of life, but only as in our secret hearts we dream that life might be. For surely the audience that watched him with their hearts in their throats, could well believe now in lovers being able triumphantly to find one another, behind the misfortunes of life, or even its cessation!

To watch the immeasurable beauty of this artist in his work—at home at last, mounted to some point where it seemed he could create and realize all the amazing poetry of his personality! But then how mortally depressing it often was to watch his deformation from art back into life.

The following autumn he played "The Jest," arranged from the Italian by Sheldon. Thinking in terms of Jack's career, this was a choice in brilliant contrast to what had gone before. For the role of Gianotto required none of the

passivity of Falder, nor sheer romance of Peter, but colo-
ratura in acting, dynamics of sensuosity, giving Jack an
opportunity to show in decorative cinquecento sets, and in
tights that met nearly under his chin and left no faintest
fragment of his anatomy to the imagination, an exotic, an
erotic, who so boiled and frothed either in the presence of
his beloved (Ginevra), or of her lover, that on the matinee
I visited the show, two ladies—after the bull's eye of
epileptic sensuosity had been squarely hit a couple of times
—rose from their seats and sternly withdrew from the
theatre.

After this portrayal, men, women and children left Jack
in no doubt as to their intentions if only they could get hold
of him. For he had looked as arresting as Lucifer, in his
dynamic beauty, and bravura evil, and seemed emotionally
to project a startling degree of promise. Again "The Jest"
was pictorially magnificent! Something of the massive exquisite beauty of the Renaissance had been brought into
the sets. And the play had successfully captured at least one
slant of Renaissance atmosphere—its bacchanalian attitude
toward the passions of Love and Hate.

Never will any one who saw it forget the savage rant-
ing and groaning of Lionel, while Jack skipped about him
like a malicious blade of green lightning, robbing him of
his girl, his manhood, and his life.

Sandwiched between the frenzies of Lionel and Jack,
Ginevra, the bone of contention (played by Maude Hanna-
ford), moved with a plastic caution, her hands usually
crossed on a slightly protruding belly, her eyes downcast,
mysteriously seeming to portray by her presence and in her
detachment, a kind of stylization of contempt for the in-
sane virility of these passions she had impishly aroused.

I remember very much later when Jack and I were thinking of getting married, that Tibi (my mother), at her wits' end to stop me from taking what she conceived to be an incongruous risk with my happiness, rushed in a very handsome distinguished priest from one of the first dioceses in New York, to vent his mind on us, in my apartment at the Ritz. But when Father X, having conjured up every anathema in the decalogue, saw he was not achieving his point, he suddenly cried out: "How could any woman in her senses marry a man who played 'The Jest' as Mr. Barrymore played it?"

"Why, Father, you didn't see 'The Jest' yourself, did you?" said Jack coming to life in a chair!

"Five times! Five times!" shouted our visitor, in a vast excess of disgruntled fury, directed I thought at us and himself, and the buoyant magnetism of forbidden fruit.

After a long and successful "run" in "the Jest," building up Jack's reputation with audiences all over the country, it was decided—and again I think on Edward Sheldon's advice—that he should next play "Fedya" in "The Living Corpse" by Tolstoi, and I was asked to adapt this great but turgid drama.

So I went to my Russian friend, Ray Rosenbaum (sister of that jovial opportunist sculptor Jo Davidson), for a literal translation, knowing that from Ray's vital and sensitive mind I would get something of what Tolstoi was driving at.

And through hot August days and evenings we sat in the basement of her Russian restaurant while she read me the play, translating as she went along, and I took down her lively speech, went home and worked it up by myself.

But when I read it to Jack he said, looking eerily off into

space, "Oh, it's all right, only I want more sensuousness for Fedya. Now, have him the kind of man who, when he lies beside his wife in bed, feels, senses her lover wriggling in under the door on his belly, and getting into bed with them. Have Fedya tortured, driven mad"—and Jack's arm described the very cycle of madness—"by the thought of that man around his wife!"

"But Jack, remember when the play starts, Fedya has already left his wife, only hopes her lover will be able to come across, and finally shoots himself to legalize their union." "Never mind," said Jack. "But Jack, from the beginning Fedya is beyond the physical, and only wants to lie in a gypsy café, inviting the inconclusiveness of his Russian soul to balalaika music, while Masha, the beautiful gypsy girl, keeps on kissing him and hoping she can bring him to." "What?" cried Jack increduously, "Why, you can't play a fellow like that. I tell you," and he rolled his eyes downward in a terrifying manner, "to give me something to tear out my liver with in front of those So-and-Sos!"

So I went ahead and gave him all I could; and never dared read what I was doing to Ray. The great night came. We went down together to the theatre and sat remotely in the gallery. My name was not on the program, as matters weren't officially arranged between Jack and myself, and the curtain rose. And for the first time I heard with terror, delight, and a sense of guilt, whole sentences of mine spoken from the stage. The audience was enraptured; Jack played an adorable Fedya with a slight Russian Jew accent that stood out with exotic poignancy from the simple midwestern voices that surrounded him.

During the first entr'acte, when the lights went up, I saw a very stout man sitting in the stage box angrily searching the program and waving his arms in controversy with the usher. Vaguely uncomfortable, I went down to ask her, "What's the matter with the fat man? Why is he so angry?"

"He is Count Tolstoi! He is the son of the author," she replied, "and wants to know immediately who adapted the play. He cannot find a name on the program."

"He'll have to wait some time, thank God!" I thought to myself as I crept back to Ray.

After a successful run of "Redemption," Jack's mind turned to Shakespeare, also guided by Edward Sheldon, and at this point I was able to contribute a little something.

A few months previously I had been sent on a trip to California, to see if I couldn't recover from Jack and determine never to see or think of him again. This had been difficult from the start, as when the train was only at 125th Street, a box was handed to me containing scarlet camellias with, beneath them, enclosed in a leather case from Cartier, an exquisite picture of Jack in a small triangular frame of jade embossed with diamonds and sapphires that he had designed himself.

But the train ruthlessly persisting, after an emotional farewell with my sister who had clung to it as far as 125th Street in order to talk sense until the last possible moment, I journeyed on with my dear friend Louise Burleigh to Santa Barbara, where at some juncture of my visit, I met Mrs. William Carrington, now Mrs. Robert Edmond Jones. I was writing "Clair de Lune" and some of the music for it at the time, and singing a great deal. And Mrs. Carrington had me come and work with her in a charming music room, telling me flattering things about my vocal apparatus, even announcing it to be one of the four or five "great speaking voices in the world." Her pleasant exaggerations in no way detracted from the liking I had conceived for this sturdy mystic Scotchwoman, with quite a defined expression of second sight in her riveting blue eyes, that looked at you, through you, and seemed to revise you against the vision of some distant oracle.

During my hours with her I saw that she had a unique knowledge concerning the use of the voice. She provided you with no routine of voice production, yet gave you elementary ideas concerning the liaison of breath and sound. These would never allow you to force yourself, or harm yourself, only release yourself (if you got what she was driving at, which was not always easy, as you had to be able to take notice of hints). As we worked together I thought how wonderful if she could practice on Jack, now that he was going to square up to Shakespeare, and lower the breath out of his nose into his chest, or whatever else was necessary to efface the nasal, and bring out the natural tonal beauty I felt to be lurking in his vocal cords.

So one day, as Mrs. Carrington was engaged in teaching me to draw out the vowel sounds in my own poetry, and I stood fantastically crooning on a sustained pitch:
"I am Sol-i-tude
The Ma-a-a-ster of Thought
The Mo-o-o-d of Sorrow
The Whi-i-i-stler for Dreams"
Jack nipped, bladelike into the room. They were introduced. Mrs. Carrington threw him a hint about the effect of breath on tone to which he responded with an imaginative leap in the right direction. Indeed, while trying to keep a stern hold on herself and continue to pay some attention to the matter in hand, Mrs. Carrington was immediately

[159]

captivated by his charm and his intelligence about breath control. And they worked hard together before his "Richard III," she being largely responsible for bringing out of his naturally fine voice the necessary dignity and music. But unfortunately for me, from that moment her interest in one of the "four or five great speaking voices in the world," sank into enduring silence.

I think that along with "Peter Ibbetson" went "Richard III" as Jack's finest work. There was no stop in the melodramatic malevolence of Richard's character not gracefully within his reach. But the exquisite distinction with which he played, the delicate deadliness of his irony, the unfathomable, unpredictable wrath against the whole human race which one felt to be seething in the twisted heart of the cripple—all of it came across with a thoroughness, a finality seldom or never seen in the theatre. Indeed, when the curtain fell, you were willing to concede the last word to Jack in this role.

One evening several months after I had met Jack, he took me to supper with Ethel and Lionel. Ethel had always seemed to me a brilliantly fortunate person, for since my childhood I carried about with me a memory of seeing her one day at the height of her youth and beauty, already famous, bewitchingly tilting herself forward in a hansom cab as she called out directions to the cabby through the trap. And there had fluttered into my forever lonely brooding receptivity an impression of beauty, charm and celebrity, and wonder—as if I already knew something of the meagre rationings of fate—at their coincidence. So now we all sat around a little table, Ethel being gracious and amusing, but I liked best the silent Lionel with his slightly hunched shoulders and lined face. He seemed to belong less to the theatre than the others. He did not bother to project anything, and was blithely unconscious as to whether he was being responsive or not. Indeed, in the unassuming thoughtfulness with which he sat amongst us, he might have been a writer or a painter, some one intent only on the self-effacement of reception.

His wife Doris Rankin was with him, a striking looking young woman with huge gray eyes, shot, I thought, with glints of green in a very white face. And in what seemed her rather intentionally old-fashioned clothes she resembled Emily Brontë or Lorna Doone in a sombre mood. Jack told me, and I could see, that Lionel adored his wife —for when they stood up to go I saw him surreptitiously kiss her cloak as he laid it across her shoulders—and yet a few moments earlier Ethel had asked this beloved sprite: "Da, where did Mrs. Thomas put her rubbers?" to which "Da" had replied "Behind the umbrella stand."

Probably she's a kind of Pirandello character, I concluded—a sort of "As You Desire Me" woman—and yet it seemed she must have been inured to some extraordinarily rich form of self-effacement to appear so "consciously patient," so alert and yet withdrawn, so determined "not to be anybody."

And now in another attempt to prevent our marriage, I had a visit from the distinguished lawyer, Mr. John Milburn, ruggedly handsome, dark-haired and in black. He looked as if starting off in the Lincoln tradition, he had ended up with William Jennings Bryan—or rather sold out a powerful integrity for the sake of believing in "fairies" and the divine right of the very rich. And pacing my beautiful Elizabethan library Mr. Milburn promised me no less than shipwreck with all hands lost if I married Jack. When as a *comble* to these warnings, one night, after I had called late for some necessity at my country chemist's—an old pal of mine—and was just starting up the car to leave, a window was violently flung open over the street and a voice cried out, "Now don't you go and marry John Barrymore."

CHAPTER XV

The Four Horsemen
Shout "Don't"

BUT JACK and I got married that summer in spite of the Four Horsemen shouting "Don't!" During the event Papa remained entrenched in the Reading Room at Newport, with, I dare say, a stiff drink beside him. But Tibi was there, seeing to the beauty of the floral arrangements around the cross in Vadah's sitting room at the Ritz, where our marriage took place.

Directly after the ceremony Tibi, her face flushed with apprehension and tears, took Lionel aside to ask, "But has he married the Baby at all? I heard no mention of the name Barrymore!" And it had to be explained to her that Barrymore was an assumed name given to handsome Maurice Blythe, when he went on the stage, by an old actor, in deference to Blythe's family feeling. And Tibi told us in a fresh outburst, "You both look like children, and have no business to get married!"

I wonder if any one ever really liked being the wife of an actor. Of course they might say they had because it would show them up in a very superior light. I have seen a few actors' wives here and in London. They had about them a kind of anonymity that probably came from giving and giving and not even getting back as much reaction as an audience, until they had come to look quite blurred and indistinct.

I have seen Doris standing in the wings while Lionel rehearsed, laden with everything he might need from a pencil to a sandwich. And the wife of another very famous actor sitting in her husband's dressing room with a sullen nullified look, surrounded by his mash mail and thermoses of hot milk.

Surely, the wives of actors are on duty longer than other wives. And can it be possible that any woman gets a sense of rich enjoyment out of seeing her husband mobbed for his sex appeal? I remember one young lady was so enamored of Jack that she ordered a costume in duplicate of any part he might be playing to—whenever her feelings got the better of her, as they did on a couple of occasions—appear in the public lobby of his hotel, confronting him as he dove for the lift, with extravagant gestures of worship and abandon. To add to this situation, in which I think I detect a delicate aura of martyrdom, goes the envy of the whole of womankind because of those unspecifiable advantages one is assumed more continually to enjoy.

Iris, looking like an Elizabethan jackanapes, in whom mirth and irony for the whole human race is tantamount, would tell me: "My dear, in the end actors always give in. I know!" And she unfolded—to a morbidly attentive ear —stories of actors who, having at first been worshipped from afar, written to every day, and waited for outside the stage door with no effect, had gradually surrendered to the impassioned vitality of their hunters, even going so far, in some instances, as to set up a second illegitimate family nearer the theatre than their regular home.

"But that is the Theatre," said Iris, "and it ought to be like that—richly sensuous, full of passion before and behind the curtain! The Theatre will probably die out with these English actresses snubbing their lovers to preserve their reputations, and learning how to carve the Sunday roast as if that were their real business in life."

On my first trip abroad with Jack, until we were lost in the anonymity of travel, ladies would waylay him at every point, demanding an autograph; or just planting themselves in his path, their faces would suffuse with a slow smile, to be replaced when their eyes fell upon me, the accompanying bulk, by an expression of sour embarrassment. And again when I went into the writing room to jot down a poem, it was not unusual for some young woman to pop up opposite me, and leaning her face on her elbows, suddenly exclaim: "It must be wonderful to be you—the wife of John Barry-more!"

Jack was very dignified and humorous about all this adulation, and avoided the outbursts as much as he could. But I thought somehow that without his knowing it, this passionate surge of approval kept him in a good humor, for sometimes knocking around restaurants in Europe where no one knew him by sight, it seemed to me that his eye roved over the averted eaters and drinkers, with the ironic displeasure of an unrecognized king.

We set up housekeeping in a charming house in 67th

[165]

Street and it was delightful to have some one in the "home" at last whom the servants considered more temperamental than myself.

There were splendid nurseries for the children and a tiny isolated room in the back to which Jack could retire and draw. He amazed me by the facility and imaginative power of his designs, and I noticed that when he was at them he always seemed peaceful and happy, the reverse of the way he was when acting. His attitude to the stage bewildered me, for when he told me how he hated to act, I never knew whether he was fooling me, or himself, or was genuinely right, although I had observed again and again that his contact with an audience did not revive or elate him, but rather depressed him. It would really seem that there was something hateful to him in the exercise of his surpassing gift. And as I knew him better I wondered: Was it because the Theatre, together with all it played up in his nature, had cost him his inner contentment, frayed his nerves, unsettled him toward that life in which he would have found peace and happiness and, I believe, the possibility of real recognition—the purely creative life of the painter?

Jack often told me that his friend Lawrence Irving of London had believed in his painting and wanted him to stick to it. But he had been practically without funds as a student at the Slade School—sleeping on books was not always a pleasure—so when Ethel turned up one spring at the height of her loveliness, he had accepted a place in her company and a good check every Saturday night.

But the first year of our marriage Jack did not act at all. He had found a fascinating little farmhouse near White

Plains where great clusters of lilacs "stood in the dooryard near the whitewashed palings," and he presented me outright with this lovely little place and its fifteen acres of land. We then proceeded to turn a sane little thimbleful of a New England home into a bizarre medieval studio. The hearth was typical of both of us, of a kind of crazed spirituality that crept very early into our relationship; for the andirons tapered into Holy Grail cups that were sheathed in wings, and drawn down at the ends into serpent's claws, while above the fireplace, to seal the bewilderment of the visitor, was printed in the stone, "Behold I send my angel before thy face."

Our Hidden House
As an haunted reflection thrown in the subterranean
circlet of a well—
A mound of mischievous plaster set in a gnarl of
still strange green—
Built by sprites by angels in an elfin mood
To be seen by lightning moonlight never forgotten
Perfect for memory.

~~~~~~

CHAPTER XVI

Clair de Lune

ABOUT a year before my marriage to Jack, I had read Victor Hugo's *L'Homme Qui Rit* and was fascinated by the stupendous baroque imbroglios of the story. But I had forgotten it, or thought I had, when some months later at Santa Barbara, I began writing a play, or rather letting something out of my mind that had evidently been cooked for some time inside it, for two acts were finished in a week, and the third exited quite painlessly some months later. Nor did I realize until two acts were completed that in a sense, what I had written was a dramatic fantasy whose source was *L'Homme Qui Rit*.

It seemed as I walked into the Empire Theatre with Lionel on the first night of "Clair de Lune" that I could smell the tanbark of the Arena. There was such a crowd, all jostling each other and talking loudly, and dressed in their best. Fantastic rumors were afloat that some tickets had sold for seventy-five dollars apiece, that the production had cost $200,000 and all "for the love of Mike," as Emily

Stevens was amusingly quoted as having said. I was so dreadfully nervous that I had put on my dark blue dress with red chiffon sleeves, bought especially for the occasion, hind-side foremost, which, fortunately, I never discovered —even when I got pushed out on the stage to take my curtain calls between Ethel and Jack. The saleslady, however, who had sold me my dress, and was sitting in the second row, had a seizure.

Of that opening night Jack said, "Now you will show those s.o.b's., those society friends of yours, what you are made of! This is your justification!" "Justification": I thought, rather sadly to myself. "Always so much need to be justified for doing something if you don't have to." "Now they have to accept you for what you are," he would rave on, telling me many sweet and extravagant things, for indeed there is no doubt that by this production he wanted to see me stanced forever on a prow of safety and respect, high above all the ignominious wavelashings that cried out "amateur," "poseur," "society woman taking up poetry," etc. Dear Jack, a memory is not less touching because there is in it so much of childishness.

And how he had worked for this production, even deciding to dance the ballet of the play within a play himself, so that he went nearly every day to Kosloff, the great ballet master, for weeks on end. He conducted interminable rehearsals, and cast the play with a care I have never seen him lavish before or since on my production. Indeed toward "Clair de Lune," Jack behaved with a frenzy of generosity, dowering it in every way he could conceive, while poor Mr. Alf Heyman, head of the Frohman office, who must stand the cost, lost more of his health with each day, and did actually die shortly after the opening night.

When finalities in luxurious contracts had been signed, when magnificent costumes had been executed by Helen Dryden for every member of the cast, when set designs that were really magical had been achieved, mostly by Jack himself, and a fabulous music score selected by me from Faure, Debussy and some of my own compositions (for which I was paid the glorious sum of $1,000) had been orchestrated by Frank Tours, from a piano script by Dominico Savino and myself, then Jack would rush in to Heyman's office, crying out "Now Alf, I've got to have another couple of dwarfs dressed in gold brocade by tomorrow afternoon!"

That first night I sat in one of the back rows with Lionel so as not to be noticed, and the curtain rose on my play. I saw with my first pang of horror that whenever the music played, my lines were smothered! And then in some breathtaking lapses of any sound whatever from the stage, I was forced to conclude that Miss Barrymore as Queen Anne —regal in her many-tier'd necklace of aquamarine, looking as beautiful in her powdered hair, hoop skirts of white tulle, and diaphanous picture hat, the long plumes of which clasped her feather-light waist, as a poet's dream of a queen appearing in the moonlit pools of his imagination—still did not know anything like all of her lines. "Don't worry," Lionel would whisper, "a first night is always like this. No one will notice." "All right," I muttered, nearly sinking on his shoulder in a coma of apprehensive terror, for it appeared to me that if whole gobs of lines were skipped, then the ones to follow would be incomprehensible. But undoubtedly the ones who gave the play everything were Jack, as the clown Gwynplaine, and Violet Kemble Cooper, as the Duchess of Vaucluse. How good Violet Kemble Cooper was! While Jack with his true beauty on one side of his face, and his disfiguring make-up on the other, was superbly volatile and touching.

When the curtain fell, drunk with confusion and hope, I caught hold of a sensitive friend of mine, Gerald Murphy, whom I saw leaving his box, and knew to have a heart as well as a mind, to ask him what did he think of it. "Michael, it is wonderful," he told me, "but you have given them so much too much!"

Next morning I could see from the face of Miss Jones, the children's governess and staunch friend of the family fortunes, that all was not well. However, Jack kept all the papers to himself, reading them, I noticed, with an expression of glacial incredulity, till he suddenly pushed up from the breakfast table, and disappeared into the sanctum of our own back bedroom, to emerge several hours later with a speech he planned to deliver before the curtain that night.

Apparently the morning paper had dealt with the play in salvos of hilarious abuse, and there was an extraordinary amount about me personally, unattached to my playwriting, or to what might have been assumed to be the "métier" of criticism.

But the evening papers were without exception better. There were kind words, praise even began to seep in here and there. And then it developed that the dean of dramatic critics, Mr. H. T. Parker, having evidently read the play as well as seen it, had delivered a paean of praise in *The Boston Transcript* concerning the writing, the acting and the whole production of "Clair de Lune," and in the manner of Henry James, "Such matter, so placed, comes seldom to a stage as closely wedded to reality—or the pre-

tense of reality—as is ours, with so little room for the cast
of mind and spirit that courts such hazard or for the literary
and theatrical skill that may achieve it," etc., etc. And oddly
enough the weekly reviews without exception were splendid, including such distinguished pens as that of Ludwig
Lewisohn, and at this my spirits picked up. To be honest
they had never sunk very low—it was all so obvious that
it couldn't have helped happening.

The rehearsals of "Clair de Lune" were magically interesting to me. In fact I think I enjoyed them more than I
did the production; to see the actors under a single light
in the dark and empty theatre, stand up and assume in
their everyday clothes the characters of my play, was an
extraordinary experience. To watch the spirit's expansion
along the ruled markings of art, instead of the chaotic
diffusions of life, was something that struck my heart with
an emotion seemingly more pure than could be received
from what was actual. The fact of there being no stage
lights, nor costumes, nor sets, gave fancy all the more
freedom to concentrate upon the delicate strong fusion
between the actors and their parts.

I remember Jack at one of these rehearsals, in the boat
scene with his dying love "Dea" and the philosopher. I
shall never forget the almost insupportable beauty of his
pathos, and the girl's also—and that "coming to" after the
scene—I noticed one of the stage hands, sitting in the wings
cross-legged on a chair, had bowed his head over the back
of it.

And somehow at rehearsals the music in such a dreamy
twilight could not soar, and drown out speech, but was only
a thrilling undertone exploiting the qualities of the play.

CHAPTER XVII

eeeeeeeeeeeeeeeeeeeeeeeeeeeeeeeeeeeeeeeeeeeeeeeeeee

Wild Oats

I SUPPOSE it was a little unfortunate for my marriage with Jack that up to the time I met him my vagrant knockabout type of youth had never had its fling. Domestic life (I was 19 when my son was born) and social life had not permitted it to rear what might be called its gypsy head; as Charles Shaw wrote, "She is always marvellously unkempt!" However, the variety of emotions contributed by life with Jack produced enough gas to explode the cork from the bottle. And it was to be seen that I loved travelling by myself, with no critical Psyche to supervise, and was not averse to sitting out the hours at the sidewalk cafés of Paris, piling up the little white dishes, while I wafted myself out in possessive reverie to the indescribable miscellany of people who passed.

All through those lovely inspired, disorderly, and sometimes tragic days, Iris was my boon companion. I loved her courage with life. She had what the poet should have, consciously or unconsciously, an absolute inability to turn away

from what was true in her emotions, a fidelity toward birth
and rebirth, as if her wisdom knew that if you are really
imaginative, you are in sacred luck to be able to feel genuinely, and go fully forth from yourself, at all! Her personality was set apart, extraordinary because through her
real poetry had passed. And she was preserved through
some of her tragedies by this same poet quality, for there
were points in her nature where she could not be reached,
nor in consequence destroyed. It was only the weight of
what she took on in memory that could silence her, and
that is what did silence her, and looking at her I would
often think of the old Irish saying, "It is death to wound a
poet—it is death to love a poet—it is death to be a poet."

Some one has remarked that happiness has no history,
neither has egomania—or at best a short one. And if ever
two egotists crashed down in one field it was Jack and I.

We were all right; our reactions were marvellously similar about all that did not concern us personally. We agreed
about Christ and war, Walt Whitman and the critics. But
let our argument touch some channel where the ego lurked,
with its burning demon eyes, and all was up. Indeed we
went in holy terror of our pride in each other's hands—a
pardonable apprehension, as it often turned out—and
needed most urgently some mutual confidence in which to
mature and take care of the often inspiring beauty of our
emotions toward one another.

But it was too late when we started to try for first base,
or happiness. We should have met when we were two!
And I think if Jack were here he would probably add: "In
that case only one of us would have grown up!"

The spectacle we presented was both tragic and comic,

and what a charge we were to our friends! Many interesting doors in Paris, London and New York were opened to us—but either we were too weak, after our bouts of eternal discussion—(as Iris said, "It's a tennis game in hell, darling, where nobody misses a ball!")—to answer our invitations, or if we got there, were apt in a bad mood to continue our dynamic desire to get one another down, in every one's astounded and disgruntled face.

The summer after "Clair de Lune" I planned to go abroad alone, for by this time I felt the necessity of "coming up for air." And I went to Newport to say good-by to my family before sailing.

Jack had decided to be on a fishing trip while this occurred, as he and Papa had never met. But, when I was at Newport, Jack called up on the long distance to tell me he had stopped off in Boston, was feeling lonely and might he come down to see me? Of course I welcomed the idea, telling my father, "As I know you don't want to see Jack, I'm going down to meet him at his hotel." "Nonsense," said Papa. "As long as he's in Newport he might as well come here. And," he added, "I'll keep out of the way."

A few hours later the bell rang and I waited for him to be shown upstairs to my sitting room. Time passed, no one came. "Someone else must have rung," I thought. Hours elapsed, and I went downstairs to find Jack and Papa sitting on the yellow side porch drinking whiskies and soda together, having cemented a friendship that was to become real affection on both sides and last as long as my father lived. Indeed, Papa would never hear anything said against Jack from that time onward. He had been utterly charmed, but there was more to it than that. With older men of whom he was really fond, Jack was at his best. He was his true self, modest, good-natured and the most amusing company in the world. He had a manliness, a reality in these relationships that would have made any friend with whom he had shared such hours absolutely incredulous of another kind of report.

Again some one has remarked—some one who was undoubtedly flung into the mill race gagged and bound—that "there is nothing so dead as a dead love."

So that in retrospect this part of my life necessarily takes on somewhat the character of fiction. Where it is preserved in its emotional integrity is in my poetry.

"In God's green earth what's the matter with you, Baby?" said dapper Aunt Tessie Oelrichs to me one morning in Morgan Harjes, "and with your husbnd?" she added after a distressing gasp. "Why you look like a couple of equestrians." And it was true that Jack and I dressed in a manner never affected before or since. Pleatings and flutings had appeared on his trousers, duplicates of the ones on my skirt. We wore exactly the same felt hats, cocked at a similar devastating angle. Jack let his hair grow longer, and considerably lowered his shirt collars, of which I instantly had a dozen copies made. And although his acting continued to be superb, my poetry took a strange slant, it grew convulsed with angels and fakes.

We were suffering—something was being demanded of us. Integrity—mercy, which we were not adult enough to pass one another, and suffering I have always thought, after a certain point, makes people unreal, and unreality

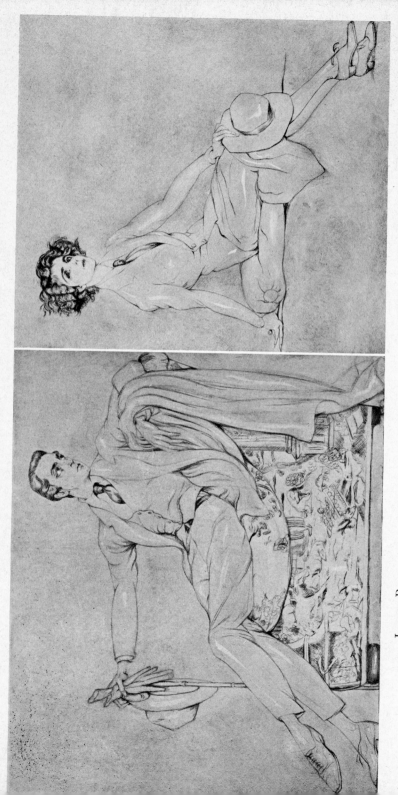

JOHN BARRYMORE

"Jack and I dressed in a manner never affected before or since. Pleatings and flutings appeared on his trousers, duplication of the ones on my skirt. We wore the same felt hats cocked at a devastating angle; he considerably lowered his shirt-collars, of which I instantly had a dozen copies made."

MICHAEL STRANGE (when she was Mrs. John Barrymore)

DIANA BARRYMORE

prolonged enough can reach madness; and it is a common trait of madness to make a legend of its pain. So that after a bad night, you are apt, in good faith, to ring for breakfast and no longer keep it from any one that it is Saint Sebastian who is hungry.

What is madness, what is that sly secret amusement in the eyes of a madman but the knowledge of place and power, which the poor rascals he contacts are not fit to perceive?

Under the automatic beneficence of Nature, he has made a fairy tale of his anguish that is at least consistent with a pride so mighty now that it is mortally damaged—and of course only the heightened story is a vast enough receptacle to absorb an agony that has brimmed over human endurance and flooded the system with poison.

Suicide was a favorite topic and threat; and one afternoon, in our lovely apartment in the Impasse de Conti over the River Seine (lent us for a couple of weeks by our friend Mrs. William Astor Chanler, as a sort of honeymoon gift), Jack fled from the particular dispute, announcing that this time he was going to do it! "Go ahead," I shouted after his running figure, to remain taut, with the beginnings of agony and remorse. A few minutes later I darted out hatless, and ran desperately along toward Notre Dame, colliding with ruminative readers at the book stalls and furious pedestrians, when suddenly I thought I saw, in the distance, standing on a cobbled road that runs beneath the Quai, on a level with the river, and already looking into it—Jack! Putting on speed and yelling with my hands cupped to my lips, a spectacle of bewilderment and horror to the essentially formal French, I made for what I supposed to be him, to find, long before I drew up, only a rather poetic-looking individual baiting his fish hook as he stared into the Seine.

Slowly I returned; evidently he had drowned himself in another direction. There was nothing to do but go home and wait for the police or something. And into the flat I dragged, and into his room, worn to a pulp by my emotions. And there lay Jack on his bed. There he had been all the time, beautifully and poetically asleep!

My own attempts at suicide were less impressive—a few calls from behind the bathroom doors of various hotels, that I had swallowed iodine, and a wonderful act from Jack on the other side, crying out that he would break his head against the door unless I opened it. And once I remember, after a terrific crash, followed by silence, that, flinging the door open, I found him stretched out on the floor. "He's brained himself," I thought, as I knelt over him searching his breast for some evidence of breathing; and that hideous blank sensation of its being all too late now was savored by me to the full, before Jack's knowledge of how to hold his breath and look dead—as the curtain slowly falls—gave out before the reality of my alarm, that kept me gazing and crying out over him until morosely he had to sit up and breathe.

But one night we were outdone by superior players. It was in Paris at the Hotel Crillon during that black hour before dawn when vitality ebbs and you are apt to admit anything. We were having one of our arguments which, though they might begin calmly enough, would sooner or later reveal the lamp of the third degree, searing my eyeballs. "So," said Jack, "you do not care that a poet whom you admire above all others—am I to understand above all others—"

"You are!"

"—is rumored to have had homosexual relationships?"

"Why not?"

"Why not! Is there nothing ridiculous to you in the idea of a venerable poet with a long white beard—and a bus-boy?"

"What have his pleasures to do with his greatness? What concern are they of mine? I'm not the bus-boy! I'm his reader!"

"You are a poet," said Jack (the district attorney now coming gravely to the fore), "and no doubt you feel that a poet should follow his emotions wherever they might lead him."

"Of course!"

"Then in God's name," said he, sweeping all the glasses off the table, "what security is there in life with such a person?"

At this point, however, so horrible a blow struck the ceiling over us, that it seemed to be no less than the rest of the Crillon, when Jack, after a startled pause, and throwing an unforgettable look of eerie camaraderie at the ceiling remarked, "Ah, Professionals!" Poking our heads out the door, we saw scurrying figures, and the manager, in his frock coat, ascending in an open lift toward the "After Silence" to learn that Isadora Duncan and her Russian poet husband, having anchored over us, the poet, no doubt in some frenzy of despairing realization anent the inefficacy of words, had leapt into the air, and catching hold of the chandelier, borne it to the ground with him—so bringing their argument to a full stop.

ecccecceccecceccecceccecceccecceccecceccecce

Crashes and Confusion

Now I HAD often said to Jack, "You go on acting, as the whole world wants you to, and although I can't say I know who wants me to write poetry, and my books don't sell, still I feel I must, and it's difficult to, in the sort of life we have!"

"I know," said Jack, mischief breaking up his face into the finest subtleties of Greek sculpture. "You have to change a line here and there before I see your poems, because after all, my lips are not as red as 'holly berries seen against the snow'."

However, there being a maniacal strength in the egotism of poets as well as actors, I pushed the discussion back over the old ground, telling him that the life of a recluse which I now led was giving me a case, practically speaking, of malnutrition.

"I suppose you want to have people in to tea again," said Jack.

"Why not?"

"Is tea any other thing than a sex projection?"

"Sex projection? Oh, my God! And I suppose there was no sex projection in 'The Jest' now, was there?"

(Crashes and Confusion!)

However, the end of these negotiations was that if I were to accept Jack's being the dream lover of the entire world, and who could tell when, according to Iris, he might not be outsped and brought down by his hunters, then he must at least allow me to project myself as I liked across the tea table.

Venice hanging in the air like a blast of music—
Disappearing in whiffs of opal mother o'pearl—

At Venice the fates played into my hand, commencing to forge an exit from my life with Jack. After a sojourn at St. Moritz, to which chilly playground Iris had been dragooned from Paris, in order to serve as umpire to our diabolic bouts of repartee, I decided Jack and I must now have a long spell of separate air. So Iris and I started a walking trip from St. Moritz into Italy (which called for initiative from the first day, when she left her only pair of shoes drying on a bush from which they instantly disappeared) and Jack went off to Chamonix, from where he soon wrote that he had achieved Mt. Blanc sustained only by a couple of aspirins. And a most wonderful picture of him arrived hanging from the rungs of an iron ladder, his extraordinary face backed by a tremendous declivity; a haze of distant earth and stretch of sky.

When my friend and I, dressed in the picturesque remnants of what we had on when we left St. Moritz, drew up in our gondola littered with rucksacks before the Grand Hotel, the Baron de Meyer and Rollie Cottenet, who were idling on the terrace, sprang from their chairs as if something bizarre as the barge of Elaine, manned by its deaf mute, were once more negotiating Westminster Bridge.

But Iris soon strung up to the breaking point by the languorous air of Venice—for in Venice you must be with your lover or obsessed by him—had fled back to Paris. Jack was still crossing the Alps, and one night, filled with the mild elation of being left alone in a beautiful adventurous place, I strolled in (as *Time* would say), to "cosmopolitan Molly Lloyd's" for dinner and there met a blond young man with a pale poetic face, who carried his head thrown back and his chest pushed out, as if he had been running against a wind to deliver tidings of sacred moment. Increasing my favorable reactions, he told me, "Yes, I saw you crossing the Piazza this morning with Geoffrey Carr and his dog, and I said 'There goes an angel crossing the Piazza!'"

After this we got on famously, and gliding down the Picole Canales past the half-macabre splendor of Venetian thresholds, it seemed that the young man was becoming attached to me. "Let him," I thought. "Here is really something for Jack to endure!" My disreputable egotism quite lost on me.

But one blazing day, the cowed Alps behind him, Jack arrived, looking nervous and sunburnt, and we got only as far as our charming apartment on the Grand Canal, hung with yellow damask and loaded with heavily white Venetian flowers, before the eventual "blow."

"Is he in love with you?" asked Jack, the second after I had mentioned my new friend, looking as if his pulses might easily throb him out of his skin. "I'm not in love with him," I replied, adding with the diplomacy of a falling rock, "and that's the only part of it that concerns you."

"I wonder," said Jack, and he threw a look toward the Canal.

Going into my room, I banged the door, then paused in terror behind it, listening for curses and pursuit, or maybe just a splash, when suddenly I heard, drifting in through the open windows, a sound to make any one pause and be set apart from his obsessions, Jack's marvellous voice commencing the soliloquy "Oh that this too, too solid flesh would melt. . . ." And raptly listening to him I felt again how much more touching in its reality Art was than Life could ever be.

Artists are amazing people. Their imaginative pride can so utterly fool them into believing they would be able to behave like mature merciful people in the light of noon. And now there followed days of breathless excitement, and also incredible misery, during which my unfortunate friend, used as a decoy and bait, on the battleground of our flaming egomanias, lunched with me, pale as a sheet, in some remote restaurant during those hours in which it was assigned to Jack to learn how to trust me, and give me my freedom—described to him as being in the poet's case, the necessity we all had to follow up each fresh opportunity of getting to know people very well indeed. And at twilight I went to my rendezvous on the "Bridge of Sighs" with Jack, who leapt out from the giant shadows looking as if nerves had taken the place of bones.

One night our obsessed wandering anchored us beneath the windows of the Grand Hotel, from which furious heads and voices were soon seen and heard telling us, in various languages, to "shut up." A friend of ours looked out and, seeing with horror who we were, rushed down in his pyjamas, and still tells of how we each took hold of an arm and walked him about all night until sunrise, listening to our infuriated résumé of wrongs.

I think my poor young friend's point of view is the only one worthy of comment. He liked me, not only for his personal motives, but for whatever he was generous enough to believe I was or could be. He saw with distaste and apprehension the somewhat hysterical falsity of my existence with Jack. And he felt that if our emotional seesaw were prolonged long enough, they might have to back up the wagon, and that it would not be for Jack, whom he rightly felt to be my superior in discipline and adroitness.

I think it is true that the most awkward gestures, the most absurdly maneuvered situations can sometimes expose a real yearning; and apparently I was ready to bring on anything, even disaster, rather than not know if there was —what my instinct daily asserted with tocsin clangor there was not—any essential fairness from Jack toward me: "Who tells me true, tho' in his tale lie death, I hear him as he flattered" must have been printed on the lung through which I breathed.

So then this incident ended badly, although both gentlemen showed up magnificently during a scene, a few weeks later in Paris, when they leaned against Beatrice Chanler's mantel. Then Terence, after a fine harangue in which he asked Jack to set me free for both our sakes, paused suddenly, to consider the man standing before him, a being so boyishly fragile, so poetic-looking, that when Jack told him, in his most limpid style, and using the touching registers in his beautiful voice, that of course I was utterly,

utterly free, and that all he wanted on earth was my happiness, I could see, from where I lurked in the door, that Terence was not only moved and disarmed but was beginning to wonder if this poor young man, standing so genuinely shaken before him, might not be the victim of some cruel hoax perpetrated by *my* infernal imagination.

However, while Terence was struggling in the coils of what was surely supermagnetism, and the conversation becoming a series of bows, and gifts of my future from hand to hand, I threw in that all I wanted on earth was to go home alone on the steamer and sleep the trip through, while Jack did Sherlock Holmes in England and Terence remained where he was.

But next spring, feeling that the winter had led only to the usual arch seclusion for me, and a single cinema for Jack, and that it was still impossible to know how he would react to a few tea parties, I was off to Europe with my sister-in-law Doris, whose tragic sadness anent the possibility of her coming separation from Lionel needed some attempt at recreation. And Jack, in an extraordinary mood of sublimation, bade me farewell in my cabin, having left with the steward a series of exquisite bouquets to be delivered on each day of the trip.

"Be as fascinating as you can," I told him, "and do great things!"

"You too," he replied, generously. "I'll wire all your friends to meet you in Paris and this time we'll learn how to trust one another."

Doris was also sanguine; she felt that here was the opportunity of our lives to achieve a foundation of confidence.

Once in Paris, Doris, in her green-eyed wisdom, saw I

had bitten off a great deal more than I could chew, as attempting to fill the part of the carefree artist, the unobsessed observer, another George Sand, etc. I fell off curbs and missed flights of steps, wondering just how much my freedom was costing Jack's peace of mind.

"Freedom for what?" I would ask myself wretchedly, in the words of Nietzsche, as the acacia blossoms in the Bois fell over Terence's feet and mine. Poor Terence, who, imagining that his affection had pushed me out once more into God's light and air, had now to listen to the confused apprehensions of some one quite raw with tenderness, and to conclusions about personal freedom which might have emanated from Queen Victoria's breakfast table.

However, we all forged ahead, united at any rate by suspense; Doris wondering if Lionel would come back to her; I if Jack would stick by me; and Terence with his head flung back toward a race for the ideal, his wonderful eyes strained with their reflections, already envisaging the smoke of the sacrifice, the placated deity, and a better life for all.

Well agonized, but each one with his hopes, we arrived on a bright summer afternoon at May Norris' superb château in the mountains above Grasse. Then—despite our complicated address, and wretched facilities for wire transmission, all telegrams having to ascend *"par loup,"* or alongside the crisscross of a mountain torrent—a long telegram from Jack arrived, which described that in allowing me to go on this jaunt he had forced himself to go too desperately against his grain, that apparently he could not give me what I wanted, so it would be better if we never met again.

I opened Jack's wire to find that, innocent as I was of any offense, it was impossible for him to trust me. Because, as I never doubted from that moment, he knew himself so well.

I remember Doris standing with the cable in her hand in the somber shadows of her spacious red-tiled, white-plastered room while the doves cooed outside the closed shutters. And I wept hard before her as if I were being seasick, and she kept on saying, "I never thought Jack would do such a cruel thing. He will pay for it."

And looking back, I believe, although we still had some years left together, that any genuine vitality of hope I had towards a mutually happy, successful life, fled on that day, in that wonderfully spacious house that was like a Shrine of Peace.

CHAPTER XIX

The Oswald Mosleys

SOMETIMES it has happened that people who were going to mean a great deal to me have cast their shadows across my consciousness before we actually met.

So, dining with Jack one night in the Casino at Deauville, in a state of heightened sensitivity because he was accusing me of trying to catch the eye of an old friend, the still extraordinarily beautiful Lord Cholmondeley (Horatio Rocksavage), and I was denouncing him for having attracted upon himself the full, level glance of buxom Kitty Schoenbrunn (now Baroness Eugene Rothschild), I saw enter at the far end of the room an amazing-looking couple. Both were tall and dark and slim. I noticed the casual arrogance of the man's poise, and the regal loveliness of the woman as she went towards her table with a grace that did not need pride to set it off; and I heard some murmur of "the Mosleys," and thought to myself with naïve *empressement*, "how wonderful to look like that and be Lady Cynthia Mosley."

But it was not until October that I met them. Jack had returned to America to reopen in "Hamlet," and I was coming back to life with some morbid indifference at the Hotel Trianon at Versailles when, arriving late for dinner one night, at the impeccable Villa Trianon of Elsie de Wolfe's, there they were, across the table from me.

I caught Tom's stare first, a Byronic eyeful of hauteur, romance, and whimsical salute, and then I saw his wife's sweet face turned to me with a childlike sort of recognition and pleasure.

And I did not dare to look too much at the Mosleys, for amongst the rest of the company which might have been recruited from the ranks of Peter Arno, Cruikshank and the Vogue Pattern Book, they stood out before my astonished eyes like a couple of "Martians."

Then later, when I was alone and passing a comb through my hair before a mirror in the dressing room, I looked into Mr. Mosley's eyes standing directly behind me.

Like a magic carpet, for which we had no further use, the party, and every one at it, rolled up and faded away. We three were so glad to have met, and we went from plush-garish café to café, Tom dancing with us in turn, and Cynthia watching Tom and me drink without rancor. Finally, I remember, as he and I were executing a waltz somewhere in the old bouncing manner, we tripped and fell to the floor, pulling the cloth off the table nearest us, together with everything on it!

A couple of laughing gentlemen rose and helped us to our feet, one of them, a short, squarely built fellow with great style to his head, asking me in French, "But where have I seen you before?" And opening my mouth to reply, "I can't imagine," I saw that he was Moskvin, one of the principals of the Moscow Art Theatre. "Ah, I remember just where—on Mr. Barrymore's dressing table, and you are Mrs. Barrymore," he went on alarmingly, for Jack was liable to be disturbed over something less than a rumor of my having fallen to the floor with a Byronic stranger in a festive mood at 3 A. M. in Paris. So I swore Moskvin to secrecy, and after some Russian toast drinking, we returned to Cynthia, who was blazing with laughter.

That night, the first of our friendship, we did not want to separate, so the Mosleys drove back with me to Versailles. St. Cloud went flying by, the tunnels roared in our ears, and then came that shakeup on the cobblestones at Versailles; and we said good night in that fake marble hallway of the Trianon Palace, dim with the dawn, and usually consecrated to gigolos, poodles and their fat shameless proprietresses.

It rained, and it misted, and the autumnal forests of Versailles were marvellous that year—great Gothic alleyways of moist black-iron branches hung with lemon-yellow leaves that came fluttering down with every breath from the gray sky, and touched you with gentle evanescence, making of your walking a kind of disembodied *shushura*; until distinctly you heard in that veiled atmosphere some nocturne, in which spoke the mournful eternities of passionate memory and forsaken loveliness.

Tom and I walked through those moist Cathedral aisles, pausing by the disused fountains, stirring with languid fingers the dark rain water to its brownish depths, until we brought a strange tremulous, reflected life to the o'er leaning satyr faces ornamenting the classic stone base. How magical that afternoon is in memory.

I found Mosley an interesting, romantic, bitterly impatient man. In those days he was a member of that Labor Party which contrived somehow to go on hoping that Ramsay MacDonald would not forget the interests of the British workman, now that he saw so much of Lord and Lady Londonderry. But Mosley was the last man you could envisage as a Socialist. He was an aristocrat, angered by the stupidities, procrastinations and muddlings (a word he often used), of his own class; yet you did not feel that his contemptuous wrath for one lot of people drew him nearer to the others for whom he fought.

He could easily persuade me how outrageous it was "for that jackass, the Duke of X," to discover coal under his lawns and woods, and become, through this happy coincidence of ownership, a millionaire on a gigantic scale. Yet when I drove in his Mercedes car to hear him speak in drab quarters of London, I did not feel that he gave to his anæmic, oppressed audience any warmth whatsoever.

But Tom was in love with his own "will to power" and certain scruples went down before the avidity of his vanity, and the philosophy that it needed to flourish in; for he had to have all sorts of stimulants to keep his self-confidence up to the scratch, and with subtlety and irony he sought these out. His humor was immensely elated by the absurdity of people. He was stirred by beauty, warmed and shattered by whatsoever was really rare, and he had great charm in spite of his egotism, perhaps because of it.

Cynthia loved people and had a child's fresh delight in pleasure of every sort—good food, lovely clothes, charming people. Her gusto about sun bathing at Cap Ferrat, American cocktails, and movie celebrities was as genuine as her desire that the poor should be told not only how to reach the necessities of life, but also some of its glamour. If only they would organize and protest! And so she would go speech-making and distributing her pamphlets in her most lovely clothes,—coming in for lunch one day laughing and soaking wet because some sour conservative had hosed her off the stoop. "But not before I had thrown all my literature in at the door," she told us as she fled to her room.

Her indignation with the selfish ignorance and ascetic evasions of her own set had in it none of the barbed irony of Tom's. It had the purity and beauty of an angel's wrath, and her laughter was so tenderly infectious! directed as it always was, not upon what was pitiable or ridiculous, but on the crookedness of values.

"Imagine," she would say; "poor Nannie is in despair because Nick and Viv (her two small children) aren't going to be asked to join So-and-so's dancing class because we're Socialists. Isn't it too absurd, when we're making all this fuss simply for her!" And Cynthia loved her husband with all her heart. Her life mirrored his wishes, and in those early days she saw his mounting egotism generously and without alarm.

Ramsay MacDonald was a frequent visitor at 8 Smith Square and before elections Cynthia's face and his would divide a post card. With her chronic kindliness she was fond of Mr. MacDonald, but in the slight acquaintance-ship we had I was not as impressed as I had looked forward to being; I thought him handsome, but in a harsh and hollow sort of way. You would theatrically cast him for the "Man with a Noble Head." And I wondered how this dry, rather haughty individual could speak courageously and warmly enough for British Labor, for surely people battling for the necessities of life, work and food, plus self-respect, would need more warmth and courage to give them heart than it seemed to me he had.

I admired these friends of mine so much. They had love and children and a fight on their hands that they were making together; and as I listened to their Socialist premise I grew bewitched by its logic and was glad to take some people at the values I heard voiced in their house "that arch-conservative Lady Astor with all her liberal tomfoolery, etc., etc."

Because Tom has since become Sir Oswald Mosley, leader of the Fascist movement in Great Britain, certain slants of our conversations that had no particular significance then stand out now in memory. And I think from the emotional, intellectual viewpoint he was a Fascist long before quitting the Socialist ranks. I remember our talk one night over dinner in a restaurant when Cim had gone off to speak somewhere. He showed such a brilliant knowledge of the gods and goddesses of German mythology, praising the heroic structure of the Wagner operas, which seemed natural enough to me, considering the sublime composer's "Ring" was said to have been created during his socialist days, and friendship with the anarchist Mikail Bakunin. Nor do I recall at what point I realized that the theme of the "Ring," concerned as it is with the bad news that can brand even immortals when they reach after treasure, passed Tom by. It was the pagan strength, not the moral he admired. Then Cæsar came on as a topic, to stay right with us, and I was amused to hear the great militarist described as the most exotically imaginative of lovers, and the most obliging, where the opportunism of his ambitions was concerned. Cæsar seemed to have obliged "every day in every way better and better."

And Tom described with the vividness of heartfelt alignment a path of striding warriors and heroes, paramountly concerned with the triumph of the empires they served, who, although accepting the consolations of beautiful and submissive creatures, at intervals, never yielded to these frail emblems of their necessity any right whatever to detain them on the march to new conquests and joys.

Listening to him, it became evident that he considered the whole A. D. period one long depressing drift into degeneracy. Mercy did not seem to intrigue him at all, nor the wonderful Creator of its consideration in the world.

Much of his attitude to women was out of the old Nietzschean theory, "When you go to a woman, take your whip," and I thought his insistence on manhood's right to egoistic brutality rather suggestive of what the gentlemen with bulging brows call "a deficiency neurosis."

But there was more to it than that! Tom felt that the "time sense" of his contemporaries was archaic, that they allowed intrigue, adroitness and debate to interfere with all straight thinking and acting. The machinery of government was perilously old-fashioned if the other European countries were to get into modern gear. Palliations of the wretched political confusion and the eternal palaver of liberals sickened him. He longed for a spirited readjustment from the bottom up, and to carry forward clear-cut convictions with unyielding courage. The miserable lives of a large percentage of the English people, which he had seen as a Socialist, had long persuaded him that a democracy which could leave so much to be desired for the majority was hiding an opposite idea, under a stooge title.

Again and again he would repeat, "The character of time has changed, we must know exactly for what we stand, there must be unity and realism behind our convictions, for if we cannot get things done as quickly as the day demands what will become of us?" And I thought he is saying exactly what Julian Huxley wrote, "This age differs from all ages preceding it—as no two ages have differed from one another."

There was, and is, in Tom something of the martyr, of the man whose particular wisdom is destined to become against his background, such as it is, an agony, only to be endured by a straight advance upon danger.

And yet he was stimulating and fascinating to be with. His advice to me to be myself—to be all the selves I could trump up—burnt into my ears with a kind of infernal charm. After listening to him I felt richer in daring, more bound not to be duped by conscience, cowardice, nor any inferiority complexes. I did not realize, then, how dangerous such a viewpoint might be to the happiness of Cynthia, who practiced daily, and with all her heart's intensity, devotion and mercy and common sense, and had also the high, fine, youthful spirits, demanding and believing in responses on her own terms.

And not often enough I thought that, strong as she seemed to be because of the vitality of her heart, too much was being put upon her, always on the run between her work, her family and holidays abroad. These could be fairly hectic, with Tom's behavior modelled, apparently, on the precepts of Wotan, Alcibiades and Cæsar.

In those days we all went about quite a lot with that odd miscellany of successful artists of the musical comedy and farce variety, rich travellers in a bright mood, and titled people somewhat chastened by events, who clustered around the buoyant overemphasis of Elsa Maxwell. I found Elsa very diverting; she took a childish, uproarious pleasure in cracking the whip over this ring in which she had persuaded so many prominent people to posture. And she had her disarming contrasts too, for on a night table by her bed could always be found the latest that was worthwhile in fiction, drama and poetry; as I recall it, her literary avidity only reined in before philosophy and mysticism; but I am unfailingly grateful to Elsa Maxwell for showing me a side that is not the one usually selected for report— the side of a serious friend, worried by my pangs and casting about with sensibility and intelligence to restore my attention to real duties instead of doomed hysterias.

Cynthia was pleased by my being struck, one afternoon as we were leaving the House of Commons, by a man with an extraordinary face, the transparent nobility of which seemed to have been actually lit up by some blast furnace of anguished dreams. "That is Maxton," I was told, "and English Labor has not got a more genuine friend." "Why doesn't he lead it?" I asked her. "He has the finest revolutionary head and face I have ever seen!" "But we don't want a revolution," said Cynthia, in her lilting, caressing voice. "Besides, I think Maxton is burnt out. He lost his wife and children in some hideously avoidable accident, due to the system's chicanery. He won't be met, either, and lives only for his work." And I thought to myself, "That would be it, for this man is even terrifyingly unconscious of himself, of the glow he presents, of menace and salvation." Only great anguish could set a man as free from himself as that, and energies all focussed on a single retributive point.

In the December of the autumn I met Cynthia I came over to see Heinemann about publishing some of my new poems. Pale Terence, with his harassed priest-poet's face, companioned me with that unhappy servitude it assuaged him still to give, and we burst into the Eiffel Tower for supper where in Herr Stoolig's small rooms the most famous successes and failures in the London world of art and letters gathered expansively, boastfully or in a drugged and picturesque silence.

Lunching next day with Tom and Cim, I met a thin, sensitive individual with visionary eyes and it seemed to greatly please my friends that Mr. Massingham, editor of the *Fortnightly Review* appeared to like me.

At the request of Mr. Massingham I sent him some books of my poems and "Clair de Lune," and wish I had not lost the letter he wrote me after he had read them, for in those drab hours "when no glorious conviction appearing unannounced across the portals of reverie," it would be good to have such a letter to reread; and perhaps consoled, strengthened by its eloquence and clarity and faith, make yet another dash at the hurdles.

Mr. Massingham asked me that day if there was any one in London that I would especially care to meet? And I said, "Of course! Bernard Shaw," and the very next morning I found, shoved under my door, a message from Mr. Shaw inviting me for lunch that very day! Instantly I cancelled a luncheon engagement with Lady Colfax and I remember swallowing a good-sized noggin of gin at a corner "pub" on my way from the British Museum, where I had been working all morning, to his house in Adelphi Terrace. I arrived there, ignominiously the first, in a simple, white, book-lined study overlooking the fog-wreathed terrace.

In a few seconds in came tall, thin Mr. Shaw, in a dark blue suit, with such a domelike forehead and such bright blue eyes, white hair and fresh complexion. "He is an adolescent, and a Druid," I thought, as he shook me warmly by the hand, and told me, in a fine brogue, "Massingham wouldn't let me go back to the country 'til I'd seen you!" And then Mr. Massingham and his daughter arrived, and we had a most pleasant luncheon with Mr. Shaw getting younger and younger, and airing his prejudices with a spendthrift brilliance. At one moment, having added something of my own to a great paean of his abuse, he leaned over and, clapping me on the shoulder, announced, "But you have a fine sense of invective yourself! You ought to be in the House of Commons!"

As his talk ranged from music to drama, to politics, illuminating every subject with an impish caricaturing of wisdom that you could not contradict, or top, my first impression deepened, that he was both a very young and a very ancient man, but that some serious thing had been left out between. Was it possibly this void which he must sense as a limitation, that made for cruelty in him, a cruelty keeping his superb instincts concerning humanity, and demoniacally fluent intellect from their fullest, deepest development? And gazing at him I wondered if that Mephistophelian tusklike look, which appeared at the corners of his mouth, came from the way his beard grew, or from the character of his smile.

Was he, perhaps, compelled to caricature this wisdom

of life, that intellectually he sensed so fully, because life had not allowed him to know her quite well enough through a man's emotion? However, he was a charming, a great man, sparkling with sanity and right about everything, whether he showed it to you in reverse English or not. And when I was leaving, he invited me to come again, and asked me with the most candid inconsequence, "Why on earth did you marry an actor?"

Lady Colfax was one of the great London hostesses of that moment. She collected celebrities, mostly by means of short notes in a large, clear hand, and infinite reminders on post cards. And lunching with her one day, surrounded by fame—and as I was the very least of anything in the celebrity line and had already remarked a famous peer and writer on my left, with Vita Sackville West on his left, Miss West, looking like "Orlando" and also the last word in breeding and remoteness—it seemed to me probable, that the deeply lined coffee-colored gentleman on my right, with the incredibly thick mustache, might be the one letdown that can happen anywhere! And looking at his heavily spectacled face, which somehow resembled a cocoanut, I decided to mingle our nonentities, telling him, "I'm afraid I didn't catch your name." "Rudyard Kipling," he answered. "The marvellous author of *Without Benefit of Clergy*," I thought to myself, bursting into a sweat of reverential embarrassment.

Another great English friend of mine was Bridget Guinness, who lived in a state of Titianesque and Renaissance splendor and disorder, at Carlton House Terrace. The artist, mother and society hostess fought together for supremacy in this red-haired, green-eyed, pale and beautiful Bridget, giving to her household contrasts that were dynamically picturesque. Card parties, boasting the *éclat* of royalty's Presence, would be shattered by the dancing entrance of her three small children, quite nude but for their Bacchante wreaths. Huge easels set up in the drawing room, and containing vague designs to be consummated on that *manana* of amateurs, tripped up the footmen; while there were often workmanlike stains of thick paint on the brocade curtains. Bridget's capacity for friendship, however, was contradicted by nothing, and I have fled to her house at the most inauspicious hours, even putting her husband out of her bed—if an especial cataclysm with Jack were on—never to be disappointed in her gift for consolation.

Dining with her one night I found myself beside a very old gentleman who seemed, because of the tender pink of his complexion, and the gentle whiteness of his hair, to be well on in his second childhood. And I was immensely pleased when Mr. George Moore invited me for luncheon at his house in Ebury Street, feeling certain that in the home of this great stylist whose *Memories of my Dead Life* had been one of the *accoucheurs* of my intellect, I would meet with the most distinguished representatives of Literature in London.

On that December day the long shaft of Ebury Street was lost in a dismal haze of fog, as I rang the bell of one of the uniform houses, and stood palpitating on the stoop.

Mr. Moore met me in his small green-white sitting room, and after a while it grew apparent that we were lunching alone. Our meal was of the good old English variety, greens immersed in water, tender meat, and I remember a delicious bottle of white wine. As Mr. Moore placidly reminisced, a suspicion I had had as his reader returned and grew, that his attitude to sex was really very Latin, extremely un-English. For one felt, as the conversation riveted itself upon a hundred facets of the relationship between men and women—as if nothing else could be thought of for a luncheon *à deux*—that the pleasure of what might be called such contacts had always been more talked about than experienced. And, I wondered, could Mr. Moore ever have loved suddenly, wildly, and fallen amuck of all the innuendoes! From his talk I couldn't make out, filled as it was with the repercussions of an era of cut-glass, repoussée silver, and beautiful, blond, well-corseted ladies in dresses of princess lace, pursuing intrigues on yachting parties, along the glamorous coast of the Riviera.

After luncheon we went up to a simple library for coffee, when Mr. Moore, who had fallen silent on a sofa, as I dreamed along about him, while I tried to work my back into a spot of heat from the coal grate, suddenly—and no doubt rousing himself to the gallantry of an old formula— asked me if I would mind . . . undressing! I looked at the old gentleman with a horror that was entirely apologetic, and from which even in his balmiest days he could have reaped no savor of indignant coquetry, as I answered with a naïveté that must have revolted and disgusted him, "No, of course I don't, Mr. Moore, but it's so cold in here do you mind if I only take off my shirtwaist?" After an embarrassing interval Mr. Moore, changing gears, produced a roll of his manuscript, the sketch for a play he was writing on St. Paul. I took it, appreciating the compliment he paid me, but with misgiving, since I had not cared a great deal for *The Brook Kerith* (his book on Christ).

What a piece of *volu marginalia* it had appeared to me
to be, on the most touching, tragic and hauntingly beautiful
subject ever to challenge the imagination. So I said good-
by to Mr. Moore and lost his manuscript and two of his
letters, but continued to hold much of his earlier work in
admiration unchanged by the somewhat appalling experience of having met this great writer too nearly ready for
his eternal sleep.

In those days, and of course without our knowing it,
Fate was loosening the foundations of ways in which all
three of us, Cim, Tom, and I, thought we were set forever.
And looking back I wonder how I could have been so in-
sulated as to catch nothing of the drift of this mounting
murmur of change in which there was to be much grief.
Tom's discontent was growing, since the Labor Party did
not seem able to spring "full-fledged from the brow of
Jove" and taking the field in triumph press the baton onto
him for the rest of the performance. Labor was somewhat
in retreat, led there by Ramsay MacDonald, who, palpitating like a débutante upon the brink of the King and his
Circle's good will, began to trouble less about the chief
point in the platform that had elected him, government
ownership of mines. So it grew less endurable for Tom to
be jeered at by his former friends for allegiance to a party
with which he was losing sympathy.

As Tom grew riled with his party, Cynthia gave ever
more devotion to him in his irritation, and to me in the
throes of finding out that life with Jack was becoming one
long stretch of listening for the next crash. And always
through the confusion of those years I knew I could go to
Cynthia and bring her my children (as I did on several

occasions) and that her friendship was a certain, bright, limitless fixture in the darkening of what seemed to me, then, a large part of my horizon.

ee

This Army of Agonies

"O you to whom I stretched forth my arms
Radiantly—as a child at last finding himself
In fairyland—awake
O you into whom I sinking my glance
Have become exalted! refreshed!
As a thirst-dying traveller
Stopped finally before his pool of dreams.
Tell me how should I with outstretched arms,
Vulnerable eyes,
With nerves suddenly relaxed as a child's
(From nightmare waking into the sweetness
Of his own little room)
How should I so disarmed,
Have heard through the soaring flutes of our caresses
The viol's increasing of pain!

IN PARIS a few weeks before Jack was expected back from "Hamlet," I had been dining with Mrs. William Randolph Hearst, and sitting next to, and exchanging salvos of laughter with, a marvellously gay, chesty blond fellow with a tapering protrusion of chest and slimness of leg that made him fantastically resemble a pouter pigeon. Suddenly his shirt stud burst from its setting and, flying across the table, hit in the face a dark, swarthy man whom I seemed to have noticed screwing up his eyes at me in a peculiar manner.

Lord Castleross, the pouter pigeon, leant across the table to apologize for the accident; and the dark man, getting up, came over to our side to assure him that it was all nothing at all. Then turning to me he said: "I am Zuloaga, and I would like you to pose for me. There will be no responsibility on your part. I would just like to paint your portrait. What is your name and telephone number?" Much impressed, I gave them.

When I went to Zuloaga's studio I brought with me a lovely pink and silver dress which the famous designer Edward Molyneaux had practically given me on the theory of "Michael, you can't go to any more balls in Paris in your sister-in-law's red gingham beach dress, no one understands it!" and also a medieval boy's costume. But the painter waved aside the Molyneaux dress. "No, no! I want to do a dramatic portrait of you," he cried, "put on the costume!" I did. "That's it, that's it!" he said and wheeled up a long canvas. I enjoyed my hours with him. He had the sturdy pride, the delightful childlike arrogance of many artists, and I inordinately admired his canvases of Spanish peasant types. How well he knew the skeleton of his nation in all its haggard variety. And there was such drama in his work, or perhaps in the Spanish weather, that I understood his penchant for theatrical pictures. I did not much care for his portraits of society women, however, with the single exception of a likeness of the young Duchess of Alba, herself a typical beauty in the Spanish-Moorish manner.

[205]

Seeing my impressions, he grew ribald over his reasons
for painting American society women. "What would you
have me do?" he cried, lifting his shoulders and his brushes
toward heaven, "resist ten thousand dollars?" "No, of
course, not, you couldn't," I told him, looking at his
greedy, strong peasant's face. But I did feel some pity for
the paper-doll treatment he had given a few of our prominent social lights, especially it seemed when they had insisted on being done in a Spanish costume.

When Jack arrived in the bijou house of Elsie de
Wolfe's which I had rented, servants, secretary, and all,
for the winter—having hardly recognized me at the station
in my Molyneaux smartness; for Molyneaux had again
remarked, "You can't always meet John Barrymore in
sneakers and a turtle-neck sweater"—he had cried out to
the white satin walls of my bedroom, "Who is He! Who is
your lover! You might as well tell me!" And for the next
few days, before my new habit of gaiety had slipped back
into the old one of strictest seclusion (I don't think Jack
and I dined out together a dozen times in the years we
were together), he was apt to come up to me at the few
dances we attended, and gesturing toward some inoffensive
man indicate: "That's him, isn't it?" which was enough to
make any one trip up their partner. Something in Jack's
own nature showed him no mercy. He seemed condemned
to look forever and feverishly for his peace in the last possible place that he, as he was, would be able to find it, in
the moral conduct of people with whom he was in love.

A few days after Jack's arrival I caught flu and appeared
at my sittings with Zuloaga looking a ghost, with whom the
master seemed much discontented. "And as for your hus-

Left: L'Aiglon. *Right:* In medieval page's dress. This was the costume Zuloaga used for his portrait, calling it "Hamlet" for publicity reasons.

Cynthia 1924 b.

LADY CYNTHIA MOSLEY

band," he told me, "*il est un malade*." The pleasure seemed to be quite gone out of our friendship, and a few days later he said, "Now you may look at your portrait!" "Do you like it?" I asked him, afraid to open my eyes before the immense canvas.

"Whoever sees it will say '*voilà quelqu'un*'." Encouraged, I opened my eyes upon a monstrous canvas, a resemblance exaggerated and distorted to an amazing point, a gangling, ghostly nightmare of a page, a wraith from "malarial moats and unclean dreams."

"You do not seem to like it," said Zuloaga. "I don't—not at all . . ." There was a pause, and he replied: "Then, because we are such friends, I shall never exhibit it." And thanking him for that, I left.

A few days later my friend, Winnie Polignac, saw the portrait, which she detested at once, and she further told me that the Duke of Alba, who had accompanied her there and with whom I had but a slight acquaintance, had said directly to Zuloaga, "It is a libel of Mrs. Barrymore."

Zuloaga's promise not ever to show the portrait ended by his including it among a dozen or so of his canvases for exhibition in New York, and he called my portrait, "Hamlet," no doubt for publicity reasons, since Jack was playing "Hamlet" at the time, which gave every one a chance to utter a laugh from the bowels.

When I had returned to New York the year before, my gills throbbing with indignation at having been cast off by Jack for moral turpitude, I found his friends rallying about him, occupied in eliminating me, with suave delighted sweeps, from the picture. But it had been difficult to keep

Jack propped up in his stand against me—doubt kept creeping in, as to whether I really wore the scarlet letter under my shirt. And then one woman, friendly to both of us, had made him gnash his teeth with disquiet, when she told him that far from seeing me as an unerring seductress she thought me peculiarly lacking in the flirtatious instinct, and no more than a lost and bewildered child. Now this was stealing Jack's thunder, for to be lost and bewildered were among the most salient points in his own performance; so that now without vigilance, he was apt to lunge back toward what was represented to him by every one as being his destruction. Indeed, one day this recessional dalliance got him as far as my house, when we hurled our truths at one another until the roof chattered, no one daring to announce several of our meals, and it all began over again. And of course in the rose-glow of reconciliation, some of the poor friends who had been working like draught horses to keep Jack on the right track, well apart from mine, got called up on the telephone and told off in the most brutal fashion for their pains.

Around this time, because of all our dartings to Europe and back—for the reason that Jack was in the habit of closing to packed houses, either to rejoin me there, thus dealing the bile-duct of Arthur Hopkins a square blow, or to indulge in a nervous breakdown—I remember one occurred in the middle of Richard or Redemption after a brilliantly inquisitorial display of Jack's in front of his dressing-table mirror as he made up for Richard or Fedya (during which, unsavory facts had been unearthed about my conduct)—that going into a revue at the Neighborhood Playhouse one night, I saw the talented Mr. Carroll on the stage just starting a Hamlet take-off, which began,

"To sail or not to sail—that is the question." And there had followed an amusing résumé of our private situation.

However, the acrostic of two superlatively immature people, kept so largely by their blind selfishness attempting the give and take of everyday life, had begun to be a spectacle so distressing to every one that we had the world pretty much to ourselves—a world, incidentally, about which I now knew and cared so little, that I made a friend of mine wince one day by asking who this Mr. Harding in Washington was. . . .

"O from where erupting this army of agonies
At whose outposts already thou art slain, O my soul—
Slain in such earliness—in such bright cool air smoking yet
With the deep-shaded perfume of night—"

England. Much of my real living, much of my birth and death and rebirth is concerned with England. In England I heard my first poetry. Cynthia my best friend was English. I said good-by to Jack in England (and Jack was purely English-Irish). I married Harry in England, and Harry is altogether British, no matter how long his ancestors had been cracking ice in their water pitchers in Vermont.

It is very curious how, from nowhere, apparently, comes suddenly the capacity to put an end to something. It is as if in every human being the measure of endurance is just so great. You are as unconscious of the power in yourself to commit such an act as unpremeditated murder. Indeed you are as carelessly unconscious of the consequences to yourself as a madman.

But the habit of pain is one of the most difficult to put an end to, and there were still a few tragic intervals for

Jack and me to get through. One, in the dearest little Normandie farmhouse with a great stone-flagged living room and kitchen, and a huge fireplace, haunted by the smell of wonderful marmites. Diana stayed with Tibi at nearby Trouville, exercising her tiny toes and fingers in the sand. The boys were with their father at Dinard, and in this little house with its trim pink and white, blue and white bedrooms, its deep enclosing orchard trees, filtered by perpetual sunlight, I would listen in that legendary quiet to the woodpecker sharpening his beak on the sun-spotted tree trunks, and think: "What will bring this misery to an end?"

Then the sound of our voices and the heaviness of our sad silences went on at Tintagel, St. Ives, and at St. Michael's Mount in Cornwall. But we did not find, as some of the Knights had, "peace, glory and honor" in the fulfillment of tasks beyond ourselves. We were far from being up to Cornwall, so wonderful in early April, with the primroses coming out under the hedges, and such a grand roll to the country, as it dipped hugely down to where the Atlantic Ocean swept its clear green into the coves—and turned to blue and purple behind the surf.

The following Christmas we were living in Cheyne Walk. Leonard had commenced St. Paul's, Robin was at school in England, and the baby Diana upstairs in a nursery heated by the usual spot of coal fire.

The London streets were swallowed up in fog and the carol singers looking like tallow-faced marionettes, stood about on the well-scrubbed thresholds, drearily singing of the Messiah's birth. I went Christmas shopping while Jack painted the closet door in the cook's room with macabre characters representing the Louis XI period, and a wonderful Christmas card for me in which I appeared in a silver armor, scarlet wings and a blond head of hair.

I think it was Christmas night and we were returning from a large dinner party at Bridget Guinness' where Jack had all evening seemed to be his old tender self, looking very young and beautiful. And he told me as we drove home that he had just had such a nice talk with Mme. Edvina, whom he had sat next to at dinner. Edvina had told him, "You have everything, the love of the person you love, great talents, and every opportunity to use them." Heartily he had subscribed to her optimism, and now told me that he really felt we had got to make a go of it, and with childish swiftness I reacted once more to the happiness of his mood, and started to believe in everything all over again. But that night there was one more flight from happiness to infernal misery, and next morning I was up very early ready to put into action a decision that must have been reached subconsciously long ago, for there was so little hysteria now in my readiness to leave Jack, for always.

Certainly, in retrospect, the best of Jack's beauty, the best of his thought, came through far more poignantly in his art than in his life. In his art it seemed he could surmount an essential exhaustion, or was it an exhaustion with essential things, that was very apparent in his life. In his art he could go deep and bring up all the beauty and fire and meaning of life with its majesty of reasoning justice, its smiling mercy and its poetry, and be, before his public, the incarnation of those things which now, apparently, he knew so well. Yet in life, I think, he was the victim, never the master, of an ailing unrest which forbade him from ever achieving that calm in which things come to be understood. But that the full capacity was there, or seemed to be there, since it did actually appear in his work, made the matter of life with him all the more tantalizing and tragic.

The years with him gave me great inspiration, because there was so much that was beautiful connected with him. They gave me discipline because I watched work being done that had to be finished in spite of exhaustion, illness or disinclination. They sharpened whatever grains of humor I possessed, because in order not to go mad, or perhaps stay as mad as we sometimes were, you had at least to try to stand a little aside from yourself. And then the spectacle of our terrified egos linked in an infernal debate about the rights of each to get everything out of life and each other as well, would have broken up a corpse.

And the years brought me the knowledge of what is tragic, for I saw a splendor of talented youth, tenderness and personal beauty gradually destroy itself, and the hopes of those around it, through what seemed to be a refusal to grow, or perhaps an impossibility of growth, because of certain traits partially visible—of vanity, of an almost feminine inability to intellectualize, spiritualize, those ideas that, starting in the emotions, finally needed more permanent supports if they were to be brought into the practice of living.

But surely there are in all of us tendencies, deficiencies preordained, that psychoanalysis, with all its fussily obscene hands, can never diddle into the truth. For I think it is only the deep-eyed fates who are worthy to weigh for final judgment the merits of those rarely gifted individuals in the race, with a knowledge of what handicaps were imposed upon them through inheritance and experience. Surely only they could have told what pressure, strain or block it was in the spirit of Jack that prevented him from being the abettor in any true sense of his wonderful genius. As for me, when I look back, I know the scales tipped favorably and that he did me infinitely more good than harm.

"But now your figure is walking off there into the vast
night
With pain—age—death ahead of you—of you so familiar
to me
Who am nevertheless debarred from sharing these things
with you—
O how will contrast be sustained
Between orchards dusting the inclining spring sky
With their pink foam
And my threadbare shivering past—
Between music rippling out across the shoulders of
dancers
Reaching—inviting my excluded feet
So brightening into luminous shame
The silence of my jaded step—
Or when—or when—upon reading some loveliness be-
side the fire
I look up already speaking—into your empty chair—
O for another sun—another sky—another earth out of
other tides."

CHAPTER XXI

To Live Again as Some One Else

THAT spring after I left Jack in London, there seemed quite a lot of pain to be endured, and I discovered if I reverted to a childhood habit and memorized the lines of a special character in some play, that soon I began thinking the thoughts of the person who was speaking, instead of my own—a brilliant exchange.

So one day as I was stamping up and down in my library in Cheyne Walk—Jack had already moved to the Ritz—giving forth the "If—if—if" speech of Shaw's "Saint Joan," with Betty for audience, she said to me, "You must do that for Mr. Shaw himself!" and in another moment my intrepid friend had arranged that I should. Of course what I did in the presence of the master was merely to read a little from the book. He was kind to me, however, expressing an attitude toward acting that was half jocose, half serious. "It's all right if they come in on their cues," he said in his tremendous brogue, but ceased smiling entirely and was simple and impressive, when he told me that Joan had "written herself," adding "and you have the right voice for her," after which he remarked, "if your husband lets you have the Haymarket I will rehearse you in some matinées of 'Candida.'"

I don't know what of mischief or malice made me entertain the idea for a moment; or want to put Jack on the spot by even asking him for the Haymarket, since all my intuition knew utterly well that it would have been impossible for him to allow such a thing to go through. He could simply not have borne it, nor could he have endured showing that he could not have borne it. Therefore to make such a suggestion was merely to throw an extra theme into the conglomerate agony.

But I did, and there was, out of the integrity that made him touching as well as infuriating, a blank pause, filled with the sullen incredulity of a small boy who suddenly finds himself pelted with his own marbles, and during this interval I left.

In the small hours of the morning I heard an odd noise that came apparently from the library, which turned out to be gravel hitting the window. Looking out I saw Jack in the half light of dawn, standing under the bleak tree with its crooked sign "To Let," his overcoat collar turned up to his ears, his hat pulled down, his hands in his pockets. And I thought, "Here is an illustration in black and white of the End of All Things, of the numbness and dreariness of death without its dramatic extinction. For that little business note of the 'To Let' sign there makes you know you are not a comfortable leisurely shade in Hades, but in Cheyne Walk, with the hand of Real Estate emphasizing the remains, reminding you of all there will be to clear up, and reorganize, after the obsequies."

I went down and opened the door and Jack practically fell in through it, telling me, with the desperate haste of a general's surrender with all his army, "You can have the Haymarket." And of course I knew that he knew that the answer to that, by this time, was "Hell! I wouldn't take it for a million dollars."

So I did not play "Candida" at the Haymarket, but instead crossed the channel with Betty on a rough sea beneath an embattled sky to France, where I fetched up with my children and sailed for America. I remember nothing of that trip. It is a fairly flat stretch of gray.

But on my walks after we had arrived in New York and were all installed in a hotel, when I came across stage doors wide open onto side streets in the bright May weather, and could see the watchman sitting in his shirt sleeves, derby hat cocked over one eye, chair tilted back, feet against the wall, I would pause, avidly breathing in the theatre atmosphere of grease-paint and staleness, and long—as I stared into that empty darkness, and watched the sun motes alive with dust— to have a job in the theatre, and be going there to work, and live again, but as some one else.

Salem, Mass., . . . the Theatre . . . and I was to live again as some one else; in the character of Sally Negly in Clyde Fitch's bit of old rep "Barbara Frietchie."

Thank God my cues are all on one page, I thought, when next morning I joined the assembled company in a dusty theatre smelling of the grease-paint of previous performers.

For a week this *chef d'oeuvre* of Clyde Fitch awaited its public in vain, only a shrouded figure here and there in the orchestra standing out with mortuary clarity. Then one night, having faithfully counted, I thought, the couple of recalcitrant shapes in the first row, and just about to enunciate one of my two lines which halts the advance of Stonewall Jackson's army, I suddenly heard very close to me a startled whisper of "No—it can't be Blanche!" Apparently some friends just a few feet off, and equipped with binoculars, had been unable to assure themselves that this gawk in pink taffeta with hoop, pompadour, ringlets and a fantastic smear of makeup was I.

After this interpretation, there was little talk of a part for me. I told MacFadden I would get demoralized with this waiting about, I might even leave! He seemed distressed; the publicity of entertaining what Charlie Shaw had just written up as "the current wife of John Barrymore" had been enormous. "Would you like to play Jo in the 'Eight Cousins' or that brilliant adventuress Mrs. Erylinne in 'Lady Windermere's Fan'? An adroit society woman ought to be well within your compass," he added, taking care to look past me.

A few weeks later, however, our manager who had begun to look off his feed, told me that now I should have a real chance. Would I play Gwendolyn in "The Importance of Being Earnest"? "Is it the lead?" I asked. "Of course," he replied and made a strange request for that hour, for he asked the entire company to step out onto the stage. No doubt he's going to announce that after all this waiting, I'm to have the lead next week, I thought. But our manager, squarely facing his company—some of whom sat down, our leading man Gilbert Emery on a valise—declared, "Folks, I'm bust. I need a thousand dollars before I can put up the curtain again." And somehow I felt he was looking at me. So my week needed a thousand dollars! Gilbert Emery had done his "Pygmalion," Blanche Yurka her "Enter Madame!" Well, I would raise the thousand dollars, and MacFadden accepted my proposal with a first-class show of astonished gratitude.

To have persuaded a group of vacationing society people, nearly all of them strangers, and with their money in the banks of Boston, to give me a thousand dollars to avert a crisis in my acting career, I still consider to have been a major feat. However, I owe nearly all of my success to Margaret Sargeant McKean, the lovely sculptress who accompanied me on my visits with the whimsical determination to make her friends and admirers see my point of view.

Then, only a few hours later, with the $1000 in Mr. MacFadden's pocket, Mr. Emery and his friend Mr. X —who resembled with grotesque exactitude a celluloid bath doll—suddenly announced that they had no intention of acting in "The Importance of Being Earnest." No, if they remained they would do some other play and give me a part in it, only perhaps!

What a betrayal! It was Mr. Emery who had instigated my descent on Salem, since one day, having just finished an interpretation of Oscar Wilde's Salome in the Troubetzkoys' sitting room, he had told me, "Miss Strange, I know just the comedy for you—'Love in a Mist.' If you like you can open in it with me next autumn in Boston." Then on the theory that some training before a lead—even if I was the current Mrs. Barrymore—might be just as well, the stock company at Salem had been suggested. This genial actor's interest in me, however, had perceptibly cooled since after reading "Love in a Mist" I had told him I thought the play a bit of sugared tripe from start to finish, whereas his friend Mr. X had, I suspected upon two occasions, fastened on the reverse side, the papier-mâché colonial doorway through which I must rush, in order not to be trampled to dust by the advance of the Confederate Army.

So now I stood paralyzed with indignation; for the roles of Mr. Emery and Mr. X were unfortunately the only two male parts in "The Importance of Being Earnest"; when recovering I told MacFadden to choose between the value of these gentlemen and myself to the company. I remember he walked the length of the stage in distraction, and returning voted for me. The comrades left.

And it was only Thursday morning, five days before the opening, that the cast was complete, with an actor dispatched from the New York office of the agile Johnson Briscoe, and a rich, very good-looking young man, Leslie Buswell, who, occasionally interesting himself in theatre matters, had consented to accommodate us in this crisis.

"Michael, don't worry, I dreamt of you last night standing in the prow of a ship and crying out: 'Everything's under control!'" said Alice Johns, the mainstay of my existence in the company. So now she took me distraught over to Nathaniel Hawthorne's "House of the Seven Gables," and pouring coffee down me at intervals—as I stared suicidally at the sluggish Salem tides—she told me in a brisk, cosy, comforting voice, "Now, my dear, I shall cue you, and cue you, until you know your part so thoroughly that you may give the rest of your time to interpretation."

"Rest of my time! Interpretation!" Late Saturday afternoon I was still being cued under an apple tree (I will never forget the pale, tortured faces of actors under apple trees, what a travesty they made of summer!), and knowing only about a third of my part sketchily, for the necessity to keep speeded up seemed to be paralyzing such faculties as I had —and then so many reporters kept dashing in to ask me what did I suppose John Barrymore thought of my going on the stage—when MacFadden appeared in the distance shouting and beaming. "Miss Strange," he called. "What do you suppose! We have a wonderful break—the President of the United States and Mrs. Coolidge are coming to your début on Monday night!"

I received this news in petrified silence. Later on I grew sullen and the troupers, who were all my friends by this time, gathered around. I had lost three days that went to make the ordinary stock week in getting funds and actors. Now they told me I should ask Mr. MacFadden to give me one day extra for the three I had lost, and announce that he would open Tuesday night.

But Mr. MacFadden told me to go home and get a good sleep, I would feel differently about everything in the morning. Next day, however, the company told him, and so did I, that he must make some suitable excuse for opening Tuesday, and after that work swamped everything. Tuesday night came. Mrs. Coolidge was present, guarded by marines. The President had wisely seen fit to stay away. The theatre was crowded, and there was good-natured tolerance by all for my performance, which I should say was one hundred per cent without merit, and through which I passed like a somnambulist weirdly aware that he is balancing a truck over Niagara Falls.

Next day, coming to, with a telegram from Jack in my hand, which expressed his conviction that in taking to the theatre I had found the high spot in my career, I learned from a friend, who had religiously kept it from me until that moment, that on the day of my opening some newspapers had carried headlines (syndicated throughout the country) "Michael Strange Shows Barrymore Temperament." And there had followed a succinct account of how, acting on a unique preference for opening Tuesday, I had kept the theatre dark through Monday night.

Just what had I learned at Salem? How to make a life-boat when the prow of the steamer is pointing its nose to the sky! How to take a wholesome dose of exploitation *à la Américaine.* But without doubt I had discovered more about acting from hearing Jack repeating his lines while he shaved.

Mr. Al Woods, the veteran New York manager, who had for some time been wiring his desire to see me to Hamilton MacFadden, now suddenly requested that I should instantly materialize in New York. So during the course of a stifling August morning I entered his office in a costume as startlingly trim as I could make it, for Alice Johns had told me, "Now Michael, look as snappy as you can when you visit a manager and give him the devil of a time before you sign up."

So, looking rakish and carefree, and heavily disguised in makeup, I entered the office of Mr. Woods. He was a strongly built fellow with a massive head crowned with gray wavy hair and a skin sallow as yellow marble. "A wonderful head," I thought, "like the death-mask of some great orator in Revolutionary France." He roused himself from his desk to greet me, a half-chewed cigar well over in one side of his mouth and considering me in profound silence for some moments, suddenly remarked in an astounding nasal, "Dearie, you'll do!" And he handed me a manuscript, telling me "You play Poppy, a society bitch, at $250 a week." And I took "The Shanghai Gesture" by John Colton under my arm, black spots of fury and amusement floating before my eyes, when, after another sharp perusal of my entire person, Mr. Woods added "Jesus! I wish I'd seen you before I gave the lead in 'The Green Hat' to Cornell!"

Betty Vaucour, my devoted English friend, had come all the way to America to look out for my theatrical career, in which she believed as firmly as the Polar Star. But her ideas for suitable vehicles for me, to quote Dorothy Parker, ranged "all the way from a to b—," or "Only on the needle-points of the mountain tops! It must be Galahad, Parsifal or nothing!" And I listened to her, charmed, blind to the point of imbecility about the conditions through which I must carry this banner which she conceived was in my hand, plus astuteness, persistence and a knowledge of jiu-jitsu. She read "The Shanghai Gesture," and considered it obscenely unsuited to my efforts. So I discarded this opportunity without even reading the manuscript myself.

Mr. Woods then offered me another script in which I was invited to play a Parisian *cocotte* who reclaims a drug fiend only to lose him to a virgin. I refused this, and from then onward the Woods office exuded toward me a breath of frost.

How deeply confused I was! This theatre I had only glanced at was poles apart from the one my years of functioning as a poet, and experience of living beside—and watching America's first actor through four or five years of his finest productions—had led me to expect, to say nothing of the work I had done as adapter of his scripts.

Salem had been a lesson in the unscrupulousness of exploitation, and also in the weakness of my own capacity to defend a position so anomalous as my own. And nowhere could I discern a wise training to give me the things I needed, and to bring out those which could be seen, by any unprejudiced and un-theory crammed observer, to be already somewhat developed.

Mr. Woods had, with perfect geniality, cast me in routine fashion. I had been a poet. What of that? Possibly he did not even know it. What had concerned him was that a society woman, widely publicized, had gone into the theatre and not been reported too bad, and might easily, from the safe teaching of practice, know how to play a broad part with taste.

Around January, after as much telephonic energy as would galvanize the *Bremen* between New York and Cherbourg, it appeared that Edward Goodman, the director of The Stagers, would be interested in directing me in "Easter," by August Strindberg. And this play contained an aura of poetry and mysticism which it seemed to me, despite my theatrical inexperience, I might be able to project. My part, Eleanora, played some years earlier by the lovely Gwen Franchon Davies in London, was that of a young girl suffering from no less than insanity, who breaks away from an asylum where she has been detained by her poverty-stricken family during the dark dawn of Good Friday, hearing, as it were, through the thinness of her proximity to the Spiritual World, the Great Act of the Last Supper. And, luminous with such a vision, she arrives at her family's house, having unfortunately complicated her escape by stealing an Easter lily on the way.

The critics were amazingly kind to my performance. Even *The New Yorker* brightly patted me on the back for having won through "the influenza addicts of March with a performance of merit." Nor was I ever unhappy playing "Eleanora," for always I felt the brow of a great genius, August Strindberg, turned in a transfigured manner towards truths that were perhaps too profound to be successfully held within the limitations of language. At least the critics remarked that it was well to remember, in view of the incomprehensibility of most of the play, that Strindberg was mad when he wrote it.

During an entr'acte on the opening night Edward Goodman rushed into my dressing room, his loyalty incensed by what he termed the impertinence of my society friends. Still far too submerged in my part to pick him up on what I thought might be a contradiction in terms, I added more pallor while he told me—"Do you know what Miss X said? 'Couldn't some one have taught Blanche to walk at least like a human being? And what on earth does she look like in that brown uniform with black cotton stockings and slippers without any heels!' What does she suppose," shouted Eddie, "that a lunatic child escaped from an asylum, who comes onto the stage thinking about the Last Supper, ought to be gowned by Bergdorf Goodman, and affect the sexual slump of a 'kept girl' out of the 'Ziegfeld Follies'? And Michael, I hope it doesn't put you off, but Ethel Barrymore and John Drew are in the stage box." "No," I told him, "I hadn't any idea they were coming. I don't see faces when I look out or, when I do, I can't recognize them if I am really thinking the other person's thoughts!" And I asked Eddie had I looked all right, been all right? "You looked like Eleanora," he told me, "because you know her!"

But during Edward Goodman's sensitive direction and the four weeks run of "Easter" I began to appreciate a little of what it might mean really to act, to make a character live; through some mysterious submergence, transfusion, accentuation of myself, to become lost in the thoughts and tears and laughter of some one you could understand; to build the fabric of that sympathy so tight and strong that no waft from the outer world could pierce it. Why when it happened, it was like walking on water, a thing of magical excitement; for the tears you shed in the shoes of some one else had in them a thrill of the outer world, and a bewitching cleanliness!

CHAPTER XXII

Electra

A FEW weeks after "Easter" closed I was rung up by a brisk manager, who invited me to play the lead in a road revival of Jane Cowl's "Within the Law," but still undetached from the mysticism and touching poetry of Eleanora, I could not stomach the idea. So I turned my interest eagerly to fulfilling a contract that Elizabeth Marbury had just negotiated for me with Gabriele d'Annunzio.

And, while I worked at this script, I listened to Miss Marbury, who had managed that Margaret Anglin should invite me to take part in her "Electra," my impersonation being that of Chrysothemis, Electra's sister, and Orestes' sister, and the daughter of Agamemnon, King of Mycenae. And since all this sounded up to Betty's standards, without inquiries as to which version they were going to play or even reading the "Electra," I accepted.

It turned out, unfortunately, to be the Sophocles version,

a rather heavily turned piece, but then, as Alexander Woollcott said, "Michael Strange knows how to give a bad line
its full value"; and soon we were plunged into rehearsals
taking place here, there and everywhere, until finally we
had crossed the Hudson River and were motoring up the
Palisades before we could find room enough for the dignity
of our classic grief.

It was fun to try to stand up to Miss Anglin in two
spirited scenes, and I was somewhat nonplussed one day
to find a reader substituting on her dais, and Miss Anglin
herself watching me from the audience.

Of this stupendous tragedy there was only a fortnight's
rehearsal and we never saw the boards of the Metropolitan
Opera House, where it was to take place—nor the impressive gates of the "House of Atreus," from which issued a
flight of steps hammered together by the carpenter during
a fit of spleen against the human race, nor the bit of pleated
chiffon with which I was to try to cover myself as I fled
across the stage of the Metropolitan—until twenty-four
hours before the curtain rose.

Came the opening night and the Metropolitan Opera
House was sold out. Miss Anglin surmounted the crazed
unfamiliarity of her company with every detail and position. And though the unfortunates had stepped from their
"chalk lines" on a flat surface in the studio barn, and were
poised instead on a flight of the steepest steps hell ever contrived, to say nothing of musical cues which burst upon our
crazed ears from a huge orchestra that was only able to give
us a single part-time rehearsal before the opening, they
gave, as Sarah Bernhardt would say, "*quand même*," a
superb performance. The critics broke down a silence of
years between Jack and me, and he wired me his pleasure

at my good notices. But I was most impressed by the favorable comments of John McCormack, who told me he had left his seat and walked to the back of the Opera House in order to assure himself of the carrying quality of my voice.

D'Annunzio's "Daughter of Jorio" was a beautiful play, having a melodramatic plot based on the swarthy bodies and nostalgic, sensuous, half-pagan souls of the Abruzzi peasants. There was earth under your feet in it, while the beams of an authentic spirituality played over your head. Moreover, d'Annunzio's Mila was a reasonable part for a poet to play, who had already been cast twice as a harlot. For the whoredom to which Mr. Woods had consigned me was of the vicious, insolent, innately cold brothel variety, needing the murder which does occur to retrieve it, but Mila's was the real thing. She was a pagan girl, revelling gracefully in her promiscuity, a mischievous, passionate, sunstained, breathless figure, caught unawares and writhing at first in the snares of love. And then, as love gains and her heart comes into blossom—in the finest transports of language too—she takes on the ailing wonder, and the immortal wound of heartbreak, accepting false judgment for the sake of the beautiful shepherd she loves and going to stand in the flames for him, accompanied by a frantic Bacchanal of Roman Catholic litanies. It was all superb drama, pictorial to the nth degree, and filled with the ecstasies of pagan passion, religious frenzy and pure love.

Arthur Hopkins seemed the right person to show it to, for it appeared he was always looking for Art. I even thought, as I considered him, that his compact bulky little person expressed a kind of pugilistic readiness to ram fine things down the throats of those who would be shallow at any price. So forgetting that his reaction toward me was bound to be slightly psychiatric after the indirect blows I had dealt his box-office receipts, I asked him to dine with me at East End Avenue and read him the play.

He was very enthusiastic, indeed I thought he complimented me too profusely on my abilities as an adapter. Then suddenly after a solemn pause he vouchsafed: "And you belong in the theatre as an actress too!" Now this was where I could rush in: "Oh, Arthur, I have only adapted the damn play to play Mila myself." But at this bit of news my guest seemed to sink into a kind of mournful embarrassment, from which I tried to rouse him by saying "Oh, all right then, if you think Mila's too much of a part, shall I play Aligi's sister Ornella? She's a blonde and has only a few lines." But now Arthur, looking me straight in the eye, announced with Delphic finality, "No, you must not play Mila, but I do know the part for you: Cleopatra, in 'Antony and Cleopatra,' "—at which I went down to the cellar to fetch up another bottle.

What was I up against? The people to whose judgment I must turn for a job seemed to get the wildest notions, and the most crazily different, about what I ought to do. My own logic or intuition about what I should at least be allowed to try to do they put in the wash, for even after all the enthusiasm aroused in Arthur Hopkins by my reading of Mila he would not let me go down to the theatre and give him a real reading of it on the stage. Was he afraid he might be persuaded to do something against his better judgment by what the women's clubs call my "dynamic personality" and, if so, how deep was his self-confidence?

A few weeks later, however, during a telephone call from

Palm Beach he bought the play—God only knows why he called me all the way from Florida, since no one else was after my piece that I knew of, except to uphold I suppose one of the unwritten laws of the theatre—that all must be hectic. And so I let beautiful Mila go, regretfully, but with the thought that salvage is salvage.

CHAPTER XXIII

L'Aiglon

B Y FAR the most exciting venture in my odyssey of being some one else was the acting of "L'Aiglon." And "L'Aiglon" came about like this. The summer before, I had played in Bernard Shaw's "Man of Destiny" the role of that girl who bedevils Napoleon (then First Consul) with dispatches and disguises. My costumes were superb. As the lady I wore a directoire white dress extravagantly moulded to the form, and a diaphanous purple scarf embroidered with silver flowers, while my officer's get-up was a blue coat with golden epaulettes, a tricolor sash and white trousers into which I had literally to be poured, not to pass over magnificent boots.

Arrived at Dennis, Cape Cod, it seemed that scenic desolation could go no farther. A windmill in action croaked outside my window and was evidently in league with a cesspool just beyond the threshold of my door, for, whenever its noise stopped, horror erupted, while a tearoom opposite furnished us with that sterile marginalia of food that only women over seventy convalescing from typhoid could be supposed to want. And when bright-faced, short, dapper Clarence Derwent, who was to play Napoleon opposite me, said, after glancing at the Company: "Well, Michael, there is nothing for us to find out here except who can break up whom during an act," I thought to myself "That's the spirit!"

After the performance that I got through somehow—for I could never imagine liking to play Shaw as much as one wants to read him, his actors being continually embarrassed, cut off from the effect of their climaxes by the merry antic of the only person who is really on the stage—Shaw himself—Helen Westley, a trouper whom I have always greatly admired, brought her cloudy-haired seeress' presence into my dressing-room while the loudspeaker roared a last gramophone record to the departing audience. She sat down heavily, her knees wide apart, exuding accretions of coarseness, kindliness and witch's insight, evidently getting ready to utter. I went on removing grease paint and feeling the glamour of Napoleon fade from me, when Miss Westley said: "You were perfectly terrible! That is, my child," she went on in a softer tone, "you were awful when you played the girl, so awkward. No one could hear you either! But when you were dressed as the young man everything went splendidly. Your head looked right, your voice came out, you walked properly. My dear, if I were you I would play nothing but boys' parts in the theatre."

"Just Parsifal and Sir Galahad?" I asked bitterly. "No, I think you might even do boys' parts in modern clothes," she replied insanely, and then left me to stare into my light-lined mirror while the loudspeaker continued to murder a waltz. Indeed, the obstacles to my career as an actress were getting insuperable, so with this "coup de grâce" ringing in my ears I got into a motor and drove off to visit Hermann Oelrichs at Newport.

Subsequent to the strange sights and sounds of Dennis, it was amusing to come across another way of life again in my cousin's beautiful house, "Rose Cliff." After wandering among his guests, however—so seriously dotted over their bridge along the huge expanses of marble terrace, the only human sound to be detected on this exquisite set, a muttering of scores accompanied by a distant clatter of gin and ice in the shaker, the only expression a secret smile or wry twist of the mouth to indicate the palpitations of fortune—I solaced myself with memories of gay flirtations in my 'teens in the starlight on Mrs. Goelet's terrace and lawns. For then the cliff walk was thronged with couples exchanging not the monosyllabics of scores but conversations leading who knew where; but even as a child, to watch them gave you ideas. And a picture flashed up in my mind of the great coal magnate Mr. Ned Berwind, with his upright carriage, mane of white hair, heavy mustache, and eternal cutaway coat and striped trousers, and his queer straw hat turned up all around with its heavy black band. Always pale and stately was Mr. Ned Berwind as he loitered on the cliff walk above the Forty Steps, with piquant Mrs. Whitney Warren (who reminded me always of the French actress Réjane). And on one distant summer afternoon I remember she was bewilderingly hatted, and wore a princess gown of lace, as she stood listening to Mr. Berwind with downcast eyes, and dug the point of a flounced chiffon parasol into the gravel.

Hermann spent most of his time in his library, where were his true and only intimates. And on this marble terrace that, as a child, I had thought so luxuriously glamorous, sat many of the same people, gone a little more aquiline or stout or gray; but they were curiously quieter than of yore! Were they practising a kind of understatement I wondered, or had their continuous association with games and machinery worn perilously thin the fabric of vitality. For it seemed to me that they had been caught and had been put aside from life, and were crystallizing somewhere out of reach of humanity. Did they know this or care? And what was the matter? "For the matter," as "Le Grand Will" would say, "seemed to be grave."

And watching them I knew I was far more at home in Dennis with the the windmill and the sewer, and the intellectual skipping of Bernard Shaw, and with my friend Harry Winston (who had directed my performance in a spirit of disapprobation and amusement) bounding up the stairs to where I lay on my bed, trying to force the evasive caul of one of the master's characters over my being, while he grasped me by both hands and cried out, "Michael, are you getting it!" And that in retrospect I never did, doesn't seem to matter.

So, with Helen Westley's denunciation and strange advice ringing in my ears, and another long distance call from the offices of the Commercial Theatre which informed me that "The Daughter of Jorio" had been released by Mr. Hopkins (who had failed to interest the somber fire of Judith Anderson in the part) and was now tied up to the intrepid Eva LeGallienne for Madame Nazimova's favorable consideration, I turned my attention to what had been actually written for boys in costume to discover this field to be as comically narrow as I had expected.

It is perhaps a curious provision of nature, or possibly just a bizarre part of my own make-up, that when Destiny, or sometimes the smallness of one's reputation, throws fantastic obstacles in the way of creating interest, or getting proper material for a desired and possibly legitimate end, I am apt to cry out "All right then, I'll put everything on the red." And this is what I did when I let John Williams buy "L'Aiglon" for me, before I had put any of the scenes to the test of study.

After the urbane Mr. Wynne of Morgan Harjes had concluded matters with the nervous system of Maurice Rostand, and the script was put into my hands and I had read through the pyrotechnics of language, strung upon a few languishing sentiments—a dozen or so affected scenes —I began to feel a degree of numb terror which was not dissipated by John's telling me that the play was already cast and the company sitting about ready to go into rehearsal!

On this I retired to bed with fever and a severe cold, and some good books on Napoleon, deciding, after another perusal of "L'Aiglon," that if I must take the fatal plunge into Rostand, critical anathema, public condemnation, and possibly a hanging scene in Times Square, it simply could not be with this little nit-wit, forever changing his uniforms, coughing, and dredging for tears, but with Napoleon himself.

So what I attempted to do was to recharge every sentence of mauve theatre within theatre plotting, artificially arranged confusion of sentiments, and wretched crumbling of backbone before mischance, with the cunning heroic stamina of the Napoleonic will. Indeed what I wanted to present was a L'Aiglon thwarted, so to speak on the side, and not in the main, by consumption and the ruses of Metternich.

When I first met the company, however, I decided to keep this interpretation to myself, so I gave a conventional reading, listened to by all with a marked degree of relief, while John remained aloof from the group shading his eyes with his hand.

And it was not until we got up out of our circle of chairs, and into action in an Armory, that I began to reveal the plan of my reading. Then—surprisingly, astoundingly and miraculously to me—the company which had justifiably stood aside from me in a state of polite but marked apprehension, containing as it did such distinguished veterans of the theatre as George Marion (Flambeau), Effie Shannon (the Empress Marie Louise), Hubert Wilke (the Emperor), accepted me. And how terribly grateful I was, for it seemed you could prove something to people you worked with, when they were strangers to you.

One day, I fully exhibited my point of view about L'Aiglon in that frothing rhodomontade, with Rostand at his worst and best in the "Mirror Scene." Then it is that L'Aiglon's hopes for himself are ground into powder by the sardonic Metternich, who, collaring the unfortunate youth, dangles him in front of a long pier glass while he forces him to hold up in one shaking hand a lighted candelabra, and admit, in a duet of yelling, that the caviling softness of his chin comes from bawdy Karl, the unnatural popping of his eyes from crazy Johanna, and so on down a line of rickety ancestors; until the maddened boy hurls the candelabra into the mirror, thus destroying, with a magnificent crash, this prophetically frustrated image of himself before, as usual, collapsing. Well, when on that day, egged on by Napoleon's spirit, I had turned the tables on Metternich and very nearly killed him, to the delight of the company, while making as little as possible of the collapse, I saw George Marion smiling at me and making a gesture of applause. Pleased enough with that, I turned to hear Hubert Wilke telling me, "My dear child, all your company know what you can do now; but in another week you will have your success and every one will know, and I want to be the first to congratulate you!" Perhaps it is vain of me to repeat this because "L'Aiglon" was not a success, but to remember the kindliness of this faith, given on its glorious own, to relate how it fortified and touched me in rather a grim moment, seems to be something I want to do.

We opened in Baltimore to a sold-out house and my maid rushed back, her brogue incomprehensible with excitement, to tell me, "You had thirteen curtain calls after Wagram."

The night before the opening we had one of those into-the-dawn rehearsals with the company working at pitches of fever and stupor; when, returning ossified with fatigue to the hotel around five A.M., I was told to call the Hollywood operator. In a few moments Jack's voice, more nasal than during the Great Days, but affable, sounded at the other end: "Ned (Sheldon) says they all say you're all right, and in such a rotten play too! What did you want to do it for? I thought about it for myself once but then I did 'Hamlet' instead. It was so much easier!" "Easier?" "Of course. In L'Aiglon you're on for the evening with a ninny (didn't I know it), whereas in Hamlet you have the greatest soul, etc., etc." "But, Jack, I go on with Napoleon's soul." And as Jack was shouting, "Why, what on earth did you say?" my darling John (John D. Williams) entered with aspirin tablets and commands that I should instantly retire.

The critics in Baltimore and Washington were extremely kind. In Baltimore, by some heaven-born chance, they had not even caught on to the spectacular side of my private connections; in fine, they did not know who I was, the best paper alluding to "the dark, slender, personable young woman who had played L'Aiglon very well indeed."

After a week L'Aiglon began to emerge from the hectic chaos and overpowering dread of an opening. The wistful caul of the unfortunate boy's spirit really began to descend and blot out the conscious me. And I looked from the tall brocade-hung windows of my dark-panelled room in the Palace of Schoenbrunn, out at that tremendously royal garden running uphill to the "Gloriette," to see, against a warlike sky, the grim pageantry of my father's life passing in a clatter of artillery, in fields of saluting sabers under Victorious Arches, and in coils of smoke through which the "Grande Armée" catapulted itself across Europe to victory.

"L'Aiglon" played to fair business on the road. But I learned that current expenses had been totted up to over-reach those of Jack's "Hamlet" production, and that fair business wasn't half enough. In New York we went into the huge Cosmopolitan Theatre on Columbus Circle, with a seating capacity of two thousand five hundred, which was, moreover, considered by the actors a place of "hoodoo." And by this time apparently there wasn't enough money left to advertise properly the bewildering fact that an actress almost entirely unknown was just about to imitate Sarah Bernhardt and essay the title role of "L'Aiglon."

But there we were with all our trunks and there was nothing to do but go on. Effie Shannon, so lovely with her gentleness, the blond ringleted daintiness of her head and her calm blue eyes reflecting a heart which has fully and beautifully lived, consoled and encouraged me. And the curtain rose.

Next morning, in the "Captain's Cabin," telegrams arrived from friends, congratulating me on my success, so I assumed from their overstatements that probably after all there were no machine guns mounted on the stoop. I picked up first, as always, *The New York Times*, and was amazed to see a guardedly good review which, while dealing me a few compliments in a discreet manner, left the writer open to no charge of madness from his confrères. But naturally, such a calisthenic could hardly help producing a quaint impression on the reader: "As a matter of fact, L'Aiglon might have been played much worse than it was last night by actresses of much more experience and infinitely greater technical equipment than Miss Strange. The very lack of command of that technique helped, in fact, to give the performance of the boy's part something of the quality of which a perfected technique might have robbed it utterly. . . . Miss Strange may easily become a greater actress, but when she does, she will probably not play L'Aiglon half as well—supposing by that time she cares to play it at all."

After a few weeks in New York, during which it became certain that running expenses were still over half the take-in, and with people continually calling me up to ask, "Are you really playing L'Aiglon? Where? I can't find it in the papers," it was decided that we would close on Saturday, giving over the theatre to Max Reinhardt, although toward the end of the week the box-office barometer had shown a slight rise. And I heard that Otto Kahn, then the "Lorenzo Il Magnifico" of Art, had, after visiting the show, declared for me, though adding that I had ranged myself against "formidable obstacles!"

It was after the Saturday matinée, Clarence Mackay had just visited me, with congratulations that I knew him too well not to know were sincere, and had left. And dearest Tibi had come into the dressing room and sat down without speaking, to say finally with tears that it was a great pity I had not gone into the theatre earlier. "I didn't know you, not once! You were never my baby," she told me. She too had left; and my maid was looking about her with the appraising, stowing eye of departure, for we planned to leave that night, when the members of my company came in and a nice thing happened,—"very," as Jack said, "outside the usual experience of the theatre."

For the proposition that George Marion and Effie Shannon made to me was, that I must not close, but get one of my rich friends to put up money in order to move the production of "L'Aiglon" into a smaller theatre, where they felt the business would grow. "At least," they told me, "you will have the chance of going on for another fortnight, and of proving what you can do." "Expenses must be cut, and then," said Effie, "I have come to tell you, Michael, that I represent all the company in saying that if you will continue your production we will all go on with you, on half pay."

When Jack heard of this at the Lambs Club some time afterward he told me, "That is the greatest tribute you could have had." But on that night I felt too numb and crushed, too utterly unable to be buoyant, to go to my friends about a proposition which had already lost so much money. And so "L'Aiglon" closed on a glacial January night and I watched the romantic costumes and beautiful tall boots being crushed down into the death of trunks which were bound for the attic at home, and not for the night express and another span of life.

But, with all the tragic disappointment of such an early closing, what a splendid experience the twelve weeks of really gruelling work had been for me! The endurance chart of my temperament had been jacked up permanently, I felt.

A sinister note, which I thought very little of at the time, was struck one evening at the Park Lane Hotel in Washington when, petrified with exhaustion (after two performances on a Saturday night), I had allowed the daintily minute danseuse of the "ballet masque" scene to go back with me to my room in an effort to untie some of the Houdini knots settled on my throat and shoulders. The danseuse, who was also a masseuse, and could cry very prettily and flatteringly night after night, perched on a trunk offstage during L'Aiglon's death scene, now, as I lay pitched over on my face, informed me that another side of her equipment was fortune telling: "And Miss Strange, you are about to go through a long, serious illness," she remarked soothingly. "But it will not be fatal." No, not fatal, I thought, starting to go to sleep. Not fatal!—what could be, after Jack and "L'Aiglon"!

Burble and murmur
Your subterranean resignation and advice
River at night—
Your muscular life
Abruptly manifest
Between weird syncopating columns of gauze
Shed forth from the passing boats—
Your looping finger of harbor
Dreamily buoying the hulks—
Somehow lending the slant of shore derrick or drill
In consonance with you—
A look of tremendous etching—

Night river
Enwrapped in your own sure terms
Furling back so swift
After surface pyramidal scrawl of ferries and ships
River preoccupied
Until over your brooding rest is shed . . .
The inquisitive flush
Of another dawn.

CHAPTER XXIV

Downpour and Convalescence

I HAD been living for three years with my children at
142 East End Avenue, a tiny house smothered with
a gargantuan wistaria vine and fronting one of the last
cobblestone streets in New York, with just opposite, the
Gracie Square Park, that shimmered its leaves or tossed its
dark branches always between one's self and the great
sparkling sash of the East River. I loved my house, rented
from my dear friend Maude Eliot, quite passionately, for
it was all my own. I had tweaked the portières into shape
from pencilled sketches, and practically built by hand with
the carpenter my strange bed that hung from the wall by
whitewashed chains in a little coved lantern-lit room on
the top floor which I christened the "Captain's Cabin."
And when I came home from disconcerting interviews,
journeys or parties, I would stand in my vestibule, my face
pressed to the glass for some minutes before ringing, just
to look in through the gold and flame-threaded cherry silk

[243]

curtains and think "this is really my home," a refuge with nothing in it to bore or to hurt me.

Indeed, for the first time at East End Avenue I felt free to breathe an atmosphere that belonged to me. I could read and write as long as I pleased without feeling apologetic as in my first marriage, or without having to pause and wrestle with Dr. Jekyll and Mr. Hyde. How I loved waking up in the "Captain's Cabin," looking across to Gracie Square, beyond which the great river rolled swiftly by under the blazing silver sheath of morning. Diana would be chirruping her lessons to frosty old Gerdes below, there would be letters in minute writing from the boys at school on my breakfast tray; and now past the theatric tragicality of my pent-up egotism, or it might be easier to say free at last to try for as much as you could take on the chin and elsewhere, I wrote my poems again, and they were once more real, which made a difference impossible to describe.

At East End Avenue I sensed for the first time how desperately at odds I had always been with my environment. And I thought it was only because of my youth and vitality, and the absorbing, transfiguring voice of my poetry that I had ever been able to push what was all around me aside, and make it wait until I had completed the spate of my thought, for never in the atmosphere directly surrounding me had there been any welcome whatever for what alone was my reality.

During the years at 142, I received many interesting people in my front parlor with its seasonal window boxes, booklined shelves, and plaster copies (but you would never know it) of favorite epochs in sculpture represented by the archaic Greeks and the subtle asceticism of Donatello.

Elisabeth Marbury—hostess par excellence to the nearest thing to a salon that I have seen in New York, and agent for many of the world's best writers for over a quarter of a century—would come in after her Mass on Sunday morning. Then leaning the planes of her amazingly heavy face, riven by such expressive lines, on the snout of her cane (a subject for François Clouet at his best), she told me: "Michael, now is your moment. You are living as you always should have lived, and I hope to last long enough to see the success that ought to be yours";—and curiously enough she repeated what Charlie Chaplin had said to me from the depths of a chair in the "Captain's Cabin": "Michael, you would be wonderful with success, you must try and do the things that will bring it to you!"

How frenzied the neighborhood of East End Avenue would become over Charlie's visits. And when he came down my front stoop there was always a small crowd of boys whom we called "sea wall savages" hanging about to cry: "Charlie! Charlie! Write us out passes for your movie!"

I liked Charlie Chaplin, and sold a fair poem about him to *Vanity Fair*. Some loathing for the injustice of the way things were ordered rankled in him, and was concealed by whimsicality, by humor that called upon a vein of sheer tragicality so obvious in him, never to exhibit itself straight, seeing that the world was what it was, and his shoulders so narrow. However, I thought the secret arrogance and wistfulness of terrible experience was in Chaplin, and that no wonder the complete reversal of so much turned toward the public became dynamically funny and touching.

Jester standing to me
Through grayish criss-cross lightning
Of tears . . . lost
From downward pondering on disc faces of a waning moon
For beauty Sheer. . . .
The Uncaught Flying Child.

Carlotta Monterey (afterwards Mrs. Eugene O'Neill) often brightened my sitting room with the finesse of her beauty. I enjoyed her one hundred per cent femininity and little girl's solemnity over the great books she was always reading, and then her features seemed to have been painted in by the flash of a blackbird's wing. However, her looks, so finely drawn and striking, were, I thought, the outer envelope of a rather sternly romantic attitude toward what she conceived to be the balanced beauties of living. And sometimes I felt her to be rather dangerously theatric, not as the artist, who is always getting it off his chest in work, but as some one who not being an artist is perhaps inclined to dramatize herself and the people around her:—so putting life into the cast-iron shackles of some artifice of mood that has no drop of the curtain to put an end to it. Once or twice she brought in Eugene O'Neill, a profoundly sympathetic-looking fellow, and with a set jaw he would sit with his back to the fire for hours in a state of marvellously prolonged and dogged inarticulation.

And how peculiarly temperamental my small sons were during those East End Avenue years. I remember asking Leonard to put on an extra sweater when we were starting off for a walk on a damp afternoon, to have him retort, with his arms folded "a la Coquelin," "I will not put on that sweater—I will kill myself first!" And Robin, who worshipped the epoch of Marie Antoinette, and spent all his time rigging up cardboard theatres upon which he would present for me an imitation of the fêtes at Versailles, Robin, smelling the cooking which permeated now so easily through our tiny house, told me "How tawdrily you live, Mother." And on one occasion he became so frenzied by our lack of grandeur that he dressed up in parts of my costume from the "Man of Destiny" to which he added a wreath of gold bay leaves, and opening the front door took an attitude on the stoop proclaiming to the mob of roughnecks that nearly instantly gathered, "I am Nero and I command you to stop your screeching in our street." As the jeers and catcalls rose, however, he fell back gratefully into my arms when, carried away myself by the scene, I told him, "Now go and stand behind the portières and mutter 'Canaille'."

In the spring after "L'Aiglon," there was fulfilled over my head that dreary sentence about it never rains but it pours. Running away from a bull in a New England field littered with rocks, indeed, leaping a stone wall with the abandon of Nijinsky in order to leave the monster on the other side (and while musing on the career of Joan of Arc), I had wrenched myself off stance, suddenly to find I couldn't straighten out my leg without excruciating pain.

So I lay marooned in the "Captain's Cabin," visited by distinguished doctors who, resembling portraits by Van Dyck, still didn't seem able to pin their attention on the matter at hand without frantic efforts on the part of the frantic patient. And when their opinions could get by their obviously strained sense of being late for the next appointment, these were alarmingly diverse. During these sterile interviews, Robin, on the floor below in a set-to with his tutor, screeched himself into an attack of appendicitis which called for an immediate operation. The roof over our heads was suddenly sold for an enormous price (it was the beginning of the boom of 1928). And what might be called my nearest and dearest friend became convulsed with his major attack of doubt as to whether he could ever make me happy, which ended in a departure from under my roasting roof that must be construed as final. Around this time, too, Leonard threw himself on his knees beside me in the parlor to swear he would not go abroad with his father—a trip on which he had greatly counted—until some of the doctors found out what was wrong with me. And Diana's English nurse, Gerdes, who had lived in the family for nearly twenty years and was excusably pessimistic, told me in her icy tremolo that it was a good thing for me that some one stood by.

Then with the July heat striking through walls and windows, the children and I living mostly on containers of pineapple and orange juice which Leonard fetched from the corner drug store, while explosions from the river where they were dredging (in that eternal breaking up of whatever is that occurs in America between 8 A.M. and 5) rattled the windows until one of them broke—then through this miasma of misfortunes appeared Jack from Hollywood. He told me that the divorce which I had asked him for some months ago, and which he had not himself wanted at the time, must now go through, and we considered how, in view of my illness, this could be done.

It was a strange conversation that might have taken place between shadows in Limbo, and, after it, I hopped downstairs on one foot and let him out into an airless night.

At this point Ned said to me on the telephone in his fine deep voice, "Now is the time for your pen, Michael," and it seemed that I must be proven to myself a curiously superficial insensible character, for these blows of misfortune didn't seem to stimulate anything but my appetite. I ate and slept remarkably well, and was only conscious of numbness, of an inability to feel on any account. Apparently, if I was to have no further part in life on the one hundred per cent terms I had known,—of course without that appreciation which is probably only to be discovered in retrospect—then life had no further part in me, and painlessly I sensed my own wholesale dullness, my engulfment in the gray.

What numb sadness there is in a long illness, after those first hysterias of comparison between what has been and what is are over. Resignation creeps up through you like stone advancing upon living tissue!

A couple of years before, while I was still careening around on my legs, the Mosleys had arrived in New York, when I was in the thick of rehearsing "Easter," and had been overcome with amused astonishment. Reporters followed Tom even into his bathroom at the Hotel St. Regis, barraging him with questions—not, as he said, about anything he might possibly know of, but on subjects so inanely diffuse that he needed Alice in Wonderland to see him through. Movies appeared almost instantly of them coming down the gangplank of their ship, looking extraordinarily distinguished, and they were childishly delighted to have these run off at a large party given in their honor by Mrs. William Randolph Hearst.

They made rousing speeches at Cooper Union Hall,

attended by great crowds, and Cynthia really enjoyed herself in America. Her celebrity in Society was reduced to the
fact that she was Lord Curzon's daughter, and a very beautiful woman, and this was a good deal more than enough
to make them put into a dark void any reports on the convictions for which she lived. As for the Socialists, to them
she was a prophet out of her own country with exuberant
results.

"Ducky," she told me one day, her eyes sparkling with
mischief, "did you know you are very '*mal vue*' in New
York?" I did, and the news left me where it found me,
although I would have been delighted to have had it
otherwise.

Before sailing they both spoke of a fishing trip taken
lately with Franklin Delano Roosevelt, then Governor of
New York, and gave me enthusiastic accounts of him. "He
has the most extraordinary charm, and he does stand out,"
said Cynthia, "for he seems to be the only person we have
met who is on to what we think is happening in America!"
And I learnt from my friend what she thought about our
tenement districts, growing unemployment, unique lack
of insurance for workers, sinister evasion of the tired business specialist, and of the specialist in law who protected
him from universal human values.

"Right next to your Babylonian skyscrapers such blocks
of miserable drained want, joined to every one of your
cities, such a no-man's-land of desolation and nothingness!
—all of it, considering your wealth and technical genius,
absolutely unnecessary to a degree that is unparalleled in
history. You will see. It will not go on."

And I thought, as she looked past me, her eyes filled with
defiant prophecy, tenderness and strength, that she rather

resembled that heroic statue by Jo Davidson, which he
intended to have placed at that point on the Marne where
the Germans were driven back. It represents a woman in
a corselet of steel, her feet planted wide apart and strongly
in the earth, her skirt blowing roughly back against her legs,
arms flung up, head back, mouth wide open to cry: "They
shall not pass!"

And now recovering from a cartilage operation in Liverpool to which I had come for the distinguished services
of my favorite doctor in all the world, Sir Robert Jones—
who had asked me as I was coming out of my anæsthetic,
"My dear Mrs. Barrymore, won't you let me send you in
a glass of champagne?" I really saw Cynthia again. She
had come down from London to be with me all she could
during my convalescence, and one November day I took
my first walk down the fog-dimmed brick alleys of Liverpool, leaning heavily on her arm.

In those quiet days of routine with hours between each
thing that had to be done, I sensed that now Tom's conduct, was becoming more and more of a strain. Also
I noticed that when Cim stood up to say good-by she
seemed not to be able to hold herself erect any more. But
I knew well enough there was no counsel to give her; you
could not approach so noble and changeless a heart with
any American idioms about "not standing it," "making
one's own life," etc. She was utterly a woman with all the
alleged trickery of femininity left out. Her happiness was
up to the man she loved. But she was still strong, young,
lovely, and had the pride of her qualities—pride which
must never be too deeply damaged if her life's core was to
remain intact.

I returned triumphantly from Liverpool, with a leg I could walk on—and oh! how little anything else on earth mattered—and was met at the station by Cim and Tom. Smith Square again with Queen Anne's footstool sprawling its stone legs into the fog, again blade-thin maniacally efficient Mabel in her trim brown and white uniform clicking back the door of Number 8, letting me into bright warm rooms, savory with a dinner in preparation, flower scents, children's voices, and the argumentative nasal of Mr. John Strachey raised over some problems of state.

And again Mr. Ramsay MacDonald came for dinner, dilating this time on his pleasant entertainment lately in Paris at the house of Princess Murat.

And once more we stopped in front of Lady Sybil Colfax's door in King's Cross Road. But even though we saw the muffled, classic profile of a celebrated actor just dashing off into the fog, and were sure there would be more of his ilk inside, still I surprised my friends by not consenting to go in with them. I was not ready for all these people yet. I felt a little Lazarus-like, as though I had not quite shaken off the mould of some late acceptance of death. I wanted to go back to my rooms at the hotel by myself to practice with such a numb feeling of gratitude, being alive again!

So telling my friends I would return with Robin to spend Christmas with them at Denham, I went off to the Riviera, to convalesce at Gourdon with May Norris. . . .

Gourdon was the reincarnation of Englehaus, that fortress castle in Bohemia toward which, at sixteen, I had run away, leaving my parents asleep in Carlsbad. You reached Gourdon from Cannes by spiralling up and around mountains, by crossing the chaste, radiant racket of dozens of waterfalls, and still ascending, until the gray olive orchards could no longer balance their roots in the steepness of the earth;—then at length you arrived on a vast plateau, a kind of tableland of the gods, on which boulders of every size had been strewn as counters—and saw Gourdon just opposite you!

And the Château itself, which had appeared as you climbed toward it in guises enlarging from a thimbleful of vision in a crusader's dream, to a tremendous fortress clamped by tier upon tier of Roman arches to the side of sheer abyss—the Château itself! With all its rich formation of walls, dark exclamation of cypress, rolled green terraces resting upon the arches, murmur of doves fluttering to their cotes, rude strength of the Romanesque court, and delicacy of iron grilles admitting you to a perfected maze of white arched halls and lofty rooms, the Château itself announced: "Now you are crossing the threshold of the greatest strength and beauty you have ever met with in a human habitation, so cheer up and get well!"

And where was the world? As you stood on the terrace and looked down, it depended on the weather if it put in an appearance or not. On fine days you saw infinitely below you the whiteness of Nice, Cannes, Monte Carlo, like spots of architectural sugar touched by moveless expanses of the tides; and sometimes the earth evaporated entirely, for which you were not ungrateful, and again it put in a syncopated appearance between rifts of the passing clouds, taking on in such moments a corn-yellow light.

The place was like a cry of drama and aspiration—a superhuman stage set for that whispering of the devil at the shoulder of Christ—and it possessed too a serene calm, like the peace of a knight's spirit, who returns in triumph from the last and greatest quest.

If there could have been a chatelaine for such a place, it was my dear friend May Norris, for she saw Gourdon with the only attitude toward anything superb—passion. She had craved it and bought it just after the war, and with mad indiscretion, according to those informed of her circumstances. She had planned to live there with a friend who was fairly well off, but who had departed to get married before May was properly installed. So Miss Norris continued alone on her mountain top, receiving only a few guests, walking the boulder-strewn heights with her shaggy dog, gathering according to seasons in the heroic fields narcissus, lavender and snow to cool her fruits; and watching often from a turret window in the corner of her bedroom, the light shifting across the passing of time in a massive panorama of such reassuring loveliness that I know it could never have failed to give her companionship and consolation.

Nearly every morning sunlight lay across the white counterpane of my enormous bed. I read desultorily, listened to the flight of doves with its sound—as of a wet cloth being slapped on a stone—saw the shadows move across the cypress; and letters dropped on my bed from the outside world, which would have excoriated my heart a few months earlier, were as impotent to disturb me as if in reality I were "leaning down from the gold bar of Heaven."

One day, however, I was nudged off the "gold bar of Heaven" by a phalanx of American reporters. "Miss Strange, Miss Strange, we have been looking for you all over London, Paris, the Riviera." "For weeks!" they cried out in the good old tempo. "But why—why?"

"Mr. Barrymore has just been married to Dolores Costello and the Women's Clubs say it isn't legal, for he's never been divorced from you. What do you think of that? What have you got to say?"

So Jack had gotten married and some strange imitation of a nervous throb of pain—the last I was ever to feel—emerged uncannily for a second from its burial wrapping. "Why, Miss Strange, didn't you know about Mr. Barrymore's marriage?" "Of course," I told the agitated young men, "and he's been divorced too for months, only you didn't know it because the action was carried on under Blythe, his legal name, and I never told my friends, so no one found out." "Then there's no story," they cried out, even with beautiful drinks of May's best white wine in their hands. Then by the grace of God somebody remembered that there was a nudist colony reported to be sheltering in the prehistoric caves just above Gourdon, and restored to a glow of optimism—since sensationalism had not utterly passed them up—off they rushed.

After they had gone John Strachey, also May's guest at the time, whom I called "Erasmus" because he so greatly resembled the Holbein portrait, and who called me by some Greek name that epitomized earth and fire, shook his head and asked me, "Dear Michael, must you go *out* to America to lecture?"

Profoundly Gourdon made up to my friend May for life's ineptitude at furnishing a rarely sensitive person with companionship for all moods and occasions. But no doubt this was too much to have found to be allowed to keep it. Gourdon ate up more than her income and left her mazed in debts which were sometimes fantastically incurred, as whenever funds grew low in the arrondissement of the Mayor's office, Mlle. Norris was told with shrugs of despair that a huge advertisement of "Cinzano" was about to be run up between Gourdon and her view of some favorite peak—that is unless matters could be arranged with the Cinzano authorities. But such a transaction would involve some thirty or forty thousand francs,—more deprecating shrugs, oily side glances, and the enamored May, on several occasions, actually did descend into the airtight speciousness of the Mayor's office and pay up.

Then suddenly when things were going wretchedly and desperately, the great singer Chaliapin wanted—and no wonder—to buy Gourdon at a fine price, and May refused the offer, still clinging to the only attachment she had ever had worthy to be rooted in her heart and soul, whereby she became, especially to her richest friends, a confounded nuisance. They had generously helped her again and again but here she was a gray-haired, frail woman, refusing a magnificent opportunity to protect herself and move off their consciences, still insanely clinging to her home and sending up cries for further assistance. It was maddening, not to be borne. So eventually, after indescribably sad struggles, May had to part with Gourdon and the rest was up to the auctioneer.

The last time I saw my dear May she did not see me. She was sitting in Notre Dame, just where the vast parallels of the aisles make a cross before the altar, just where all four magnificent windows can be seen if you turn your head. Her white hair and listening face stood clearly out of the unearthly dimness and I said to myself as I watched her: "May, you have associated yourself again with a sovereign beauty."

And now the sun setting
Behind the rose window of Notre Dame—
And casting a million opals steeped in blood
Upon the surrounding grayness—
And now—afar—through distant vaulted gloom
A shower of arrested stars—
Prayers—importunate—
Humbly attempting to warm into noticing them
Those narrow feet of the Mother of God—

CHAPTER XXV

Lecturing

T HE lecture tour, which Elisabeth Marbury had arranged for me the winter before I went to Liverpool, and to which I now returned after that Christmas with Cynthia at Denham, was the first opportunity I really had to see anything of America outside New York, Newport, Palm Beach and Long Island. And I was immensely glad to have a job all ready for me when I touched the dock, for a reason which had its melancholy side.

For many months, the first in years, I had not been able to write my poetry. Shocks from illness, and from life, had evidently vibrated to some vital depth and mesmerized the spring with stillness, so that to have some escape into definite action was oxygen from on high.

My chief lecture, written at Gourdon—discouraging to my stenographer who had ventured, "Miss Strange, do you think the American public will care for this sort of thing?" —rehearsed before the Mosleys, and worked on during those last days in Paris, contained no particular message, but was an attempt to recapture in prose some grain of my well-loved Whitman's optimism about American democracy.

Nineteen-twenty-eight was a piquant moment to have chosen to speak of Democracy—America was *en fête* riding a great surge of prosperity. And as we passed down a lead-colored river, toward the immense bulk of New York attached to the skyline at first like the ramparts of some mammoth Arabian Nights vision, and later showing up as a terrific hive of windows, through which the canyon streets cut their dismally straight shafts, I felt like calling down to a colorful group of immigrants in the prow—their faces straining with such awed wistfulness toward the myriad flashing windows of big business—"Hi! You won't all be Joseph Pulitzer or even President of the United States." However, at this point reporters were upon me to know what I thought of Jack's marriage, Hollywood styles, French ones, epilepsy, and "Alice Through the Looking Glass."

The lecturing went over marvellously after a setback in Newark next afternoon, when I discovered that one amidst hundreds of neatly ondulayed graying heads was nodding toward peaceful sleep in the front row, and had been compelled, in rage and amusement, to abandon then and there —to every one's delight—what I had thought of as my "Ten o'clock" version of Whitman's Democracy for a racy, gossipy bit written at my manager's request called "The Stage as the Actress Sees It."

"Sing me a Song of Social Significance" goes a ditty of

this season, and I don't quite know when my sense of this dynamic quality grew wakeful enough to influence my fate. Perhaps it was during that winter as a lecturer, when I covered the East and the Middle West with a couple of valises. The Grand Duchess Marie Pavlovna was allowed a maid, she also got twice my fee. But I must face those early morning blasts of icy air and racket in Kansas City, Chicago, St. Louis, etc., looking peculiarly distraught, and with only Claire's mink coat to give me caste before the reporters.

One night in Cleveland—having unexpectedly addressed so huge an audience that, my larynx faltering, there had been embarrassing shouts from the rear of "Louder Please"—when I got to sleep at last in the inevitable Statler Hotel, I was aroused around three A.M. by a stampede that took a maddening time to quiet down. "In God's name what happened in the hotel last night?" I asked the colored boy who brought me in my thermos of morning coffee, to be told that fifteen hundred salesmen had descended like locusts on Cleveland in that fragile hour, for rest, refreshment, and commercial contacts, and would depart at noon. Later I strolled down to look them over, and indeed there they were in a swarm around the magazine stand; calling out dates to each other with hysterical good-fellowship in the lift; bolting their breakfasts in the dining room with vociferous camaraderie, all looking frighteningly alike; fat bodies, faces of putty, restless anxious eyes, "sicklied o'er" with jaunty carefree optimism, all spruced up for contacts, one hundred per cent American.

What frantically juggled puppets, I thought. Their stomachs and brains are being shaken out of them. Surely the slaves building the Pyramids could have had no worse digestions. "What do they want to put across?" I asked the

Bell Captain, who told me "Mostly Breath Fresheners, but some of them have a new gadget for fastening your necktie."

Sobered, I went down to the theatre to while away the time until the next train, where I watched that ample diva, Mae West, slumbrously rocking her bosom toward a lot of sailors in the show, until the Marxian implications of the scene at the Statler faded from my mind.

Or was it not until years later, when I came back to the little house on Kay Street, the night before my father died, that some intimation dropped like a plummet into my make-up that private grief might have repercussions in thought which related a personal experience to that of millions of other people. On that evening my father had come slowly, painfully up the stairs, no longer able to stop and wind the grandfather clock; and sinking down on the edge of his bed in Lily's room, gaunt and a little wild-eyed with the half-delirious torpor of approaching death, he had feverishly plucked at my arm, and spoken the last words he was ever to address to me: "Baby! Baby! What will become of Mama—My liabilities—my liabilities———"

Was it in that sad moment, dim with repressed tears, when we covered him up and consoled him, that my heart turned to face a desire to serve some day in any capacity in which I might be allowed to do so, some form of inquiry into this juggernaut of insecurity over American life, which it seemed to me had hypnotized every member of my family with mirage values until from all of them peace had fled? Grief had gone deep enough to show me that it was not only my father's death at his ripe age that was regrettable, but his life—or was it life?—wasn't it merely an increasing confusion, evasion, of life's sanity and possibility, a systemless system of each for himself and to the devil with the hindmost which (set with some awkwardness to the prose of the Constitution) had consecutively through the years cheated his faculties, his principles, and his efforts with a return so mean and disheartening that during the years I had known him, nervousness ever on the increase was merely getting ready to be exchanged for indifferent bitterness? So I believe it was on that final evening, that there entered consciously into my mind some unyielding distaste for the moral mockery—that must long have been of the air I breathed—to ever bring such a decent and tender man as my dear father to his last farewell, distraught.

On those long Pullman journeys across the endlessly flat Middle West sparsely decorated with snow, loitering in tremendous shop-lined stations where you were entreated, beguiled, seduced to want anything, from a set of new teeth to a wardrobe, while I gazed out at sectional New Yorks rearing up fantastically from the dim winter plains every few hours, I began to think about what I saw,—although warned never to do this by Zoe Akins, who had said, "Never look out of the window on a Midwestern lecture tour. That's when I write my plays."

But the Middle West interested me. The people had such energy and hospitality, and were possessed by an earnest, if diffused, love of cultural things. Also they carried their tongues less in their cheeks than the New Yorkers, and of course it was charming to have the *crème de la crème* of every town roped in to meet me, with no effort on my part. However, the depressing uniformity of the cities with their bulking start of the skyscraper line, the Greco-Roman museums, banks, and first of all and more than all, the eternal flux of drained faces on Main Street, began to get me down. Prosperity didn't seem able to erase three puckers of startled apprehension from between their eyebrows, which gave their faces a kind of masklike similarity. I began to wonder how many people were really happy or healthy or at peace. And thoughts rimmed with thunder began to build on the horizon, so that I longed to stop gassing on about the theatre and talk of what, freshly impressed, I was thinking and feeling.

I was told from headquarters, however, that reports of my lecture, "The Stage as the Actress Sees It," were highly pleasing, that I was sold on my personality, etc., and I was left to conclude that, in my manager's mind, personality must always remain a label carrying no challenge whatever —must remain, in fact, the very opposite of itself, or of what I had thought it without reference to myself, the embodiment of conviction.

My life was full enough of contrasts. I might have dined with Mrs. X. in her beautiful Georgian home, with the napery and silver gleaming discreetly, and every sound but desultory talk ruled out (for Mrs. X was the "Lady Londonderry" of Chicago). That is, the power of wealth had been subdued into subtleties of perfection which could in no sense be termed display. One looked up from the dignity of Colonial silver and candlelight to perceive gradually that the walls were hung with priceless pictures, the lusty bright flesh tints of Renoir, elusive melancholy of Manet, and even a few canvases by that arch student of suffering —at that point where pain touches madness but cannot oust beauty—Daumier. Then afterwards, in a warm sweater and coat, I might take trails on impulse into the city where the revolving lights of chop suey joints and lunch rooms turned the slush underfoot a kind of infernal raspberry, and the houses were tenements, fragments of buildings striking eerily skyward between fields of refuse.

Into the lunch rooms, where I often took a late dose of refreshment, would come truckmen, mechanics, taxi drivers, gangsters I dare say, and near down-and-outs, and these men also had one thing in common, faces unhealthily white, the white I have seen on the bellies of dead fish, while their bones, under such pallor, had the texture of iron. "Oh, yeah!" seemed to be a laundry mark in the pit of every man's guts—disillusion "in excelsis"—as I sat about listening and occasionally had my ticket punched to a treat of ham and eggs. Every one of these fellows was the very poles apart from all the smooth talk about the opportunities that America granted "real initiative" which went on in the good houses; they were in "the know," I felt, they were "on to" the game in some ghastly and also humorous way.

Gangsters were going strong that winter in Chicago and the tourist was invited to look at the swing doors in a wooden saloon where two gangs had lately massacred one another with machine-gun fire on St. Valentine's Day. And one night, arriving back at the palatial Lake Shore Drive Hotel, I found the frock-coated gentleman in the office in a terrific dither. Apparently one of the guests had had her motor stopped at two A.M., right on Lake Shore Drive, and a string of pearls "lifted" from her neck.

Another night, dining out with Betty Field, a lovely

devotee of glamour, and at that time a columnist on *The Chicago Examiner*, it was arranged by the business editor, who was also present, that I should take a raiding drive in a police car. This consisted of piling into a small auto with machine guns hung along the roof, and a couple of detectives, who themselves looked like blood brothers of Al Capone and Jack Diamond, to whirl around the city at a great rate, while a radio voice repeated an esoteric jargon anent the movements of the criminals, who fortunately all got away that night.

But when we got back to the police station we learned that a raid had just come off on a drug joint and that the cells were crowded to capacity, and we were taken up into one of the floors of cells for women. A hideous smell of urine and lysol greeted us, and in each barred cage were huddled four or five limp grotesques, some covered by fur-collared coats bought in a more hopeful time. In their abandoned sprawling some seemed to be dead; some were being sick, others dreaming with their eyes wide open in a glassy merciful suspense from the life around them. And outside the window of the eighteenth floor, I looked and saw the dreadful night from which they had returned defeated. The incongruous scattering of skyscrapers stuck up their phallic arrogance into the dark from out the rickety rotten foundations of wooden tenements, and the great American advice "To Buy" belted and capped the huge buildings and was written in scrolls of circling, scarlet, intermittent light.

Another time, when I had been driving for a couple of hours through the Chicago slums with a couple of male escorts, we wound up in the late afternoon by crossing the bridge to the University of Chicago to take tea with Gertrude Stein in the apartment of Thornton Wilder. Miss Alice Toklas, with her fine eyes, tactful tongue and Hindoo appearance, fed me with delicious sandwiches while Gertrude Stein, looking like Buddha and the glowering hope of the steel strike, sat to one side negligently passing dictums. After she had welcomed me in the most charming manner possible, I said to this pictorial symbol of the roughest kind of revolution, "I have just been driving through twenty miles of Chicago slums." I paused, throaty with indignation and the assurance of sympathy. "Have you, my dear?" said Miss Stein. "I took the same drive myself day before yesterday. Haven't those wooden buildings an extraordinary beauty?" And she enlarged the scope of her listeners while I shut my eyes and took a deep pull at my glass.

Returning from sprints to St. Louis, St. Paul, Chicago, Milwaukee, Rockland and subsidiary cities—occasionally so small, so lost in the vague wilderness of winter that I thought the train was stopped especially for me, when I would curse my manager for this jolt to my pride—I found New York a carnival place, one hundred per cent on the up and up.

The bankers and great industrialists had become extraordinarily benign and attractive. Indeed, in the heady flush of continuously successful deals, they were not nearly so afraid of their wives, and acted now on a gay margin of self-confidence that made them great fun to associate with; while the boxes of flowers I received at that time had a generosity plus an imaginative note never sampled before.

"Big Business" was running the country with no interference from the government of Herbert Hoover; every one was making money. And one night I was taken to dine at an enchanting house on Long Island—with the "Sound" rippling at the end of the lawn,—to be told that my host, next whom I sat at dinner, and who looked and talked like a distinguished savant, was worth seven hundred million dollars. "Probably that's more than the Tsar of Russia could ever lay his hands on," I thought as I looked with social enthusiasm into the bland oval of his face, a strange face reminding me of a phrase of Whitman: "castrated of good and evil." Also around this time a friend of mine rang me up to say, "Do you know what? My cook made twenty thousand on the market last night."

It seemed that every one believed we had struck a golden era that would outlast time. Production was at full steam and no one, apparently, was inclined to stop and wonder how this terrific surge from farm and factory was to be unloaded onto a market that must sell at a profit. At a profit —there was the rub. Still, I hugely enjoyed the confetti tempo of that winter. Agreeable things happened to me from morning to night. On a couple of occasions I gave my weekly salary to a certain financier, to have three times the amount playfully returned a few days later.

And how amusing it was to go out to dinner in a tweed suit and, having dropped my valises in the hall to the austere discomfiture of the butler, be shortly obliged to rise and leave the bright vacuity of the talk, the hard-boiled wisecracks, the cultural torpor, the intimate nothings, and gather up one's luggage, to finger with rapt interest as if it were a life-belt, a ticket for Duluth. There you were going at least to talk about something that interested you to people who would not only not interrupt, but pay to listen to you. It was a stimulating exchange and, flushed with eagerness to get away, I laconically received the commiserations of my friends. "Why, Blanche, where are you off to?" "To the Middle West to give lectures." "Not really! What on earth do you lecture about?" Restraining an ever fresh pang (in those days) at the apparent impossibility of extricating myself from my social aura, I always replied, "On my career as actress, poet and playwright, and this week in Chicago, Oak Park, Lake Forest, Milwaukee, Indianapolis, Canton, Madison." Then upon the grand surge of my itinerary I left them, nonplussed, I hoped, and remorseful.

All this was in the year 1928—and already it is set aside as seen from across the flood. Between trains to Duluth, Chicago, Cleveland, Indianapolis, etc., one evening in particular stands out during that winter. I was dining at the home of one of our foremost bank presidents in the flood tide of his glory. It was a brilliant party: beautiful society women, captains of industry with overstressed jaws, some of the more brilliant extemporaneous toastmasters, and a few picked dramatists standing for that sort of success which is achieved from a blending of home humor and showmanship, but that will never pull away a chair from beneath the faculties of the average man.

The dinner seemed to have been served on a succession of gold plates—clusters of white flowers alternated with pyramids of fruit on the long refectory table. The surrounding walls were of white marble ingrained with meandering black veins and encrusted with flat decorative columnar shapes in the Roman manner. And as more champagne went down, the conversation took on an adventurous, amatory note rarely heard in such circles, while the wisecracks of the extemporary speeches had moments of brilliance. The men lost that confused wife-watched look so prevalent in America, that has been known to pass for relief into an inebriate stupor, and became flirtatiously masterful; while the women seemed rather less waiting to be looked at, and more generously ready to exchange a little something here and there. Indeed, one could feel the subtle recklessness, the self-confidence of the presence of triumph investing everything.

Dinner was ending, the pyramids of fruit had been levelled, and the white flowers, strewn from the centerpieces of gold, lay in confusion over the lace tablecloth, looking, I thought, as if a dancer had shuffled through them, while all about the table stood the jewelled bulbs of glasses half-filled with bright liqueurs.

I went upstairs to telephone, thinking, "This is the feast of a triumph. What is it that they believe has just been won?" Then, as I took the receiver from the hook, one of the more terrifyingly important financiers, utterly wife-tamed and disinterested heretofore, suddenly came up behind me and engaged in determined advances,—which Roman struggle was brought to an end by the entrance of a member of his family whose footfall he seemed to have sensed some moments before the door actually opened.

Going downstairs, jubilant with suppressed laughter and feeling that on this night, by St. George, everything was in character, I found the program for the evening was under way. Upon a platform erected against a great tapestry the journalists, dramatists, speechmakers were performing. There were take-offs and skits of private and public personages marvellously rendered, it seemed to me, while trays of champagne kept floating in front of my nose, and I surrendered myself more and more to this high-geared enchanting party.

How casual and generous success seemed to be making these men. Now they had the ability to relax, to be utterly charmed by the moment, because back of it all they had come to believe that they would be successful and powerful forever. A drama, whose theme I was not then looking for, anointed them, made them memorable. And I saw them that evening in a new light, as dangerous performers cele-brating landings that were sometimes miraculous with fra-ternal winks. They had cornered with grim astuteness the spoils of civilization and were trailing these with ignorance and jubilation before their guests, but judging from the dual tests of looking at, and listening to them, little or nothing had been digested or really perceived. There had been no normal time to digest anything; it had been too insistent a struggle to keep one's foothold in the great lavalike shiftings of high finance, where I supposed ordi-nary faculties of self-preservation were daily sharpened into something so near genius that now the line was much thinned, and the adversaries in their isolated panorama grown titanic.

Neither were their houses homes. There had been no time for that! They were the momentary tents of victory, gloriously rigged up as palaces that appropriately enough emulated the splendors of Rome and the Renaissance. Home was merely a place where you dumped the treasure and yourself in a mood of vainglory, or exhaustion, and saw your wife for a few baffling moments, while you listened to the bracing shake of gin and vermouth that would put you on your toes to receive or go out.

Suddenly I remembered all the fractional New Yorks I had been visiting with their mammoth uneasy skylines, their classic post offices, stations, art museums, the richness of the stores packed with things, things, things, the endlessly attractive invitations to spend, in the streets, in the magazines, on the ground floor corridors of the hotels that were really only closed-in streets of shops.

And I thought of the salesmen in Cleveland, of the prevalent type—short, with heavy, pasty jowls overhanging their collars, mostly carrying paunches, their eyes never resting, expressionless, dressed in hats, suits, coats that seemed to have been spewed out of a single hemorrhage of the machine. I remembered the frightening uniformity of that hive of men settled momentarily in Cleveland before rising up in a locust-like cloud to attack another selling point, obviously kept on the rush without decent time to eat or sleep or browse or think, deadened, deafened, blinded, driven by having to succeed or "so what?", rushing in day coaches or in sleepers all over the vast continent to make people want to buy their nine-tenths rubbish, personal testimonials, if ever I saw such, to the quality of their servitude.

And I thought of the great semineurotic, cowlike buying of the masses of American people that would follow the cloudburst descent of those poor chaps, of the enchantment of the advertisements, the persuasiveness of the talk filling up some half-crazed gap of their barrenness. Then finally those piles of things, things, things that had arrived at every part of the American Continent would be transmitted into counters; into stocks and bonds, over which sat the Titans—over which sat in any comparison to the great hive of people who sold and bought beneath them—a mere handful of astute men with admirable capacity to persist, to dare, and to work . . . and a few other things. But I thought with only a slight intuitive sense of the inarticulate distress, of the rising nervous disorders upon which they were resting their game. And if they had any knowledge of the prophetic values of history God knows they kept it a dark secret in their conversation.

At this time my parents were quite proud of the flattering notices I sent them of "The Stage as the Actress Sees It," and one night they motored down to Providence to hear me, and I shall never forget the still handsome face of my father, leaning on his cane in the back row, with such an expression of distinguished astonishment, as I wisecracked along.

Not having to be anywhere for a couple of days, I went back with them to the little house on Kay Street of so many memories; but now what a melancholy metamorphosis! A great Post Road with a line down the center went by our front gates, taking away at one fell swoop all silence and peace from the garden and rooms. The meadow opposite, over which I had seen the fog swim, while Miss Pam played Chopin, had been cut up into little lots upon which stood nondescript jerry-built houses, each with its concrete garage, modern plumbing, radio, telephone, etc., providing everything but one scrap of charm, individuality or peace.

And our little house—the mildew of sleep and death was upon it already. In many of the rooms the paper had started to peel from the walls; yet Tibi and Papa did not seem to notice, for they were nearly always dozing in their chairs in the library, or waking up to quarrel faintly, or to be desperately worried over trifles. And I would think, as I lay in my old nursery with the fresh white muslin curtains still tied back with enormous blue bows, that behind the peeling paper and the marks of dampness was exuding the moisture of slow heartbreak. It seemed that even the elm trees and horse-chestnuts had lost their pep, the bark looked unhealthy, and then they seemed so much smaller. "Did the vibration from the road affect them right down to the roots?" I wondered.

But I was glad, as the winter gales tore through the leafless boughs and the motors made "their anesthetizing hum of speed" outside the door, that my parents were still surrounded by all their charming things. The colors were still the same, though faded; the pictures of old friends, taken on a day of youth, still looked down on them from their white frames; the cheerful Delft pieces stood about on the bookcases with their blue scenery of a tranquil day concerned with sails and windmills; while on the blue parlor mantel shelf still stood the lovely Dresden china—cupids and shepherdesses, and the one I always called "The Tired Lady" with her powdered hair under her fragile lace head-dress, who had fallen asleep in her chair reading a love letter with a red seal, and had kicked off one of her slippers.

I supposed it was good to go toward the end amidst the consolation of familiar things. "Old age, old age flowing by, with the beautiful nearby freedom of death." If only it could have been like that, but money worries were still with my father in every waking hour. His anxious integrity and his pride left him confused and wounded. He was at that time existing on an income from that part of the money originally bequeathed to him by my uncle, but lost in the suit with Aunt Tessie. This kindly arrangement of my cousin Hermann had staved off actual ruin.

Forever of me . . .
Your chin flinging upward . . .
Face steadied, sobered
Solemnly wrought in linular cadence of beauty
Apart from me . . .
Setting its earnestness all
Toward slim clear, mounting splendor . . .
—Burning sidewise down on us
As a diamond candle . . .
Of the sickle moon . . .

Forever of me . . .
For the still pondering aloof on us both
When strikes of light over sublime stretches
Bringing out majesties so determined . . .
That Revelation's young echo
Seeming nearly to pierce . . .
Our abstracted mutual listening.

Forever of me . . .
Since reclaiming
From under the harsh treadmill wheel of life
An enchantment . . .
Wistful, rare
Curiously warm . . .
We may nurse together.

CHAPTER XXVI

Sunsets in Common

UPON my third marriage, Arthur Brisbane bet Mary Harriman Rumsey ten thousand dollars that we would not be together ten years later for our tin wedding. As this event has just been celebrated with a surprise cocktail party arranged by Harry, it is sad to think that both the sports who so generously backed their convictions are dead. Indeed, lots of people were willing to bet their shirts that we would never get married at all, as Harry and I behaved—with the idea—like a couple of maddened broncos in a rodeo.

I think Mary Harriman Rumsey was largely responsible for downing the egomaniac fears of Harry and myself, so that we were able to consent to marry one another that spring, following my lecture tour, in the registry at Kensington. Something of the determination that had helped her father E. H. Harriman lay the tracks of the Union Pacific from the east to the west coast infused her also, but she was that rare personal product of a great financier—a refinement of his own faculties. She too could select, organize, put through interesting ventures mostly to do with art, while her whimsical far-seeing eyes carried in them the tang of a spirit that I always thought was completely superb.

Mary, when I had come back from Europe to lecture, with a good leg, would look at me with elfish tenderness and inquire, "But what about Harry?" extracting, however, no consoling answer from my attitude of haughty independence. I simply stuck my nose farther into the air and went off to pack for another round of lectures. But this did not stop her, for she was determined we should marry one another and I know she felt we were quite free to do so, since I had seen Jack only twice in three years, and Harry's former wife had married several months previously.

Mary, however, had been laying for our marriage a year or more before Eleanor Tweed had married Count Palfy, and chiefly for the reason that, loving Harry dearly as she did, she was anxious that his loneliness should cease, and that he should have a more normal personal life, since Eleanor Tweed had for several years lived in Europe and Harry saw his family only at the Christmas holidays, for which he travelled to Europe, and during the summer when they returned for a couple of months to Montauk.

So one spring morning in Paris, cozily gay with the children, and ruminating once more on my theatrical career, which was at that moment commencing to interest a couple of London managers, I received a wire from Harry telling me he thought of sailing for Europe with Mary Rumsey, and did I think it was a good plan? I was, of course, elated, but having by this time sensed a couple of things about the New England temperament, I wired back coolly that I thought it would be far better if he stayed where he was.

Harrison Tweed

From the circular: MICHAEL STRANGE
Poet, Playwright, Actress

Naturally, I received word in a few hours that he had definitely decided to sail.

The last engagement as to whether we would marry or not, was fought at Orleans (a few weeks later), where we landed in a beautiful Hispano-Suiza car, grimed with battle, exhausted even beyond desire for food or sleep, just at that moment when the city was celebrating the anniversary of Joan of Arc.

The bells of the Cathedral struck their heavy fateful note over narrow streets, and the great Cathedral Square was crowded with French people, mostly in mourning for their relatives as usual. Their dismal ranks, however, were fortunately broken by the peasants from Lorraine, who, their feet still rooted in the blessedness of the soil, knew enough to retain the joyful beauty of their imaginative native costumes. I remember how their winged head-dresses soaked radiance from even that gray French day.

After falling down at the hotel for a few hours in the dreamless sleep of soldiers, we dined in my sitting room and watched from our window the torchlight procession— Joan, riding by with her generals and troops to the Cathedral to ask God's blessing on the lifting of the Siege—and afterwards I told Harry we simply had got to get in to the High Mass that was to be celebrated next day in honor of the Maid. A truce must be called long enough for that! But the concierge was hysterical with that pessimism of the French when confronted by a request that does not follow form. Hadn't we seen the notice in the lobby? Why the sale of tickets had closed two days ago.

However, surpassing hysteria and pessimism with tips and some sex appeal, we got in and were marvellously placed, right to one side of the altar behind an immense grill through which we faced Monsieur Doumergue, the gray-haired President of the French Republic, and members of his cabinet.

For me High Mass heard in a vast Gothic cathedral, which gives to a human choir and organ an unearthly echo and resonance, is one of the most beautiful experiences to be had on earth. The Mass, identical in every part of the world, dramatizing—stylizing as it does—to a Latin text the event of the Last Supper, with all the sayings and gestures of Jesus in that critical moment preserved in the only way they possibly could have been, by ritual, has never failed to clarify my mind by refreshing my spirit. And this Mass was no exception, for during it Harry and I both relaxed inside and decided without words that nothing of value in our make-ups would be blasted out of existence by marriage.

I never realized fully what pathos there was for children in the divorce of their parents until I came to Montauk in early September after my marriage. Diana had always been entirely with me, Robin almost all of the time, and when he and Leonard did visit their father, the friendship which Len and I had for one another kept me so informed of their health and doings, that I did not feel really separated from them.

I had met Harry's two lovely little daughters in Paris a few months before our marriage. Of course I was not introduced as their father's future bride, and to the very blond blue-eyed little girls with such proudly delicate modelling of head and face, I was the wife of John Barrymore and so glamorous to a degree. During the interval, however, between our meeting and months later when I returned to

Montauk as Mrs. Harrison Tweed there had naturally enough been a severe let-down.

Beautiful Montauk would not show itself for my arrival that September evening. A heavy fog with the impenetrability of wet gray drapes hung over the whole place and Harry was so disappointed, because his desire to have me love Montauk, was only second to his lovely enthusiasm at having me home.

And then Harry's daughters came to say hello, calling me "Michael" as per rehearsal. But now the poor children could not smile relaxedly into my eyes as before, for here was glamorous Mrs. Barrymore balefully costumed as that legendary figure which all fairy books had taught you to loathe—the stepmother. And although their manners were perfect, their underlips protruded very slightly and trembled, and I thought they looked exactly in their beauty, rigidity and self-control, like two little Anglo-Saxon princesses who have just been told that it was time now to take their places for the triumphal march through Rome in chains behind Cæsar's chariot. What could I say or do? Nothing! For a hundred per cent, naturally enough at first, they would have none of me. Children cannot rationalize. A picture, clear and consoling to them, that of their parents together, had suffered a collapse; nor had they faculties with which to make intellectual readjustments. And I thought to myself, time, and going to a great many more movies than they have ever done before, is the only thing.

The beauty of Montauk came out of its haze the day after my homecoming, and sparkled upon land and sea, as if the light itself had been refreshed from its submersion in mist, and when I walked through lanes cut in the shad bush and bayberry—down to the low cliffs (much like the visionary drawings of Blake) that overhung the sea—I was enraptured, for there was an almighty celestial gaiety and strength to the way the giant combers broke far out, reared up to form again, and came crashing in—in lanes—in battalions of the whitest surf I had ever seen! And when you bathed in that green crystal-clear water with wafts off the great foam patterns wetting your nose, why, you experienced an absolutely divine sense of restoration.

Concerning the whole range of political and intellectual ruminations Harry and I were in entire disagreement. Discussion of current events found us the poles apart, and yet about things which can be loved only inarticulately, such as oceans and sunsets, we were at one. And I began to see that it did not matter so much whether you saw eye to eye on the merits to the social system of John L. Lewis and J. P. Morgan & Co., if only you could both join hands and run like the wind before nearly all of the beckonings and restrictions of social life. Indeed, in such matters we possessed a kind of Indian savagery in common that was most companionable. Then perhaps it is only the things that cannot be talked about that you want to feel are seen alike by you and your lover, and how marvellously Harry's head and shoulders looked coming up out of that shining surf at Montauk!

After my marriage I popped back into the Social Register, and was visited by several friends who hadn't crossed my threshold in years. These indicated to me with a kind of beneficent clarity, that they now hoped in God's name to hear no more of Michael Strange, Poet, Playwright, Actress: "Really, dahling, it's been a little difficult sometimes, but (dipping their rapiers in sugar), as I've always said, you have such charm"; and I was left to fancy what might have occurred if charmless I had clamored to focus the world's attention on all my long list of spurious endeavors.

Indeed, some years later a cousin, always one of my favorites, wrote to me at least with admirable candor: "Why not cut out all this tomfoolery in calling yourself 'Michael Strange' and putting on airs, and come down to earth. Be human like your mother and father, and the rest of us. You are too nice and attractive for all this nonsense. If you only knew how people laugh and make fun of you, which is none too pleasant to hear by those members of your family that are fond of you. As ever, Your devoted cousin."

One evening, coming uptown in the pitiful inferno of a New York subway, I read these headlines in an evening paper: "Lady Cynthia Mosley dangerously ill." And a few days later Cynthia died of peritonitis and in a week or so came my last letter from Tom, a very dear letter.

So then I lost my dearest friend, and learned that there is something rather like spring about a great sorrow, for in it the feelings are preserved absolutely forever in their freshness.

And now Tom is the undisputed chief of a few hundreds of thousands of followers, and I read about riots against his Party in London, and see his picture, stern and taut, standing in the Albert Hall or beside Mussolini in Rome, but never smiling; and I believe that the real, the fruitful years of his life are already spent, for I think in the end that Tom will look back upon those young days when he turned away from the snobbery and deafness of his own class, breasting surge after surge of ridicule as he did so, to help British Labor, with Cynthia beside him, as the only real days of his life.

In the intervening years after my marriage I had seen very little of Cynthia, whose house had been my sanctuary. For at perhaps one of the loneliest moments in my life, when I went out to America to lecture after that Christmas at Denham, she had said—I remember she was standing and made such a lovely gesture with her arms—"I would do anything in the world you wanted me to, Michael, anything! And you could have anything of mine you wanted— always."

Her career, as long as she was well enough to pursue it, had continued eminently successful, but then there were some serious illnesses. During the first of these I was in London and went down to Denham during her convalescence. I was rushing back late from the tennis courts one night to dress for dinner when I came across them both in the fanciful double dimness of twilight and the shadow of a great tree. They were standing very close together, for I think Tom had just been arranging a scarf around her shoulders, and once more they seemed with a curious poignance to be made for one another, very tall and apparitional. Just like "Martians," I thought, as I had on the night I first met them.

In the following years there were many letters but only a few glimpses of Cynthia, and then there was another long illness before the birth of her son and my godson, Michael. He was not called after my alias, but only because Cynthia cared for the name. Then about a year after his son's birth,

Tom blossomed out into a full-fledged fascist and we had some diverting days in Paris together—our last—with Tom extraordinarily returned to his good spirits, now that he was about to assume the leadership of a fascist party in Great Britain.

Cynthia appeared happy for the change in him, for it seemed she had put aside with a strange new serenity all of her own vehement viewpoint, for which at any rate lately she had been too ill to work. And I thought how changed and stooped she was, and that instead of racing over to Paris on holidays with Tom, her lovely frailty should have been guarded with the greatest love until her strength returned.

During this last mutual stay of ours in Paris a ball was given one night by four *élegants jeunes hommes* at the house of Armand LaRochefoucauld, a *"Bal Blanc."* I had dined first at the Cole Porters' in their beautifully arranged country château in the midst of Paris—13 rue M'Sieur—and looking at the enchanting white toilettes about me became aware as usual that I might have done better for myself, if I had given some thought to the party before I started to dress for dinner.

However, I pressed on with the others and, once arrived in the thick of the scramble, felt that nothing mattered, for here was an entertainment for the *crème de la crème* of professional society: I don't mean the society of professional people, but a Simon-pure exploitation, professionally expert, of toilettes, jewels and personalities, using as a sort of theme word the term "society" (probably to give the fillip of an inviting exclusiveness) to this production of people by themselves.

Every one made *entrées* and as their names were called out, on either side a line of people were drawn up to stare with undisguised appraisal, d-rr-i-nn-king in every detail, as Noel Coward would say, of whatever degree of glamour the exhibit might show. Keeping on my coat in a spirit of contradiction, I made my *entrée,* when every one quickly looked to see who should follow me!

I walked through the ballroom and out onto the Rotunda balcony, seeing before me the stylization of green and gravel that is a French garden, softly lit with magic lanterns, while up and down the gravel walks and on the marble benches the *entrées* continued to pose, hovered over by their male escorts, in attitudes from which it might be safely said there was withdrawn the smallest part of that most interesting intention of life.

And especially I remarked one young American woman notably fashionable. She was seated on a marble bench across the garden from me, the theatre light perfectly enhancing the long-limbed grace of her pose as she leant slightly forward, her smooth head bent, one perfect brown arm heavily loaded with diamond bracelets clasped about her knee. How still she was; her oval face wore the wide-eyed imperviousness of the mask—the line of the eyes scooped up at the corners emphasizing the oriental non-human aspect. She might have been—almost was—one of the best possible of those figurines that one sometimes sees photographed now in place of a person. What a horrible time, I thought, when only the painted shell and the titles are left to sell down to Vogue at a price!

A stage show began at the end of the garden and never had I felt such cold as there was in that garden. Was the River Seine drawing closer, I wondered, the tragic River

Seine; for if there is a river dedicated to suicides it is this one. And suddenly I remembered the clumsy outline of two figures under a tarpaulin laid out on the cobblestones that led down to the river, the man's rubber boots protruding as they splayed to right and left in the relaxation of death, while the woman's soaked brown high-heeled shoes showed that she lay sideways, turned toward the man, in this death they had cheated of loneliness by breasting it together. Then in a moment I felt unendurably tired and ill, and Tom, who was standing beside me, said he would take me home. So we went first to find Cynthia to tell her that he would be right back.

She was standing on the balcony looking out at the show, very tall in her white dress and wearing rows of diamonds about her throat and a light ornament of diamonds in her hair. I kissed her goodnight telling her, "I will see you tomorrow afternoon while you rest;" and I thought "Cynthia, how radiantly you are alive, I will never get used to what there is in your face." But the next day I was ill, it was the beginning of the worst cold I ever had, and Cynthia was too tired after the party to come to me. Tom arrived instead. I had never seen him so content, so exuberantly at ease, the way a person is who at last has struck what will take the most that he is out of him and use it; and next morning they both left for London and I was compelled to return to America a few weeks later via Cherbourg.

After that Cynthia's letters grew a little strange. They seemed to tell me nothing because they were trying so hard to conceal some mortal pain,—Lady Cynthia Mosley dangerously ill. . . .

What Cynthia said, and what Tom said, and my reactions to them then, and now through retrospect, appear important to me in 1939, when apparently the battlefields of the world are convulsed with the very issues in which their opinions rooted.

To me Tom appears always to have been typically a fascist, and although he reasonably enough wanted muddling and hypocrisy to cease, and ancient methods of government to melt away before a more modern timing sense, although he certainly desired a better life for all, one hardly felt he would be modern enough to rule out arrogance and brutality in the performance of his ideas.

I think Tom's fatal political fault was his egoistic impatience, which perverted his fine intellect from that appreciation of British character which would have told him, no matter how wildly aside from a true democracy he might have considered most British lives to be led, that still, to the deepest fiber of their spiritual marrow, fascism would have been a repellent answer. And to me Tom's fatal spiritual fault was his jejune scrapping of mercy, mercy brought to us possibly at a greater cost than anything which happened to Cæsar's armies, or the vast wraiths of Valhalla.

And what is Cynthia to me across all the years besides the dearest friend I ever had? Over and above her rather frightening beauty, a man said to me in her audience one night, "You don't often hear people saying fine things, who look exactly like what they say." Cynthia from across the river is more now than my friend. She appears symbolic to me of that truth, standing back of the incredible confusion, impermanence and worse of today, toward which all things will and must tend as to a magnet.

I see now that the reason her sayings affected me so

powerfully was that they were only a by-product of what she was in herself; that it was because of her own intrinsicalities that she could believe everything of and for other people, and set out with her laughing gallantry and infinite nerve to tell them about this power they had in themselves. Not about her power over them—or the States—but about her belief that they could be so spirited, so decently fraternally intelligent, so capable of coming strongly together, that they would become invincible, not as an army, nor as a navy, but as an example of what you could do with what you had, when once you'd decided to jack yourself up to modernity, spiritually, psychically, physically, "and to use right side up instead of bottom side up the machinery already at hand." "And now we must plan and work to put in a government that will do this for us," Cynthia might add, with such a lilt in her voice that no one thought of barricades or bombs, but only of a long stream of people filing courteously in to replace the dead.

I think of her clarity with an indescribable wistfulness. Of course it came out of long apprenticeship to her task as well as high personal endowment.

Cynthia was of the chain of fulfillers. She scrapped none of her great derivatives. If the priest were corrupt in his practice then she set about changing that, but not the significance which had given him his *raison d'être*. Cynthia was neither militant conqueror nor destroyer, she was the purifier. Her sense of humor, of proportion, would always have been more interested in Jesus than in Cæsar, and I believe that her meanings destined for life will shape themselves into the acts of men, because it is through her, and those who like her believe that it is not from iron rods held over humanity's backside—but from what wells up in the spirited individual of acceptance and of rejection—that evolution is justified and history in the long run a document of hope.

And so now taking leave of her in this book, but never elsewhere, I want to quote for her the lines that describe her the best—the first ones in Walt Whitman's "Leaves of Grass":

> *"One's-Self I sing—a simple, separate Person;*
> *Yet utter the word Democratic, the word En-masse."*

And these lines, which I have loved and revered always, are my farewell to Cynthia.

e e e e e e e e e e e e e e e e e e e e e e e e e e e e e e e e e e e e e e e e e e e

The End of Johann Strauss

"A while ago when my little son was ill
Three evenings he pulled down my head to rest
on his narrow white breast—
And his light child's hands so transparent with illness
wavered in and out through my hair—
O he held me my little son did in the curve of
his unborn tenderness—
And I know in that moment his sweet child's mind was
securely forever imprinted—
With the yearning face of my love."

ROBIN had lately been very ill at his eleventh school in Phœnix, Arizona, so ill that Harry and I had taken a plane as far as Kansas City, and gone from there to Phœnix by train. It was our first plane trip and although I know how interesting Mrs. Lindbergh's writing has made flying, still when we mounted into the air, and I was imprisoned in the middle of that fearful throbbing noise, with the earth under me beginning to look like an extinct volcano, I felt more sure than ever that we ought to take machinery with a dose of salts, use it sparingly, and with plenty of counterbalances. How nervous and sallow the pilots had looked, nor was there a grain of rosy stewardess-cheer about the grim young woman with her bland nasal voice who strapped on my landing belt.

After any experience in our mammoth New York hospitals what a dream I found this Catholic hospital in which Robin was slowly recovering, where you were nursed by nuns and a priest came in for a cheery talk every day. They saw you, these nuns, and so did the priests. You registered on them and they on you, for you were able to register on such peace and hope as they bore within them. During a stay of five weeks at one of the most "hotcha" hospitals in town in the previous fall most of the trained nurses "bore within them" the latest Hollywood news as relayed by the tabloids. "Miss Strange!" as they snapped up the blinds around seven, "Did you see where Merle X shot her husband in the back, in their swimming pool at 5 A.M.? . . . Must have been some party!" a sense of their own importance, and also the pathetic psychic confusion of spinning mice. Indeed, as we talked over the often desperate condition of their personal affairs, I wondered if I oughtn't to haul myself out of bed and give them an alcohol rub for a change.

Because Robin had told me that he wanted above all things to study music in Vienna, and I thought Leonard and Diana needed a breath of change, we all found ourselves in my mother's city in the June of 1932.

But it was a strange Vienna divided in sentiment and at loose ends. The spirit of Johann Strauss, of "Tales From the Vienna Woods," which had lasted so notably from my mother's youth into mine, had vanished. All the gay uniforms were gone, the Hussars in black and gold, the Dragoons in their blue coats and red trousers with the gold stripe. For at that moment Prince Starhemberg's Storm Troopers slowly paraded the streets dragging pieces of fearsome artillery after them, and the Waltz Dream was utterly routed by those grim realistic gray-brown uniforms and terrible helmets.

And again there was the Socialist Vienna, "Gemeinde Wien," with its impressive modern housing for the workers, just ninety-nine per cent ahead in acreage and pleasantness from anything I had seen before, or that I have ever seen since.

And there was the old Vienna tragically nonplussed, whose members sat about at their clubs, and in houses which they kept a quarter open. Some of them came to call on me—Count Apponyi, Count Colorado Mansfeldt—and I put on a black silk dress and had all the children appear around the tea table to make an harmonious impression. For much water had flowed under the bridge since handsome Count Anthony Apponyi had brought me in my lunch from the Ritz while I posed in Prince Troubetzkoy's studio for portrait number nine, dressed in a white brocaded dress trimmed with sable, and wearing all my pearls.

And Count Collorado, whom I had known as a dark, slim, tall, young man, the personification of romance, during his years at the Austrian Embassy in Paris, conjured up for me, when he walked into the room—even twenty-five years later—the ballrooms of June, with those long

French mirrors reflecting what seemed to me then, and seems to me far more in the nostalgia of retrospect, to have been a great deal of genuine distinction and beauty.

"Who is that man in the doorway?" I might ask Len, who always knew every one. "His head looks good enough to be struck off on a coin." And a moment later I would be meeting my husband's friend, the Duke of Alba, an amazing-looking chap, dark-haired with somber Moorish eyes, and such a clean cut to his features and limbs that I thought his appearance the last word in that sometimes boring, but maybe always significant term, breeding.

The Duchess of Sutherland would enter in gleaming satin and rose tulle scarf, diamond tiara and pearls—Milly Sutherland, who in later years became a friend of mine, and was, I thought and think, one of the few great beauties I have ever seen. She was over six feet, blond, blue-eyed, with such a proud and smiling head, and a skin that looked literally as if it had been washed in snow, while at the risk of seeming pot-headedly redundant, her lips were the color of ripe wild strawberries. And her manners, her beautiful manners! I am overcome with a nostalgia which I will defend to the death, when I remember the manners of this great beauty and compare them with those of what might be called—but in a moment of blind staggers—her equivalent on the social scene of today.

And I was presented to the Comtesse de Noailles, just then one of the best-known women poets in France, a member of the French Academy, thin, pale, with quantities of dark hair, and that hidden agony in the eye—like smoldering embers come across in the night in some desert place, I thought. And when I was told that other members of the Academy and great statesmen were in love with her, it seemed to me perfectly wonderful to have an outstanding position before the world both in love and art.

Or it would be "Signor D'Annunzio, I want you to meet my wife," and a dark, short fellow, with a rather grim little face, looking as if commercial trepidation had him tied into a nervous knot, would come forward, and soon by the extraordinary music of his voice and the fluent roll of his words persuade me that he was indeed the great Poet Gabriele D'Annunzio.

But the visit of my old friends that afternoon did not go very well, for if I stood between two worlds, "One dead, one powerless to be born," they were, it seemed to me, with the world that was dead, while I was wishing to God for the *accouchement* of a new one. And the final *coup de grâce* was delivered to my visitors—who had been complaining bitterly about the taxes with which Socialist Vienna was built—when I told them that in a few days Leonard and I were starting for Russia. "Russia!" said Count Apponyi, rising and taking up his fawn-colored gloves and cane, "Not really! Why?" "Because I want to see for myself what is going on, surely it is an epic experiment." "I think you will dislike it very much," he told me, but I did not tell him that the air of Vienna seemed to me as stagnant as the water in the moats surrounding one of the country villas of the Hapsburgs—Laxenburg. "The whole place is asleep," I thought, and, remembering the rumble of Starhemberg's artillery, "perhaps there will be a terrible awakening."

Even modern Socialist Vienna with its marvellous miles of apartment houses and gardens seemed poised—for all the bright geranium window boxes—like a lovely noonday dream on the horizon. While behind this confused, divided

Vienna, in the depth of the country, bronze-faced girls and boys were lighting fires on the hilltops at night, and when I saw these blazing I asked Myrtle, the sturdy daughter of our innkeeper at Mondsee, what were they for? "For Herr Hitler," I was told, "for when he shall cross into Austria and unite us." "Oh, the Anschluss." "Yes," she answered. "Well," I told her, "in my mother's day they would never have wanted that, for they felt they were very different from the Germans, especially from the Prussian Germans." "But we do want the Anschluss," she told me, "we country people, we want the unity that is going to make us strong before the world and to have order here in Austria, and work for every one."

The Vienna of my youth and my mother's youth was indeed spent; the whole spirit of the city was in eclipse, and who could tell what would emerge and, impressed as I was by the unique Socialist Municipal Bulding, when I listened to the country people talk (Leonard and Robin spoke German as well as natives) I saw that the people were not behind it, that they were even bitterly antagonistic. Probably they had paid some of the taxes which went for its construction, as I knew the aristocrats had.

But for the tourist "Gemeinde Wien" was an amazing spectacle. One workman taking me through his flat in the Karl Marx Hof (it was a law in "Gemeinde Wien" that there must be three times as much garden as building) showed me his windows and porch, one for sunset, the other for sunrise. Every apartment was filled with light and spotlessly clean, while the great stretches of green and planting beneath them were really superb.

Gott erhalte unsern Kaiser, the great pageant of royalty, its flashing godlike helmets, uniforms glittering with medals, and also the often-practised unwritten laws of courage, of dutiful, tireless service to what might be called one's station in life, all of it had been swallowed up, as was 720 Wienstrasse, Baron Kubeck's residence in Vienna from which the dark-haired, wistful little girl, my mother, had sallied forth to her lessons, to the museums, to her Mass, to exercise, returning occasionally with flushed cheeks and shining eyes because she had encountered the lovely Empress at the Spanish riding school, or stood beside the curb while the Emperor drove by surrounded by his Guard.

Aunt Nancy was dead, she had wandered forth into the dusk, no doubt in fluttering white draperies, with a bunch of lilies-of-the-valley (her favorite flower) in one hand and a volume of Alfred de Musset in the other, to rejoin that love from which she had never wavered; and Baron Kubeck, her rejected husband, threadbare and precise, who must always get us to the Opera on time, was also gone.

The country estate, Leichwitz, where my mother had passed all her childhood and girlhood, had become separate from Austria and was then in Czecho-Slovakia, and the only inheritor of it, my cousin Blanche Kubeck, had also passed away. On her death came a letter from a friend of hers in Austria telling me that Blanche, even after a journalist's career, which must have sowed some seeds of sophistication, had died like a pious child, her eyes fixed upon the likenesses of her mother and father.

As I think of them all, of their sentiment, of their moderation, of the genuine consolation that their faith was to them, and of the charming order that always surrounded their lives, no matter what events, what cataclysms of emotion passed over them, I wish I could distil whatever it was they lived by into an essence—and breathe often of it.

For hours we had been passing a tremendous country with a vast roll and sweep to the landscape, broken up only by what appeared to be stretches of primeval pine and hemlock forests, and clusters of small houses that looked as though they were made of logs. Russia! The train came to a full stop and we got out and went with our bags into the first station I had ever been in that looked like a schoolroom. There were no magazine and candy stands, no indications of a restaurant, just a large buff-colored room with a frieze running round the wall near the ceiling that exclaimed in different languages, "Workers of the world, unite!"

We laid our luggage on counters and three volumes of Trotzky which I had forgotten to pitch out of the window were instantly confiscated by a female comrade with a severe expression.

I don't know if it was the custom, or if my reading matter had worked on their suspicions. Anyway, Leonard and I were taken aside and perfunctorily searched before, clutching our bags, we made our way back into the dusk and saw, at the far end of the platform through which the engine would pass, a frail arch rearing into the air and bearing in huge letters the inscription USSR.

"Look," said Leonard pointing to a group of soldiers in greatcoats poking with naked bayonets under the cars, "I just asked what they were doing [he could speak some Russian] and they're looking for spies." "How marvellous," I thought, "I knew Russia would be different!" Unfortunately so was the dinner served to us in a very

[296]

ornate top-heavy looking car (the kind the Grand Dukes must have gone to the Russo-Japanese War in, accompanied by their mistresses) by a comrade in a Russian blouse who made no secret of what he thought of having to be a waiter. However, after he had slung two carafes of straight vodka down beside our plates, Leonard was inclined to trust the morrow.

As we stepped down onto the pavements of Moscow, Leonard whispered, "Now remember, Cat, at last you are in a country where money doesn't matter, so don't tip any one." But at that moment I saw, standing behind the "Intourist Guide" who was meeting us, a woman—surely a beggar, for she was muttering the old toneless litany for alms—whose face was the worst chart of misfortune I had ever looked into. A light yellow rash covered it, her lips, blue and swollen, were contracted with sores, while her eyes moved in the terribly distended cheeks like a resigned animal's. So with a furtive look at our guide, who turned aside, I poured some coins of God knows what denomination into her shaking hand and off we hurried.

One thing struck me almost instantly about life in Russia. Nearly every one approached it with a preconceived attitude. They seemed to be all solidified as Reds or Conservatives before setting foot on the soil. And I suppose this accounted for the tourists, with whom we were herded about, standing for the most naïve interpolations of life with a straight face, and withholding applause as I did not, in front of mile after mile of free people's tennis courts.

But how terribly sad Moscow was! The great oriental city with its minarets and domes and mosques conceived in days of barbaric splendor and religious superstition possibly, but yet to the eye how eternal in dignity and strength, seemed to have averted its spirit from the building of subways and modern glass-faced apartment houses, or general jacking up into modernity by the Communist System.

I walked into "Red Square," and anything less adequate I thought than "Red Square" as a name for this vast space of mosaic pavements with the terrific Kremlin bulging along on my right in an Arabian Nights series of domes and fortress walls, and with the Cathedral of St. Basil before me, I had never heard. Moussorgsky's grand chorals rose in my ear as I looked around. They were absolutely typical of this square. They had in them the same kind of splendor and endurance, they were its true overtone.

Lenin's tomb, when I finally focused upon it, was impressive, but I thought the simplicity too conscious, and that in comparison to the ineffable richness surrounding it, it seemed strikingly arid. What made it so? Was it because it embodied a defiantly negative attitude to the mystery of death? And did something in me, whether wrong or right, range itself at once against such an attitude and think of it as naïve?

Of course I made one of the long line that goes inside Lenin's tomb and files past his softly illuminated exposed body, clad in the uniform of a Russian soldier. The remains of Lenin might have been an image of wax, but I could not help staring searchingly at the inscrutable Slavic face with its pointed beard. For certainly a strong and endlessly brave dedication to the interests of oppressed humanity had come from behind that heavy brow, so dominating the shrunken face. Why then had the power to act throughout an entire lifetime for human rights, and the power to turn a tremendous country from one system into another—why had it all so soon to subside into the undoubted bleakness of tyranny I sensed over Russia? Why the horrible liquidation of beauty, and the extraordinary lack of gaiety everywhere! Only with fear in the background could the air have tasted as it did.

How Godlike a great artist is. He sees it all so deeply, so keenly, his country and the people that live in it. He has put the case so well, and I had read and loved Tolstoy such a great deal, that when I got to Russia every duck pond in front of a manor house reminded me of some section of *Anna Karenina* or *War and Peace*. And now when I stood in his roomy red brick house in Moscow (it looked very much like an old-fashioned house in Philadelphia) and listened to a dissertation on the pros and cons of Tolstoyan philosophy (which I found maddening) by the Intourist Guide (he had been, after all, a great Christian, not something to be lightly passed over), I thought as I listened to her that it might surely take a race who were being taught to glory in their own naïveté another five hundred years to produce a Tolstoy.

"God, what a world," I thought. With us the cant of commercialism, the pleading bowel tones of the salesman, "Buy one, Honey, they're made just for you!" all just out of love for the people! And here another kind of cant; but less villainous than ours at that, for some part of it surely was intent on building up something finer than our fretful twelve-year-old pet of a public.

It was on the top floor overlooking the garden that the master had his study. And I looked around a simple rather dark little room with a low ceiling, and at the plain brown desk which had borne once the accumulating sheets of *Anna*

Karenina, while the guide told us how "comrade Tolstoy" had been an early riser, disliked city life and was always trying to break away to his country place, Yasnaya Polyana. She went on to tell us how he chopped wood every morning in the yard by the coach house, even if the weather was freezing, before he went to his writing. "Comrade Tolstoy rather fancied himself as a peasant, you know." "No, no—" I told her suddenly quite wild and irresistibly impelled, "I only know that Count Tolstoy was a great man." As I spoke a shiver of repugnance passed over her face, while the other tourists looked down their noses, and Leonard whispered, "Well, darling, you may have come into Russia as a Red, but perhaps you'll go out with your head on a pike."

Of course, this wasn't quite true. I had found many things to admire in Russia, and perhaps first of all this: I had come from a country whose cultural service to the masses through the forces of machinery and otherwise, left just a little wee something to be desired! I was now in a country where the idea of art for the masses seemed to have emerged from the sanctimonious hot air of business conferences into fact. In other words, as I undressed to go bathing at a public beach in the Gulf of Finland, and heard the strains of Beethoven's Fifth Symphony, I wondered whether the public was getting what it wanted, or what it should want. And that day I sat in my bathing suit along with hundreds of comrades, through a fine open air concert which, having started off with Beethoven, ended with Brahms. I asked if there would be any lighter touches later on for the tired business man or his little grandson, to be told "No."

It was the same if you visited the Putiliov Steel Works. You might stop a worker and ask him, through the interpreter, what was he going to do with his evening, and he would answer, "Tonight the workers have been given two hundred slips for the theatre. We will see the 'Cherry Orchard' by Anton Chekhov." Or if it was opera, it might be "Le Coq d'Or." In other words there was not, I think, at that time any second-rate entertainment of any kind for the Russian people, nor did I ever see an American movie advertised. And everywhere through the palaces, and palace gardens, through the museums and galleries, went the Russian public which seemed to me still, as I looked at them, to be the Russian peasant, with their feet tied up as ours were, in strips of sacking to keep the galleries in their spotless condition.

And at the Hermitage Museum, watching some peasant face frowning with interest over a case of jewelled snuff boxes of Catherine the Great, and knowing that that evening he would probably *have* to be sitting out a good play, I would believe that in the end something remarkable could not help coming out of so much pushing in the right direction. In fact, in their insistence on Culture for the Workers it seemed that the Leaders were putting Art in the place of God; and I thought if this were true, it would bring up a whimsical situation, since they would find out, the more they went into it, that about three-quarters of what had been greatest in painting, literature and music was religious in feeling. And I wondered if perhaps this was not how God, or the desire for a stake in your own immortality according to a ritual of beauty, would at last return to the Russian people.

St. Petersburg? The Nevsky Prospekt! The Winter Palace! Tsarksoe Selo! So much of my adolescent reading of great artists had given me the life of St. Petersburg, luxurious or desperate but always, whether it was out of Tolstoy, Turgeniev, Dostoievsky, Gogol, Sologub, Chekhov or Gorky, presented in a fascinating, memorable way.

But now the tinted baroque palaces and the tremendous Winter Palace still fronted on the Neva, but all the shutters were closed and so drearily that one could suspect no life at all to be going on behind. The streets were empty of any sort of vehicle and almost of people. St. Petersburg into Leningrad seemed to have been the turning—at some nightmare touch—of a great metropolitan city into a collection of tenements from which the color had started to peel away, reflecting into deserted waterways, standing above empty streets.

And as I walked down the Nevsky by myself I thought that the writer nearest to it as it was now was Dostoievsky. Those down-at-the-heel tenements he had depicted where half-crazed people talked incessantly of the end of the Tsar's regime and a millennium, while their own lives fell into strange forms of decay and tragedy, all of the "Possessed" had melancholy reverberations in exactly what I was looking at. But Gorky! Even in his "Lower Depths" he was too vital, too direct, for this faded *pastiche* of 18th century glory.

And then I stood with Leonard in the pathetic bedroom of the Tsarina at Tsarskoe Selo, as simple as my mother's, with its brass bedstead, and dozens of little tables crowded with family snapshots and photographs just as Tibi's had been, and I saw one thing clearly without the assistance of the Intourist Guide: which was that the splendid, fearsome, divine spectacle of royalty toward which the peasants had looked with open mouths and forgotten that they stood knee deep in mud, had ended with the 18th century, and that this last Tsar and his family living mostly for their simple family devotion had been as grimly unaware of a changing world, or of any other modern implication, as the members of millions of well-to-do American families; only for them it was more fatal to be as they were. And I thought the most savage bit of bad taste I had ever encountered was a picture of the fearfully mangled, swollen body of Rasputin after it had been dragged up from between the ice floes of the Neva, pinned onto a screen just opposite the Tsarina's bed.

If only I could have left Russia remembering the excellent theatres filled with lively audiences—every woman had stockings for the theatre—the spick and span museums, the Royal Gardens of Peterhof where the fountains played not once a month, as they do under the French Republic at Versailles, but every afternoon, the new apartment houses with their notices of lectures stuck up in the vestibules, the extraordinarily generous playgrounds for the people. If only I could have remembered these things, and forgotten the oppression in the air, the depression on the people's faces in the street. I remember seeing one woman sitting down on the curb holding her head in her hands, rocking slowly backward and forward, absolutely abandoned to her grief. And despite optimistic bulletins you would still see long queues of always poorly dressed people waiting before a small window for their rations of food.

In Russia it seemed they had commanded that spiritual hope be taboo amongst the people, because I supposed it had been found that the practice of religion in the hands of priests had shown corruption. But I wondered why none of the great Leaders had had sufficient spiritual and intellectual gifts to examine the grand legend of Christianity, and to conceive what great things it could mean for a people engaged in exactly the Soviet sort of experiment, if purged—among all the other purges—of its petrifaction in church formula, and restored to its pure meaning. It seemed to me that the Russians would then have had what they needed, the goad of a spiritual consolation, the just pride of a marvellous quest—putting a few of the actual meanings of Christ into practical legislation—to sustain them through all the terrific upheaval and readjustment.

We went out of Russia through Latvia and Estonia, travelling hard. Toward evening we got ravenous and, the stations disclosing their usual waiting herds of people and absence of restaurant service, we approached one of the train guards who out of kindness brought us in a kettle of boiling water, took from his pocket a package of tea leaves, put these in his fist, swept his hand around in the boiling water a couple of times, returned the tea leaves to his pocket, and poured us out two measures of faintly colored hot water into tin cups. And while we drank bravely, he smiled at us the broadest smile I had seen in weeks and said, "I don't live in Russia, I am an Estonian."

CHAPTER XXVIII

Social Significance

WHY did I become a Socialist? I have no wish to give out any great thesis on the subject. I think it was because, having been from my earliest youth aware of the domination of money troubles in every one's life, and of the peace-destroying, growth-destroying effects of those worries, I wondered if I should find in Socialism some solution to the tragic waste of energy and quality I had seen lived out around me.

During my connection with the Socialists, I found out what a lot of highly cultured people there are in New York. I would say that most of the audiences I spoke before in halls, schools, and old-fashioned dining halls—Adelina Patti must have sung in some of them, I used to think, as I stared around at the vast use of plush and electrified gas jets—were German Hebrews, and at their invitation I often sat down at their tables to join them in a beer. They cared for, and thoroughly knew the philosophers and litterateurs of Europe, and although they firmly believed in the triumph of Socialism, were tolerant to the last drop, and when I knew them, entirely anti-revolutionary. Social-ism would inevitably arrive, but through trade unionism and the education of the workers. The bad acting of poli-ticians, the impasses of capitalism face to face with the new era, its gradual decay, all according to them should be pointed out to the workers by Socialist speakers and writers without the brutality and waste of revolution.

I could see how they had intellectualized the whole situation to themselves, and as time wore on I began to feel that there were some angles to this party that were a little defeatist—young fellows would often get up and slam out of the room while some elderly orator was on. Also it seemed to me that sometimes they were envisaging the American Scene through applying too largely to its crises and possibilities the contents of tomes of foreign literature, and never would you be able to catch up with them in their reading. So I began to wonder if in order to really get any-where there mustn't be, alongside of their praiseworthy humanism, a more native understanding.

And it came back to me, that standing one morning in lovely Gemeinde Wien, which was shot to pieces during the Dollfuss regime, I had asked a Socialist worker, "But will all this go on with the country people against it, the aristocrats against it, and the government dominated by changing groups?" And although I don't remember his words I do recall that his reply, though genuinely uttered, sounded unrealistic, especially against the rumble of the continually parading artillery.

But any reflections of mine on Socialism, which I advance chiefly because they somewhat explain what follows, come from only a cursory knowledge of the Party's history. I

have to admit I spent a great deal more time talking to
Socialists than I ever did over their literature, for I would
always think when I opened one of those tomes: Why
is it that when extraordinary men advance truths of great
spiritual importance—truths that must strike the spirit with
a sort of wakening refreshment like water flung into the
desert traveller's face—they incline to advance their "stuff"
through language which is often involved, and very much
too difficult for the amateur, who is their potential audience,
to follow.

Two of the finest people I met in the Socialist Party
were Norman Thomas and the late Charney Vladeck.

Norman Thomas, with his noble good looks and Yankee
irony, was to me, pictorially and otherwise, a typical citi-
zen. He was what the Founding Fathers might have had
on their minds when they drew up those elastic statements
about our "liberty" and "the pursuit of happiness." With
staunch courage he questioned every infringement of human
liberty, pointed with grim humor to the mistakes of those
in power, and called some of the inhumanities and screw-
loose methods of recovery let loose over the country by
their true names. It was enchanting to hear him talk, because he made that kind of clear sense which, possibly, can
only come out of a mind when it is released from opportunism of any kind.

I was proud to sit often on the same platform with him
and to speak over the radio, with just a table between us.

Charney Vladeck, my other admiration, was a late member of Mayor LaGuardia's City Council and for many years
editor of the *Jewish Forward*, and although I never saw
much of him, what I did see impressed me greatly. Appar-

ently he had been able to carry all his integrity, and the
"long view," with its prehensile knowledge of what happens after you do so-and-so, into the politics of New York
City. It seemed to me he had brought to this country ideals
of democracy which he knew to be consistent with our real
traditions, and if these had been subjected to disillusionment, then that had not affected his faith nor persuaded
him to let down himself, nor, in consequence, us. His interesting head, the sensitive humor in his finely cut features,
his slim figure, all suggested long contact in a mood of
benign scrutiny, with the ups and downs of civilization.
He was an *intellectuel* in the best sense, and I would
think as I watched him speak, controlled by the tragic
humor of those who are very wise: "Never would he have
answered injustice in kind, with wrath, but only with the
persistent reasonableness of heart and mind." And I think
when individuals become more like Charney Vladeck there
will be no one to start persecutions or make wars. And
dimly, the great metropolis felt his loss, for on the day of his
funeral the canyon streets were lined with more than fifty
thousand mourners as the cortege passed, while even our
incorrigibly lively Mayor Fiorello LaGuardia looked forsaken as he was photographed coming from the service.

As time wore on I had read a good deal of our Revolutionary history and correspondence, and it seemed to me
that from the victorious struggle of 1776, a philosophy of
conduct had emerged which was fairly superb, and ahead of
anything to be heard in Europe at that time, and that what
the Founding Fathers had been trying to breed up and to
safeguard in every way they could think of, was the rising
shoulder-to-shoulder of a new race, free to worship and

work, but forbidden not to be brothers—forbidden to go in self-interest beyond that point where there was risk to the well-being of the whole, the average, the majority (no "self-initiative" masking monkey-jumps onto the unsuspecting traveller allowed); the majority—who were even exhorted never to allow themselves to be let down.

So that all these letters, speeches, and events began to speak a language to me that was more comprehensible, and so more attractive, than *Das Kapital* or the *Communist Manifesto*. After all, why import even the great Karl Marx, I thought, when our Manifestos, made by men indigenous to our soil, and at any rate free for several generations from any neurosis out of the tyrannies of Europe,—its packed closeness, its eternally disputed boundaries, its old sores, greeds, corruptions,—are so plain and so splendid. And I wondered if many emigrants had not psychically sensed an emanation from all these documents and events that I had been reading about, and if this was what had made them come to America, then why not let them have more "home-cooking." Or if the brigands had somewhat depleted our store, why not make up a great deal more of the same order and protect it better, for it seemed to me that with such recipes, if we had the will, courage and common sense, we couldn't go wrong.

Somewhere in his writings Emerson gives the idea that although we may have to take defeat on the chin, still for victory we were made. So now I got a full taste of this tonic beverage when, on the eve of President Roosevelt's 1936 election—I voted the Democratic ticket. I had left a dinner party to go to the radio about an hour and a half before election returns would be final. The streets were pandemonium. Paper ribbons, our signs of supreme joy, drifted from lighted windows that went incredibly up the dark side of the sky, and lay on the ground inches thick, while the people that passed, shaking their noisemaking contraptions, wore a look of elated excitement.

Harry, who with me had voted for Norman Thomas in the preceding election, and had now swung over to Alf Landon, rather resented my prophecies of unprecedented victory. However, he elbowed me through the crowd with his usual whimsical gallantry.

The radio offices were feverish; reports kept coming in through a loud speaker, from which it appeared already that Mr. Roosevelt was winning, hands down.

For my fifteen minutes on the air in such a crisis—Fords vs. Packards, and I was now on a large station—I had this time arranged a shortened version of "The Declaration of Independence," and set it to the air of "My Country, 'Tis of Thee," which segued dramatically into the "Star-Spangled Banner." I ended my program with the fewest possible comments of my own. It all went over nicely and when I got back to my dinner party—which had of course loyally listened in, although they were, every one of them, Landon's men—a charming woman came up to me with her hands outstretched. "My dear," she said, "I had no idea you could write like that! Why, you made us weep."

CHAPTER XXIX

The Golden Mask Brightens

"The theatre that one loved and could find no antidote against, like the allure of a human being that you have to find false a thousand times before the cure arrives, and then not through revelation; but out of weariness."

I HADN'T, as the years rolled by, an opportunity to find the theatre false a thousand times, but I did emerge from a few more green room predicaments.

Some years after marrying Harry I went off to play at Mt. Kisco—on the arrangement of Shubert's ex-secretary Helen Arthur—in my favorite opus "The Byrons."

I had written "The Byrons" a few years previously chiefly because it seemed to me that Jack could give a magnificent portrayal of this poet, who, with all his overstressed satanism and magnetism, had nevertheless in the end proved to be somebody by the high quality of his courage.

That Jack and I were already separated, that he had

[311]

then deserted the stage for the movies, and was presumably getting older, had not deterred me from putting my version of Byron on paper in a nostalgic play designed to be performed on three levels of fantasy, memory, and reality.

But feeling when the play was finished, that it might only interest—outside of an audience—a patron king with a touch of madness, and was bound to bewilder, distress, and even antagonize commercial managers, I kept it a secret from these gentlemen, and turned toward the less harassed experiment of the Summer Theatre to examine the qualities of "The Byrons."

Arriving, however, at the remodelled barn on a great estate which served as a theatre, it was discovered that only one level of my play could be taken on—reality. So in this instance the entire play was scrapped and we just did the prologue and epilogue joined together by a little freshly written bridge of words.

"Michael," said sturdy gallant steel-haired little Miss Arthur, "Harry Mestayer (a veteran of many years of distinguished service on Broadway) has just learned that you are going to play both Lord and Lady Byron—and he says he must see you alone at once in your room at Briar Cliff Manor—before any company rehearsals."

He came, a fine-faced, elderly artist, and well content with his appearance and reputation I put on Harry's blue flannel dressing gown (which being much too large gave me an emaciated appearance) and lying down on the bed told him I thought we'd better get right into the death-bed scene (between the poet and his valet at Missolonghi). To say he lowered himself down beside me with trepidation is a half-hearted statement. However, after he had recovered from the shock of hearing my voice drop an octave, we came along nicely and soon began really to exchange and work. And when several hours later Miss Arthur called for him, I could not resist following him out clinging unseen to the wall, to see him as he met her, wipe his brow and exclaim: "She's going to be all right. God only knows how or why."

Of course I didn't have to do any feats of hypnotic delusion, as the prologue concerned itself with Lady Byron's reception of Fletcher in her London library on the day that the poet's body arrives in England from Greece. Then the valet tells of his master's death, and of how he tried with his last breath to send a message to his wife and child, which he, Fletcher—despite Lady Byron's desperate entreaties—is unable to give her, because he could not himself understand;—while the epilogue is the actual death scene on the level of reality, in which the audience does learn what it was that Lord Byron was trying in his death agony to say. The scrapped play is Lady Byron's dream played on three levels—the first Byron's adolescent memory, the other two fantasy and reality. And in the end Lady Byron is consoled and at peace with her grief, because at last she understands its origin.

After our opening the usual discouragement to my career as an actress was voiced this time by my level-headed cousin Mrs. Arthur Iselin, who came backstage to tell me: "Why Blanche, you were quite wonderful as Byron, but I didn't like you much as his wife."

The local papers wrote up the affair nicely, but there was one furnace blast from a New York critic who had put himself to the unusual trouble of motoring out from New York through the fetid summer evening in order to be "in at the death." And yet proving that "It's always darkest before dawn," a clergyman having seen me and read him, launched a letter to the paper asking that he "be immediately dismissed for the outrageous injustice of his denunciation." This letter, although probably printed on the ninety-seventh page, was pounced on as "manna" by my publicity agent when some of the countryside journals ran fragments of the critic's abuse and the clergyman's defense side by side, the public being invited in this crisis to make up their own minds and buy seats, which they did in satisfying numbers.

I have often heard writers say that they would rather write a novel which they know will at least be published, than gamble their time away on a play which may never come to production, and of course there is a lot in that, for your unproduced works, sewn up thick in the mattress under you, often give off a nostalgic sadness on moonlight nights. But there is this to put against that: you have deeply associated for months, or years, as your own will and taste directed you, with a subject by which you were profoundly fascinated, and I felt like that about "The Byrons." In the first place it is quite possible that when the snarls and insanities of commercial considerations versus art melt away, "The Byrons" will be produced, and at any rate I have had the richness of intimately knowing an extraordinary man.

I think it might be said of great people, "By their ends ye shall know them," and in all my research and study of Byron—and his personality also came across so marvellously in his letters—I felt "that something" which still seems rarest to me in a human being—a willingness to fight, perhaps to the point of immolation and death, for that which seems to mean an increase of dignity for the human race. And I think Byron was ready for such a battle long before he went to Greece to make it. Indeed, perhaps it was this truth which made him occasionally such a cruel companion. But whatever may happen to my play, Byron was so much an adventurer in the true sense, so much of a *man*—whose "art," thank God, had never thinned his lips or shrilled his voice—that in retrospect I am glad of every hour spent in his company.

In studying lives of outstanding people, there seems usually to be a large margin of mystification that you can rationalize according to your particular faculties. The events themselves I have sometimes found less interesting than speculations about whatever could have made them take place. For example, it is on record that Joan of Arc hung about the fort at Vaucouleurs for months trying to see De Baudricourt and get him to send her to the King, meeting jeers and neglect for her pains, until one day in she walked and was immediately sent on her way. What had taken place in her to make her, after so many months of failure, so instantly successful? One man's guess is as good as another's.

I had enormously enjoyed Bernard Shaw's "St. Joan," thought the play around Joan superb, more so in fact than the girl's own part; for it seemed to me that the great master had neglected to give his heroine the one quality without which her success was not plausible, magnetism. For although she had at all times heard voices, was it not because mingled with them there had never been the voice of self-confidence which alone could have put her on the right side of fortress and palace walls; was this not why she had failed over so many months? What then had suddenly landed her with this self-confidence? I wrote my theories down in another opus, "Forever Young."

Joan had gotten under my skin like this: During those years when I travelled the Middle West and suburban towns of Eastern capitals with my couple of valises, I felt compelled in the name of sanity to cut a few capers with my lecture, "The Stage as the Actress Sees It." In fact, I had made a short acting monologue of that part of the trial scene, where Joan, faced by the torturers and momentarily terrified, retracts, recants, only to find that this will not bring her freedom but life imprisonment. Then in a magnificent tirade about the values of living while you are alive, she tears up her recantation, and goes toward the flames with a set face, her inspiration with her once more.

The "world première" of this effort took place at New Rochelle, and I suffered the worst case of stage fright before going on that I ever experienced, for there were no props, no grease paint, no other actors. You had simply to come on cold with the Maid; and imagine so vividly the priests sitting in judgment about you, that you could tell the vintage of the *vins du pays* on their breaths.

The reactions to this bit were amazingly pleasant, one gentleman writing my famous lecture manager Colston Leigh that he liked me better as Joan than the incomparable Winifred Lenihan. Indeed, his letter was so dynamically warm, that Mr. Leigh had it printed in full on my second circular.

Thus encouraged I arranged short monologues of Rosalind, chiefly because Ned had always said I should play her, and one of Portia, to whose stern whimsicality I have ever been partial. And Mr. Leigh now wrote me he had such good letters about the tour that it was clear he had begun to think it might be better to present my personality cloaked in a role, rather than straight off the bat.

So a few months later a couple of lecture managers asked me: "Miss Strange, why don't you become another Cornelia Otis Skinner or another Ruth Draper? You could, you know, easily."—"Oh, how awfully easily," I thought sardonically to myself, as I received flattering if fatuous comments on my personality in comparison to that of the other two artists, the one so good, the other so very great. Indeed, I had seen through my sweat as these tours went on, that not only could I never "easily become another Cornelia Otis Skinner or another Ruth Draper" but that I was one hundred per cent eager to leave the art of the monologist to the superb priestesses already in control. For that "extremely intermittent actress, Michael Strange"—as Alexander Woollcott once called me—likes to look into the eyes of the people with whom she acts. Indeed, a great deal of my ability to sustain a scene comes to me from the kick I get out of the other fellow.

During that period when "The Stage as the Actress Sees It" had still a few feverish monologues tacked to its dreary tail, I often got slapped back right smartly into my place if I tried to worm my way up. And one night, stopping off at some winter-shrouded skyscraper fragment of civilization, when I learnt at the station that Cornelia Otis Skinner had had a train flagged for her so that she could leave this proud spot ahead of schedule, and reach some oasis like Chicago with some hours to spare, I arranged with the station master to do the same for me. Then I foolishly confided my plan to one of the younger members of the committee who had come to meet me. "Sit in the right-hand box of the theatre," I told her, "and flag me at ten to ten so that I can make a few jumps and wind up. I'll only be cutting my performance short by twenty minutes and taking that train will give me a whole extra day in Chicago (and I thought of the warm hospitality of several new friends in that city)." My friend smilingly promised, and I never saw the gray wraith of conscience getting under way beneath her obsequious politeness.

The usual pictures were flashed of me with blowing hair and an expression of distraught amusement, before I contentedly went back to the hotel where, after all, thank God, I was not to spend the night. So I just unpacked a toothbrush, and *The New Republic,* when suddenly I was rung up to learn that a delegation of ladies—a delegation!—was calling on me. Probably an extra heavy assortment from the Press, I thought; but no, it was the entire committee which had engaged me. Most of them were a good deal older than my confidante and uniformly stern. "Miss Strange," began the spokesman—nobody used the chairs I pointed out—"we hear you have sent word to the station master to flag the Eastern 'So and So' at 10:10 this evening, so of necessity cutting your performance by twenty minutes, instead of leaving tomorrow morning as you normally would, on the 'So and So' Express."

"Ladies," I began—"I am awfully sorry"—"That we found out," interrupted a thin comrade whose nose looked as if it had been mounted on her face with an ice pick. "Well," I went on without sense or tact, "after all, Cornelia Otis Skinner did it, didn't she?" There was a silence in which shock worked first and then the blitheness of humor. "Yes, Miss Strange, I believe Miss Skinner did give us a few minutes less of her wonderful program in order to make the 10:10." "Well," I threw out, life ebbing back. "But Miss Strange," said my old belle with the sharp nose, "you are *not* Cornelia Otis Skinner——." Time ticked away the onus of this melancholy fact until it was entirely used up in embarrassment, when abruptly a second lady stepped forward with a paper and pencil as she told me with a businesslike asperity that brought us all back to what was at stake: "Miss Strange, unless you sign an order countermanding your instructions to the station master, which I will have sent for you to the station [she threw in with acrid courtesy], I think we can dispense——." "Oh, no," I cried, swamped with visions of my lost check, Mr. Leigh's displeasure, and this terrible trip all for nothing: "Please accept my apologies. I'll go on and on tonight until some one implores me to stop." There were frigid smiles and a general movement toward departure. The pretty "Judas" who betrayed me had never turned up with the committee, and I knew I would have to work like hell that night, to, as Jack would say, get "them" to go along with me.

Wonderful Joan! to me she was the most sacredly enigmatic personage in all history, and as I studied translations of the Latin text of her trial (the only authentic account of her sayings which we have) how heart-breakingly straight and to the point I found her, and I determined and somewhat succeeded, I think, in having my say about her my own way, undeterred by the imaginative conceptions and constrictions of other authors.

In Shaw's scene, laid in the Cathedral at Rheims after the coronation, and in my scene in her own room in the hostelry of Rheims, where the table is laid for two to have

supper, and into which she comes after the coronation ceremony—dressed in her silver armor with an overcape of
light blue velvet embroidered with silver *fleurs-de-lis*—the
arrowhead of her luck starts downward. Is it just the jeal-
ous antagonism of the captains whose battles she has had to
win for them, plus the machinations of the English and
the priests? Shaw makes the Archbishop on her own side
reprove her for a new pride, saying she may suffer the
"chastisement of Hubris." Pride from where? Because
she has won the battles she expected to under her Divine
guidance and military gifts? I thought that in such a miraculous personality pride from such a source was unlikely.
Again Shaw stresses her good generalship, tells us she
never really took any absurd chances, only courageous ones,
which was true. What made her then, after the coronation,
when she has been warned both in his play and mine of what
is gathering about her, go on, against the advice of her best
captains, and take mad chances one of which got her
captured?

It seemed to me there was only one sort of pride to which
she might have been vulnerable, the pride which may not
know that it is suicidal, which comes when the pressures of
an immortal spirit upon a human frame have been too
great, when there has been too much criss-crossing between
what is human and what is superhuman. Then, I thought
there might grow in such a psyche a pride, a recklessness,
which is the unconscious desire for death, together with a
mythical sense that only through sacrificial death is the
sense and meaning of great things preserved. I had my
convictions as to what could have happened in Joan's life
to bring her to such a pass, and to such a pride, and put
these into my play.

And when it was finished I did think of offering "Forever Young" on Broadway, for it seemed this script might even have some commercial value, possessing a good star part, since the heroine practically never steps back into the wings. But because my views on the Saint were not those in circulation, I thought it advisable to get a taste of the quality of whatever manager I saw, interview him, so to speak, before giving him the play.

So I was now visited, at the instance of a mutual friend, by a gentleman whom I knew only from reputation as being genuinely interested in the poetic, romantic, grand angles of drama. I filled our glasses and sat down anticipating a pleasant talk during which, relaxing, I might find courage to bring up a painful subject. Suddenly—I can't think what prompted me—I asked him why, in one of his recent enchanting productions which did not run long, Robert Edward Jones had designed a single bed for a girl who lived by her charms, only to exchange this existence for a passionate love affair which is also freely indulged in. "That single bed on the set struck me," I told Mr. C. "I wondered how—you know—." There was a deathly pause during which I took a long swallow and Mr. C. stared at me—"Well I happen really to know something about her," he said at length in a low voice. "More than what was put down in that play—she was convent bred!!! I studied her life; and her heart was never in that Parisian existence." God, what was on hand—a biographer! Some one who would study Joan's papers and take infuriated note of every infamy I had committed? Never mind, I must press on. "But, Mr. C., what about that bed? Even if the girl had lived for years in a convent she did go to Paris afterwards, and space is space—." I heard the roaring in my ears of my

[321]

own embarrassment. Mr. C.'s face flushed darkly. He rose. "In the theatre, Miss Strange," he said, "one is sometimes asked to take things from the imaginative angle." "Of course," I told him, wringing his hand. I saw it all now— that single bed expressed the isolation of the girl's spirit no matter who had crowded into it beside her; and I felt that I had failed desperately not only as a hostess, but as one who might have been assumed to have some trace of asceticism in her nature. Yet, Mr. C., at the door, with unflagging courtesy, asked me, "Wasn't there a manuscript?" "There was," I told him, "but it's in rotten shape just now. Let me send it along later." Years and years later, I thought, after we are each in a single bed of dust!

Yet "Forever Young," sewed cozily up in my mattress, did me a wonderful service, for it showed me the arrow pointing to another slit in the wall.

I had read it (at the instance of my dear friend Walter Varney) to Mr. and Mrs. Moses (part producers of the "Old Maid") and nicked the atmosphere of obsequious safety and success on which this pair were floating by remarking that to produce "Forever Young" would certainly cost some one $75,000 if he was going to do the right thing by me and the Siege of Orleans—"and furthermore," I continued in spite of their both having turned pale, "I'll get a couple of actors at my own expense and present a couple of scenes for you on the Empire stage, to convince you that the play must be done." And poor Mr. and Mrs. Moses accepted this offer, since acquiescence would get them at least through the door.

But a few weeks later, on my way to the Empire Theatre to undermine their judgment with a couple of scenes, our taxi, passing Bonwit Teller's (where two manholes fed up with the gaseous distress under the asphalt had lately exploded and were now roped off) tried to pass another in the infernally narrow thoroughfare and violently collided with the curb. Glass flew about, I landed bleeding on the floor. We all sustained minor injuries, and "Shouldn't we all go home?" was asked. But feeling I might never again be allowed to give a test reading of St. Joan on the Empire or any other stage, I gave the word to press forward. And so in a dark theatre, lit up by a laconic stagehand with a couple of bulbs, we went through our scenes, which, even allowing for the accident, I did badly. As dear old Heywood Broun once wrote: "She is now in a class with the little girl who had a little curl," and indeed my only comeback from this wretched adventure was watching a scene between Gilles de Rais—played by handsome John Emery —and Captain de Baudricourt, which I thought came over very swiftly and well.

But when my brow hit the floor of the taxi I had had "My own apocalyptic moment." Why was I forcing so gigantic a venture through the aperture of a needle? Indeed, wiping my brow, I wondered if it wouldn't be as easy to be Joan of Arc as to get her luxuriously produced on the Broadway of 1937, and by Mr. and Mrs. Moses, in a play by Michael Strange.

There must be more welcome for what you do, I thought; you cannot play to the broad, concentrated backsides of the entire reception committee. They will not take it from you, even if it's absolutely true—because your attitude has been all along too undiplomatic, too *gauche*, and too unwilling, possibly because you knew you were unable, to play the game as it must be played. (That spurious American peeress

in "Our Betters"—projected with devastating accuracy by
Ina Claire—had lately been thought of as a part for me,
which, if I had taken it on would have darkened the
theatre in a couple of nights).

Big Business, the pressure and chaos and false thinking
attendant upon it, its catastrophic influence, was as obvious when crossing some of the judgments of the theatre
as anywhere else. And where had you to retreat to, if you
wouldn't fall in line, into Artiness, into all the ballyhoo of
the amateur, the exceptional, the "just for the few" sort?
What a phrase for the theatre! A thousand times would I
have rather played a society bitch for my old friend Al
Woods, at $250 a week, than enter the frail atmosphere of
some group of painstaking nitwits, protected by a patroness
as affected as themselves.

Oh, but when you were allowed to work steadily, only
then did you feel the extent to which you might bloom, if
only you were let go on—but you never were; and I soon
saw that outside of perhaps a dozen names in all America
neither was anyone else let go on. For there being no ground
under any one's feet, if a show were not a hit, the same
battles on all fronts had to be undertaken, again and again.

Having talent, having just been in a success, having a
name, I saw again and again that all this gave no immediate surety of another job. A hundred crossed wires must
fall out of a tangle first. So that in this delay of air to the
lung—for an actor's art is no less to him than that—I saw
many famous people shrink and contract, of their enforced
idleness, into only the ghosts of their former selves, people
who had far more astuteness in self-management and in
the art of wire-pulling than I had.

No—I must lift the sharp nail, and hammer away again at the rock. If I chiselled away long enough in another direction I would find another out—and I did.

Listening to music, I feel that I am about to recall
What it is I have sought
Through generations—
Among melodies I groping my way again
Through possibilities infinitely yearning
To be awarded their dreams—
Since during music I detect that genial smile of youth
Flung back enticing over its irradiant shoulder,
And elapsing into a demure pomp of coquetry
Preceding—admission to discover.
Then finally flaring into stretches,
Into expanses sparkling with dual flight—
Mystic flight, aiming towards shrines of Supreme Love
Where certainly is donated The Sacrament of Death.
Ah, then! this cry of souls momentarily dividing—
I hear it in music!
And am racked with a whisper urging me to recall
Whom it is I have lost
Through generations.

—Poems.

CHAPTER XXX

"Fighting on the Air"

DEA

At last the Queen is gone; the night is mine. What a fragrance, what an exciting fragrance! It is as if all the rose petals in the world were fighting in the air.

PHEDRO

Fighting in the air and in the dark, but that is human destiny, my dear young lady.

—Clair de Lune.

FOR SOME TIME I had been working in a fascinating medium—an acting version of poems, set as exactly to harp music as the singer's words to his song. I would read some poem while my accompanist played what she conceived to be suitable music, and as the hushed rich notes of the harp struck my ear—From Troy! From Heaven! gradually there would be woven what seemed to me a thrilling undertone to the poem I was acting out. Everything I had ever loved was synchronized in this work—the rhythm of beautiful words, the miraculous ever-breaking heart of poetry, plus my first love, music. Undoubtedly this must go on the air—so now I involved myself in one of my major battles with more tragi-comedy in it than can be set down here.

Still largely inexperienced in the technique of handling myself upon the "No Man's Land" of Big Business, I entered into this tourney swathed in the great illusion that if you could prove you were some good then you would get somewhere.

My call to get across, and evade the barbed-wire entanglements, came about like this: During my months as a Socialist I had written a speech entitled "The Possibilities of Radio" that was delivered over WEVD during a series of lectures called the "University of the Air"—which invited such distinguished persons as John Dewey, Hendrik van Loon, Fannie Hurst, etc., to say whatever they had on their minds without radio censorship. Considering the limited acreage of this station, my speech got quite a response. Many letters said "all the personnel of the radio offices should have heard you." Finally a letter came from an important official at NBC requesting a copy. I sent it, not then divining how little it could please him. For I had called upon American humor not to stand for this insistent dribble of sales talk corrupting the day's consciousness into a crazed shopping list, not to support this mixture of laxatives and symphonies—had exhorted the Silver Fox salesmen to retreat to the fifth floor and leave radio to the artists, who unhampered by the tyranny of sponsorship in its present form, would know how to create unique uses for radio in its own right and serve the American public with cultural, inspirational material which would be certain to jack up civilization, and so in the end, make everything easier for every one.

Civilization! I knew little then of the swelling repartee of "Oh, my big toe" with which all concerned in the actual practice of making a great station achieve enormous profits would have answered such a phrase.

As one of my friends, high up in radio salesmanship, was to tell me a year or so later: "Michael, if you could just sit in on some of those conferences, and hear that bowel tone of noble intentions toward the American public fade out at the chance of making an extra dime!"

"Miss Strange," said the important official of NBC, "it is a waste of your time to write such speeches." "Maybe," I told him. "At any rate what I really want is to get an audition for my poetry with music ideas." "Ah, that's very much better," he said, rubbing his hands with relief, and called in another official, who seemed to glow with interest over my prospective half-hour.

For this audition one of our ace American harpists, Mildred Dilling, consented to be my accompanist, and we did Salome's scene before Herod when she plays upon the Emperor's anvil-white passion for her (the desire of age for youth) to get at whom she wants, St. John, whose terrible voice, repulsing her from his imprisonment in a nearby well, I incorporated into Salome's speech, the announcer briefly explaining the movements of the Princess, and of Herod and Herodias, while Mildred Dilling played a languid hypnotic air to the incessant beating of a drum.

There are so few times when you are able to do anything of what you want, that it would be false modesty not to mark them with a cross of thanks to God. And as we went downstairs Miss Dilling told me, "You made the hair rise on my scalp"; Adrienne Morrison, over from her office to listen, seemed struck into flattering silence; whereas the important official, taking me by both hands, entreated me to look out for "that wonderful instrument, your voice," and was nearly bumped by his secretary who sprang from her desk to say, "I never heard anything so exciting! Why, I felt the axe fall on the Saint's neck!"

As I perspired home in a taxi I thought, "Well, after all that, they can only send me some roses and a contract." However, a great silence now fell, through the nerve-racking surges of which I called up Miss Dilling to find that the hair which had risen from her scalp for my performance was lying down on it again. Had I heard anything from the commercial gentlemen? she asked. Then about two weeks later a crisp missive filtered in amongst the bills, which informed me that although one and all had realized "the superb art value of my program," still it had been generally conceded that very little of the "Product" would be sold on this combination of myself and Oscar.

From my astonished despair it was evident that brickbats had made no habit of falling on my skull—and with suitable poetic license I now thought of the milling, panting whirr of wheels sensed at Rockefeller Plaza, of that churning up into a vast industry of all individual outcry, until it should be lost, utterly spent, in its hopelessness, *vis à vis* a titanic automatic machinal indifference never encountered before in all the ages!

My next reaction was that I had caught hold of some true loveliness and must tilt a couple of more lances for it, in spite of a Trojan horse full of Epsom Salts.

"Michael," a friend of mine high up in radio told me, "you have only one chance. Get to some one at the top. The rest will be afraid of saying what they think of you for fear of getting sacked. For example, concerning your audition the other day at CBS, in a conference I attended, I give you my word that seven out of nine men were exuberantly for you, until they saw the Vice-President putting down his thumb, when instantly there wasn't a murmur for you left." In this case "Shades of my past at Newport," I thought, for this gentleman's wife had been a flower girl at my first wedding. Undoubtedly I was crystallized in his busily grooved mind as a socialite, so that, to have heard me drifting into his office between telephone calls, on "Annabelle Lee" with a harp accompaniment must have seemed to him far too exhausting a readjustment to make.

At this point there was an offer to go on with a famous tenor. "We will consider six minutes of you and the harp, Miss Strange, at $500 per week, if?—if you will say a few words on our product" (of course, this was in the nature of things a laxative). Apparently I was to slide coyly into poetry before the public knew what was being put across and while they were still marvelling at the low cost of Cascara "Don't do it," said the tenor, "that is, if you have anything original to sell." And a few days later, auditioning for the great advertising house of McCann-Erickson, I was told: "We have no place for such programs as you offer, but [because, it was implied, of a persuasive quality in my voice] if you will come on as a saleswoman I think a place for you at a good salary can be immediately arranged."

But just the same I landed my program a few weeks after a Town Hall recital which was excellently reviewed, and because Walter Varney did bring in "a Head" one afternoon to hear an audition in the flat.

The "Head," Jules Seebach, was young, good-looking, with eyes that possessed an earnest romanticism, and at dusk in Harry's blue library over the river, he sat listening as Lawrence Tibbett had a few weeks earlier, shading his eyes with his hand.

> *Those things we love and lose*
> *Before we learn a way to love them well enough*
>   *and keep*
> *That now are woven on the looms of sleep*
> *That now are only music of the wind.*

The "Londonderry Air" died away and there was, I remember, a pause before he sprang up. "It's enchanting," he told us, "but!" (but it won't wash, I commenced to myself). "But," continued Mr. Seebach, "I can pay you very little money, only enough for cigarettes," he offered with charming deprecation. "However, we have a very fine orchestra under Mr. Alfred Wallenstein which I shall put at your disposal if only you accept. Would seventy-five a week—???" "Give me plenty of cigarettes? Of course!" I told him, and we signed a thirteen-week contract.

Let it be understood here by Texaco, Socony and Bologny, that Mr. Seebach was not offering me a sponsored program but one that is called sustaining, because it sustains radio, and regretfully, during those hours unsold to the advertiser. I understand now why Mr. Seebach was able to offer me an opportunity he probably could not repeat. WOR was a much smaller station then, and the American disease of size not having taken possession, it was still possible for a man to know it himself when he was the boss, and so make his own decisions, instead of being— no matter where he is placed—virtually impotent on account of all the other mentalities he has to consider.

On Sunday winter nights, crossing the town to keep my rendezvous with WOR, it seemed that the westward passage inevitably led through Thirty-ninth Street where, on the downtown side of Fifth Avenue, dynamically lit up, was some store of the five and ten-cent variety—there it glared, in the midst of the deadly emptiness of the sidewalks—and the dark glass of the surrounding stores, offering stacks of paper forsythia, branches of flowering apple, accessories, perfume, china displays and souvenirs of every variety—while above it reared the bastions of Titans, cutting the sky to a remote gash that appeared grim and without peace from between those flanks of granite, perhaps because it could no longer give to men the infinity of its proportion. And I would think of the horrible weight the city had taken on since my childhood, and of the incredible panic impermanence of all its representations.

"Miss Strange, remember to take three lines out of the 'Ode on a Grecian Urn' where they won't be missed, it's forty seconds overtime" a charmingly blond young man, who had charge of producing my program, would call out as I went in to the orchestra—getting a sadistic kick, I thought, out of shifting the gears on my facial expression. But he could be softened if the subject of skiing came up, and perhaps because he usually saw me in a turtle-neck sweater with the poems of a major Immortal under my arm, he took me for a rebel against the established order, since if he had come in from dining well (my program went over the air Sunday nights at 9:30) he often posed me some question with economic overtones: "Do you know what the profits of the Bamberger Broadcasting System were last year?"—a fateful pause—"One million dollars! and I get thirty-five a week!" Longing to tell him "Well, it's too much," I would walk toward Mr. Wallenstein with clenched teeth and a beaming smile.

I often worked for a couple of days over setting a single short poem to music, but now in the larger field of orchestral endeavor I found that it was not possible for me to have more than an hour and a half rehearsal with orchestra for my thirty-minute program, and only thirty minutes' discussion of what music was to be played—and in an office with no piano in it—so that Mr. Wallenstein and I had just to hum possible arias to one another above the repercussions of Broadway traffic, with Mr. Wallenstein, as time wore on, becoming during these conferences a mere whirling blur between the telephone and door.

Mr. Wallenstein's reactions were understandable. Music, his career, in which he had won distinction, was, he had learned—during our first conference with Mr. Seebach—to be subordinated to the written word. So what was he, a seasoned musician, about to sponsor on a coast-to-coast network? And again what was there in it for him?

My convictions: that radio was a unique opportunity for the enjoyment of poetry, since the lyric mystic qualities of poetry were compensated in this loss of one sense by the doubling of that other—where it counted most—hearing; that few great poems had ever been set to music as fine as themselves, so that there might be value to narratives and symphonies directly adjusted to one another—in no way jacked up his *joie de vivre;* while the boss' enthusiasm offered from the sidelines had only kindled an ironic fire behind his lashes. And it grew evident as the weeks wore on (the boss was on a southern holiday) that Mr. Wallenstein was entirely unwilling to play up to my ideas, and I was not willing to use his fine orchestra simply as atmosphere for my readings. For I was aiming at something else, at something that had never been heard before—so that finally we relaxed into a kind of tight-lipped syncopation with Mr. Wallenstein merely furnishing orchestral interludes between my harp with poetry.

But when the boss returned the dilemma was happily solved by giving me Bela Rosa, an organist and composer of merit, to replace the orchestra, a true artist sympathetic to me from first to last—who could and did give me reasonable time in which to work out exciting relationships between symphonies and narratives.

I think of a late afternoon at one of our first rehearsals, with Rosa and me alone in the enormous studio but for Elsa Moegle, my charming young assisting artist, already quite famous on her own—who sits far to one side beside her harp. We are preparing for Lincoln's Birthday, the Lincoln Burial Hymn of Walt Whitman: and now the Beethoven Funeral March booms out eight bars, ceases, recommences softly:

"When lilacs last in the dooryard bloomed
And the great star early droop'd in the Western Sky in
the night
I mourn'd, and yet shall mourn with ever-returning
spring. . . ."

When after that beautiful statement of love and grief, along comes, like a vast gauze lifted from before another vista:

"In the dooryard, fronting an old farmhouse near the
whitewashed palings,
Stands the lilac bush, tall-growing with heart-shaped
leaves of rich green."

and under these words, shaped to them I thought as if from the beginning of time, came motifs from the Tschaikowsky Fifth and Pathetique, containing in their melodic tenderness the very solution into music of the airs of spring:

"In the swamp in secluded recesses,
A shy and hidden bird is warbling a song.
Solitary, the thrush,
The hermit, withdrawn to himself avoiding the settle-
ments,
Sings by himself a song.

"Song of the bleeding throat!
Death's outlet song of life
(For well, dear brother, I know
If thou wast not gifted to sing,
Thou would'st surely die. . . .)" etc.

And all through the bird's song, the harp alone has been accompanying the voice, the harp, which is to me celestially of the heart, as no other instrument.

So then with Beethoven, Tschaikowsky and harp interpolations, gradually was formed the accompaniment for the poem, with impressive accessories only possible to radio, of muffled drums and tolling bells.

"*Coffin that passes through lanes and streets,*
Through day and night, with the great cloud darkening
the land,
With the pomp of the inloop'd flags, with the cities draped
in black,
With the show of the States themselves, as of crape-veil'd
women standing,
With processions long and winding, and the flambeaus of
the night,
With the countless torches lit—with the silent sea of faces
and unbared heads,
With the waiting depot, the arriving coffin, and the sombre
faces,
With dirges through the night
With all the mournful voices of the dirges, pour'd around
the coffin,
The dim-lit churches and the shuddering organs—
Where amid these you journey,
With the tolling, tolling bells' perpetual clang;
Here! coffin that slowly passes,
I give you my sprig of lilac. . . ."

And on the night of production as I said this verse to the great boom of the Funeral March while the bells tolled, and the muffled drums beat, I was more elated, more utterly out of myself, than I could have been in any role that was ever written! I felt an indescribable release—for it seemed that I experienced, if intangibly, the essence of proximity to the sublime poet and musician and death of a great man being mourned for.

The very fact that it was all sounding about me—that I need not see or be seen (for usually I have memorized the script)—brought the reality so close that the words were instantly not pictures but scenes amidst which I stood myself with a pounding heart.

One snowy night with the terrible towers "Wrapt in the sky's sorrowing obscurity," indeed with only the lower half of New York visible, we did our "Poe-Chopin" program.

I thought throughout the "Raven" (which was arranged to the Raindrop Prelude of Chopin) that it was Poe's inconsolable anguish for the loss of his young wife Virginia, which spoke to him in the language of angels and demons telling him of the grief that does not pass but throws its shade "forevermore." And so my interpretation being built around this belief, when I came to the lines:

> *"Then methought the air grew denser*
> *Perfumed by an unseen censer,*
> *Swung by seraphim whose footfall*
> *Tinkled on the tufted floor—"*

I remember such excitement that my voice grew high and strange, for now it seemed it was I who "opened wide the door" upon some cloudy brink from which there might be wafted back for once, even past impenetrable death, a vision of the lost "Lenore"—Virginia.

The program was just over when I was called on the telephone; and an excited voice speaking clear, good English—something to dwell on in 1937—told me "I live opposite to Edgar Allan Poe's cottage at Fordham; if only he could have heard you! for I know that for once you have said everything, spoken for him, sometimes I thought it was Poe himself speaking!" I am so proud of this compliment that I cannot resist repeating it.

But to me the very best exhibition I gave of what I was driving at, the dramatized, musically accompanied story, was a half-hour version of Longfellow's "Hiawatha" arranged to parts of "Natoma" including the "Dagger Dance"—and the "New World Symphony" of Dvorak, with enchanting harp interpolations from "The Land of the Sky Blue Water" for Hiawatha's Wedding Feast—and of course Indian drums beat incessantly. I enacted the whole wonderful, and to me best of our folk poems, in the varying voices of Hiawatha, Laughing Water, Nokomis, with a separate voice for the one telling the story. And at that point where Hiawatha, after the death of Minnehaha and the White Man's arrival, knows that he may now seek for himself "The islands of the blessed," the symphony took a slow build that was absolutely superb; and never in all my life shall I forget the lift and sweep of that music—beneath:

> *"I am going, oh, Nokomis,*
> *On a long and distant journey*
> *To the portals of the sunset,*
> *To the regions of the home wind*
> *But these guests I leave behind me;*
> *In your watch and ward I leave them.*
> *See that never harm comes to them, . . . etc.*

> *"On the shore stood Hiawatha,*
> *Turned and waved his hand at parting,*
> *On the clear and luminous water*
> *Launched his birch canoe for sailing,*
> *From the pebbles of the margin*
> *Shoved it forth into the water,*
> *Whispered to it 'Westward, westward'*
> *And with speed it darted forward. . . .*

"And the people from the margin
Watched his floating, rising, sinking
Till the birch canoe seemed lifted
High into that sea of splendor."

(When it seemed that the music really crashed up into the Sun's center)

"And they said, 'Farewell forever!'
Said 'Farewell, oh, Hiawatha.' . . .
Thus departed Hiawatha,
Hiawatha the beloved,
In the glory of the sunset,
To the regions of the home wind,
To the islands of the blessed,
To the kingdom of Ponemah,
To the land of the Hereafter."

The towering roar of the music subsided and I stood confused and sad that I must snap out of it, and back into the generally distraught monotone of existence; and that night the boss himself called me directly after the program to congratulate all of us.

Our thirteen-week contract drew to an end; I was exhausted but happy, for I knew the program had steadily improved, and that I had been granted a fine opportunity to experiment in an absorbing medium, for which the material was endless. But I also realized, whether or not this was so, that there was such a thing as studio politics, that Mr. Wallenstein's influence in WOR was paramount, that I had irritated him by not compromising, and that I probably owed it to Mr. Seebach's extreme friendliness that I had been kept on after separating from the orchestra.

So I turned on my heel from WOR, dealing a square blow to the bile-duct of the young man who had managed my programs when I told him I would soon be surf riding instead of skiing. And so I left him poised forever, between social ambition and revolution; left the shattering savagery of Broadway with its look of some "midway pleasance" put up for a fortnight by giants with untidy minds, said *à bientot* to a real friend, Bela Rosa, and off we started for a delightful holiday with my dear friend Frances Brooks, at Nassau.

On recital tours mostly through New England the natives took to my poetry like ducks to water; they stood staunchly and even with delight for Elizabeth Barrett, Rupert Brooke, Ernest Dowson, Tennyson, Poe, Iris Tree, Eleanor Wylie, Edna St. Vincent Millay, Dorothy Parker, my own effusions and the Psalms. The old allure of language was wrapped too tightly and deeply in their natures for even 1939 to have found and erased.

And how marvellous it was now to be loose without my lecture "The Stage as the Actress Sees It" and to have the harp in its green baize cover waiting for us in the wings of each new town we came to.

And we went to the White House, where I met Mrs. Roosevelt for the first time, and liked her from the start, for her tall figure and interested kindly eyes exuded breeding, fair-mindedness; and above all you felt she possessed a genuine flair for giving new ideas a chance.

After my recital in the huge White House Ballroom Mrs. Roosevelt and the English Ambassadress Lady Lindsay were the first to come up to me, and Mrs. Roosevelt, giving me both her hands, told me with a simple sincerity that made me grateful and proud that she could not imagine a more delightful way to hear poetry—she also was good enough to put her enthusiasm into print. And then, as a *comble* to her graciousness she sent for one of her own cars to drive me away from the White House.

The tours had been going well for weeks when one February night we started out of Boston in the pouring rain, Elsa and I in my agent's, Esther Carter's, motor. Storm beat on the windshield, "flu" stalked the air, and Esther, unavoidably breathing into my face, told me she thought she had it already, and I wondered, "How can I go through with that same old program," when Esther said "Michael, darling, this may be a difficult audience. Perhaps you'll have a tough time. Mr. X refused to go on with his piano recital last month." "But why?" I asked her. "Did they do anything to him?" "No," said Esther, "but he declined to continue. . . . If anything should happen tonight, just stop." "If anything should happen—" But we had arrived.

Brockton was a factory town where they made shoes. Why on earth did they engage us or Mr. X., I thought, as standing in the wings, I saw an enormous audience packing the hall, none of whom looked as if they minded not being in evening dress. And then I heard Elsa say, "I will play for you the 'Bourree' of John Sebastian Bach." "Here's where I take it all down the front of my clothes," I thought, for it seemed that a faint titter greeted her announcement. The harp started off, but so did the feet of the audience. Elsa stopped. "If you will be quiet, I will continue, not otherwise," she said in tones through which ice-water flowed freely. They were mischievously, menacingly still, but only I felt, because they were waiting for the chief matador.

The "Bourree" ceased, I stepped out onto the stage in my black costume with its leg-o'-mutton sleeves, carrying my books, when the whole audience burst into delighted laughter—the whole audience—I looked at them, pale, nervy, intense-looking, nearly all of them under forty. These were the factory workers. The cogs and wheels had been spinning in their heads all day. These were the ones who, in that old accursed word-deceptive sense, I had always jollied myself into thinking I wanted to do my stuff before. Well, here I was, and it was obvious I couldn't rely on their manners, and that their reactions were going to be delivered neat.

I don't remember what I told them, outside of saying that I had come to Brockton on their invitation, that if, on sight, they had changed their minds, I would go, but if they wanted to give me a chance, it had to be a real one, ten minutes of utter silence; and, I told them also, without casting aspersions on my comfortable Women's Club audiences, that their sort of a crowd was the one I had always wanted to stand up to.

"Go ahead, Mike," a voice called from the hazy rear, and I started off. . . .

I will not forget the way they listened, nor the way they applauded. They were one of the best audiences I ever worked for, and the notice they wrote of me was amongst the finest I ever had, and now it is less possible than ever to tell me how you must play down to American audiences.

Because I knew that my having been let go from WOR

at the end of my contract was not an act of justice but one of politics, since my programs, without the shadow of a doubt, had improved 100 per cent from that one on which Mr. Seebach had engaged us, so still stepping on the gas, I sat, one acrid August morning, in the offices of Owen D. Young (president of the General Electric) a tall, slim, middle-aged man with gray in his dark hair and a somber fire in his remarkable eyes. He was what the French would call *très fin*. He had a kind of tapering slimness that made him look like a portrait of himself, as I told him after a winter of recitals that I wanted to go back on the air, but with a sponsor. The crude clangor of Lexington Avenue rose up perfectly preserved to where we sat on the fortieth floor! I thought you could probably have heard some one spit on the broiling pavement as I described to Mr. Young my Whitman-Beethoven, Poe-Chopin, Hiawatha-Dvorak programs.

"Whitman-Beethoven" said the great industrialist, "What a fortunate combination." He seemed impressed and tapped a button. His secretary entered, keeping a lifted shoulder between us, for I gathered she did not favor this interview. "What is the matter with the secretaries of great men?" I thought, that they behave with the cold, non-human self-assurance of queens plus a dash of Judge Jeffreys at the Bloody Assizes; and recalling her pert vagueness on the telephone I longed to put out my foot and trip her up, when Mr. Young said, "Have we signed with Stokowski and the Philadelphia Orchestra yet?" "I think he would be just the person for you to work with, Miss Strange," he added, glancing at me seriously. Stokowski— the top! One of the first leaders the world over to welcome new musical ideas! She walked off dealing impersonal hate in my direction, and I thought sadly she will return with bad news—"Miss Strange," Mr. Young was just saying, "a new idea means a very great struggle," when back she came with more pep to say that General Electric had not signed up Stokowski, and that furthermore she thought he was contemplating a winter in Hollywood.

Mr. Young now unhooked a receiver and asked to be connected with John Royal at NBC (whom I knew to be one of the tycoons of the great station) and how easily Mr. Young got Mr. Royal! I tried to do the same for eight months afterwards with no effect. "Does the name Michael Strange mean anything to you?" Mr. Young asked whimsically into the receiver. There was no ominous pause as Mr. Young smiled and listened and told Mr. Royal that he was sending me right over to tell him of a most interesting idea.

How quickly everything always went at first. I stood up and Mr. Young, towering over me, said something that was typical of my impression of him, "Do you ever read the Old Testament?" "Yes, looking for bits to set to music," I said. "Well, it's marvellous prose, isn't it?" "Marvellous," I agreed, and now I knew of what he reminded me—it was of that one of the Prophets (painted by Sargent in the Public Library at Boston) who wears a white cowl over his brooding brows, while his eyes look out with a sort of level detached irony into the affairs of men when they are about at that point where the preacher may well cry, "Vanity, vanity, all is vanity." How well such words would have sounded from Mr. Young as he stood darkly before me, with the windows behind him framing crazily spaced skyscrapers that caught the sun on their fantastic tops with a paralyzing glitter.

I had liked him. I thought there was something very

fine about him encroached upon by a tragic weariness, and even as the elevator shot past forty floors with us—for Mr. Young went down with me—I longed to say, "Oh, do stand by for a little 'in person' with all your great power; for we both love the excellence of words; so just think of what it's going to be like to push a cultural idea through the defense mechanisms of Rockefeller Plaza, and stand by for a while 'in person'!"

"Yes," said Mr. John Royal, leaning back in his chair in a modest office at NBC and looking at me out of pale blue eyes, his parched, well cut, sardonic head resembling an eighteenth-century philosopher's—"Ruth Draper was a flop at first, she did her act just before some trained seals in a vaudeville show which I was managing and it didn't go across." "Well, what did she do then?" I asked. "She was discouraged" said Mr. Royal "at first, but then she got hold of herself"; he added, I thought with severity, "she worked like hell at her act until a few days later she did put it over"—there was a pause, I felt he was wondering if my harp and poetry could ever have won against such odds. "As to your ideas, they sound good and I'll arrange for a couple of auditions," he told me. Then he pressed a button: —"In the meantime I want you to meet Dr. Frank Black." Dr. Black, the first orchestra leader of NBC, came in—a charming looking individual with a musician's sensitive head and hands. We smiled at one another and arranged dates.

After the first audition consisting of Shelley, Poe, Millay, Rupert Brooke, Ernest Dowson, and myself, Mr. Royal's office door became an impregnable fortress, al-

though I had seen Dr. Frank Black immediately afterwards. "What did you and Mr. Royal think of it?" I asked
him. Probably if Mr. Royal wasn't there it had been a great
flop! Looking me straight in the eye he replied, "We
think that you have 75 per cent more radio personality
than any one we have ever heard." Ever heard!!! "Gracious, how odd then I can't see the Chief Engineer . . .
or is anything ever odd in the industrialization of art?
Isn't it all just mad?" I thought.

However, on routine a few weeks later when I was putting in my daily call for Mr. Royal's office from a telephone
booth on the Long Island side of Penn Station, there, astoundingly on the other end, was Mr. Royal. "Mr.
Royal," I asked, perspiring freely and with a beating heart,
"how did you like my audition?" "Very much, lovely
voice, remarkable enunciation." "But, Mr. Royal, then
what?" "But, Miss Strange, they will give you the 'bum's
rush' on your sort of program." "Bum's rush!" Should I
press him about alternatives now that I had him on the
phone this once in 1937? In my alarm and excitement I
was trying to think of just the right way to use this ineffable
opportunity, when I found he had hung up.

Mr. Spitalny's office was the antechamber to Frank
Black's and sifted for Dr. Black's attention the essence of
complaints, ambitions and disputes about programs. And I
was accustomed often to waiting around there for a half hour
or so, although at first as usual the contact had been immediate, and Mr. Spitalny, a short, thickset man with very large
features, had told me in a most friendly way, as he set my
collar straight: "You will go far, Miss Strange, if Owen
D. Young is interested in you." When there had followed
a fruity pause during which I was torn between the impulse

to indignantly preserve Mr. Young's reputation and a desire to get somewhere, I surrendered to speciousness. So now there was another audition with Mr. Spitalny's orchestra, but there had not been time to rehearse any of my symphonic scores to poems before winter set in, so that there really was no reason to have had this audition with orchestra at all. But then it would have been impossible to get at any one's ear who counted, in time to explain this.

As summer cooled, Mr. Spitalny let my collar stay as it came, for now he knew Mr. Owen D. Young was only a passing acquaintance, and then it was natural to associate anybody who waited about good-naturedly in the outer offices with defeat.

Of course, long ago, Mr. Young's secretary had frozen the lines of communication when, during one of our two conversations, after telling me that Mr. Royal had written in to Mr. Young exuberantly about my audition, and I had ventured to press this good news with, "Well, then, what is going to happen next?" and she had answered "Miss Strange, do you suppose Mr. Young has nothing to do but look after your career?" Then I, appalled by this lunge into Tsarist technique, had hung up on her, to cancel definitely any further thought of effort in that direction.

However, occasionally jacking up my family's spirits, I would do guest appearances on commercial programs, receiving $500 for a spot of five minutes, and $250 for two minutes and a half. I enjoyed these programs; everything went with the dash and zip and self-confident badinage that goes with high salaries; only sometimes it was difficult to get started on a tragic poem right after hearing all the succulent ways you could use a cucumber.

Also, after Crécy and Poitiers had been fought through,

space for four fifteen-minute programs was wrested for me by the benign powers of NBC. The time was 3:30, an hour at which it is safe to say the general public is nowhere near a radio. Nor could it be announced that I would be on the following week, as I expect it was always hoped that an advertiser might—in the name of some young but coming laxative—speak up even for these inauspicious minutes.

But this time I had a charming artist to produce my program—Mr. Edwards, for many years associated with the Metropolitan Opera Company,—and what a consolation it was to hear him, as I entered the studio with my books, playing so wistfully expert, the scores of Rimsky-Korsakov and Wagner.

One day after a program devoted to English poets accompanied by popular folk music—such as Rupert Brooke's "If I should die think only this of me," scored to "Drink to Me Only with Thine Eyes," or the "Cynara" of Ernest Dowson to Strauss' "Waltz of Salome"—Mr. Edwards told me: "I have written in such a report of your work that they will say I am in love with you—I am not," he added whimsically, "but I do know you should be heard by every one." And I could just see that warm, well-intentioned note, dropped into the brass ear of the great industry—to expire like a flake of snow on the Pacific Ocean, which, as we say along Bond Street, "it jolly well did."

Often, waiting about in Mr. Spitalny's office to find out in what month or year I would be able to corner Dr. Frank Black—"Queen Bergliot," an epic poem scored to the music of Edvard Grieg was then being contemplated for his orchestra and myself—I would look into the granite faces of modern sculpture that ornamented an incredible flank of windows just opposite to where I sat, and wonder just what made me feel it was all so terrible, for I knew that to my generation Rockefeller Center was "a thing of beauty."

And one afternoon with all the time in the world to reflect, a memory of the partially ruined theatres and temples at Paestum returned to me. It was during a holiday in Sicily with Harry that we had come upon them, and a sudden smell of the ocean at sundown, just after passing swampy meadows in which white water buffalo were grazing, when there—across green meadows with the sea beyond—we saw a row of temples, their portals facing the rising and setting sun. They looked absolutely intact and ready for business, and in the gentle light were startlingly beautiful and suggestive, the character of the civilization from which they had sprung being strangely present.

And when we walked around the space surrounding the temples—with their adjacent theatres, like static ripples sunken in the earth—we came across such lovely fragments of moulding—great marble wheels of broken Doric columns which in falling had separated at the jointure, and heads with close curling hair, and with that wonderful impassive hieratic beauty of the classic times. Still after a couple of thousand years in the earth their aura stung the fancy with passionate reverence.

"Just how," I wondered, "would that plaque of barren faces and neuter limbs I was staring into at Rockefeller Plaza look after twenty-five years in the earth? How many months would those great gilded figures with their synthetic insides, striding the lines of empty zodiacs in the black polished entrance hall of spurious marble, hang together;

and what would the tourist make of the highest piles of stone ever seen on earth, together with office paraphernalia and splintered glass?"

"What sort of an idea," I wondered, "had started the Parthenon? Probably it had grown from the desire of the Greeks to put the temples of their gods and goddesses upon a hill that caught the earliest sunlight, and towards which they could look up from their own homes—when it had become, using the skill of the greatest artists, the most poignant nucleus of art ever to haunt successive generations of imaginative men. Apparently its repercussions on the creative faculty were never used up as a couple of thousand years of decoration and architecture testified."

But why had these great flanks of windows comprising Rockefeller Center gone up, putting the streets in shadow by noon! After granting the benign intentions of Mr. Rockefeller to really do something for the American public—in the way of a larger moving picture palace together with variety entertainment for the masses, and certainly by the masses—was it not chiefly out of the determination of a small group of men to rent ten thousand business offices on a few acres of ground?

Perhaps only when some form of religious worship was the reason for seeking beauty, only when some kind of worship had dominated human life, could the character of a civilization linger and be an unextinguishable light before oncoming regiments of mankind.

Anyway, our great writer, Tom Wolfe, was the only fine thing I ever saw in Rockefeller Plaza; Tom Wolfe in his long black overcoat with his strange splendid head lowered, striding along, oblivious, his shoulders above all the milling crowd, his white brooding face under his odd hat fiercely distant, remote, and—I felt as he barged by me—tragically vulnerable.

"Miss Strange," said Mr. Spitalny's secretary with bright kindliness on that particular afternoon, "Dr. Black passed through the room twice while you were looking out of the window, and says he will resume conferences about the Grieg program next week."

O Death, I am secretly in love with you—
For will you not be that arm about me
Embracing—sustaining—my long desiring to lean back—
O will there not be across your face a fused glow of re-
    semblance
To all the beloveds lost—searched for—
Along those mighty roads of the ages—

O will you not hold between your hands
A deific forge beaten cup of luminous wine—
For acclaiming the victory of great quests—
O between your hands—gentle as the hushed flutter of
    wings—
Will you not bear this wine—
And brought from its source a holy fount
Over which the image of the sun perpetually rising—
    shedding down—
And at the very end of flashing ranks of angels triumphal
Whose helmets for ever turning to mirror—
This diffusing—rearing Grail of pouring irradiance—

O Death, will you not fill me with Love again—
With Love in its resonant morning mood—
With Love once more for all those
For whom I have lost love in anguish—

O shall not those blasted holes of my wounds
With their stark-twisted clumps of raw nerve—
Be filled in—be pleated down
With joyous sprays of blossom acutely fragrant—and by
    you—

O Death, I am secretly in love with you—
Your motions suggesting—undulating—receding for
    me—
Like a ribbon of birds fading across the sky—
Your motions touching—evaporating—over me—
Like the poignancy of invisible flowers through evening
    mists—
O your movements are absorbing to watch—
And exhaling a vastly fresh perfume—
Like moon-glossed rushes and water-lilies floating—
    wavering scarcely—
Along the dreaming stir of the tides.

From *"Resurrecting Life."*

CHAPTER XXXI

Epilogue

O N THE white table in Tibi's room with its faintly baroque legs, there always stood a little pile of my books, and a stack of Edith Wharton's, and her yellow-backed foreign novels. And one winter morning I stood in her room, called suddenly from New York by my brother, Harry, as it seemed possible that she might have immediately to undergo an operation for appendicitis. I had arrived in such a nervous and distraught state of mind that, telling the chauffeur to stop outside the gate for fear of disturbing my mother, and glancing at the front door, it seemed to me that already affixed to it was a long pale sheaf of flowers.

Tibi was as frightened as a child at the eventuality of an operation—she had never strangled and snorted to sleep under an anaesthetic—and was walking up and down the room in her pink dressing gown, the morning after my arrival, looking confusedly out of her windows at the gray sick-looking branches of the trees—silent, petrified with silence, I thought—against a dim sky. "It will be nothing," I told her, "you will feel much better afterwards." All the old platitudes came out of a constricting throat, because she looked so old and seemed to have had a loneliness that nothing lifted from her since my father's death the year before. How treacherous of fate, I thought, to wait and give her some horrible modern experience so near the end.

"Oh, Tibi," I felt like calling out to her, "can't we bring back the summer mornings, with your breakfast tray coming in laden with shining silver—with fat robins hopping on the green lawn—and sweet air billowing out the muslin lace fringed curtains from surrounding meadows streaked with buttercup, daisy and clover. And within and outside of the grounds no noise! no noise! only the sound of birds and human voices, or maybe the creaking sound of the watering cart, that looked like a truncated cannon, going its rounds, throwing out its gentle semi-luna of water that made the dust smell so deliciously. God! I thought, don't tell me there is no such thing as immortality; memory, whose roots go more deeply down into the springs of feeling with every year, would be enough to prove that there was,—but I had to be strong that morning, which must have made me seem cold—and Tibi asked for her priest and told me that in any event she wanted to receive the Sacraments.

She made her confession and Communion in my old blue and white nursery and after the priest and his acolyte had gone, since she did not call me, I waited for a little and then went in to her. She was sitting in a rocker looking out of the window, her eyes slightly raised to the elm trees that stood between the two maples on the front circle of the lawn. She did not seem confused or frightened now, also she appeared to have grown up, and some of the intolerable ache I had felt for her before was assuaged.

The necessity for the operation passed away and then Tibi caught a dreadful cold that paralleled one of my own, so that I was unable to see her for a few days; and finally it was Christmas day and she was sitting up in bed in Lily's room, giving out all the marvellously tied-up attractive Christmas packages for her children and grandchildren; since her illness had not been able to keep her from all the worries and joys of being ready for Christmas. A little tree which Harry had trimmed for her stood on the table, and we talked of the most ordinary things, and of how fine it was that there need be no operation—and I stood up, anxious not to miss my train so that I would be back for Christmas dinner with the children, and next morning my old maid, Minnie, was crying outside my door as if her heart would break,—"Your mother, Mrs. Oelrichs, is dead."

When I went back to the house and really saw the white sheaf of roses tied with a purple ribbon affixed to the heavy panelled door with the brass knocker that I had remembered since I was three years old, I felt I had passed the three-quarter mark of my own life. I sensed the sound of some muffled bell of division and leave-taking and warning all in one—my father's death had been my father's death, but my mother's was in some strange way a part of my own —and I thought now the life of the house is ended, its stupendous store of memories made in the deep green time-lessness of youth will just live on in the minds of my brothers and of myself, and, because we are getting older, very much in our dreams.

[355]

And it seemed dreadful that in those last hours in the house there had to be so many people around—for outside of my angelic cousin, Dora Havemeyer Winslow and her family, Mrs. Lloyd Mayer and a few close friends who belonged with us—there seemed to be such hordes of people anxious—with that somewhat unhealthy contagious hysteria of sorrow that goes on in a house where some one lies dead—to assure us of their personal sense of bereavement in our loss.

However, at night there was a comparative silence and I went in and sat down by myself in the library where the blue Delft pieces stood on the brown bookcases and the walls were covered with photographs in their white frames. The library had always been the one room in the house where any one could reflect—and sitting before a huge brown desk to the left of the Franklin stove during his last years, Papa was also in the habit of going there to nervously ruminate on the unpaid bills while he blinked his eyes, and stacked them up in perfect order against that far-off day when something on them could be paid down. And now:—out he came from my memory, and from the library door, his gray suit hanging baggily on him, with his immaculate head and his beautifully tied pearl grey ascot, brandishing my second book of poems and shouting in fury and disappointment, "Well, Miss, do you call this genius?" And how enragedly hurt and cool I could be on such occasions. . . . "No; bilge!" I would probably have answered, but then I would find him on another day cutting out something about me and saying, "That's a very good notice, Baby, from a paper like *The Providence Journal*." And Mama would tell me that she had seen him showing a *Times* book review about me to one of his friends. I think he always felt it better to show the reviews than the poems.

And then one night, a few years before his death, he stood in the cold of January on the porch steps to welcome me after the close of "L'Aiglon"—with "Well, and how is the great actress?" He spoke fondly and affectionately, and a few weeks later showed me a letter he had written to Jack —for he had remained very fond of him and always hoped we would come together again—a letter in which he said that surely I should be congratulated on my courage in acting "L'Aiglon" and from all accounts on my perform-ance—and that if we should come together again, in view of what I had already done, Jack should leave me free to lead my own life in the matter of artistic accomplish-ment.

Tibi and Papa adored Diana, who used to be with them for months at a time. "Tell me the story of the old gray rat, Grandpa," she would say every evening in this same library from September until January, curled up in his lap, lulled by his charming voice—probably this story grew to be a sort of theme on which she built up her own imagina-tive escapades, as she eerily, and completely, in the Jack manner, gazed off into space. And so they wanted also for her sake a united family. I allowed Papa to send this letter, thinking to myself that if Jack could ever cease perma-nently from his addiction to more than one beer, and a few of the varieties of his elfin egotism, who knew what he might be like! However, he answered, it was I who had asked for the separation and that he thought matters had better re-main as they were, and there was no reference to the beer problem—I must say Jack was not to be congratulated on the quality of his pride.

My Father's favorite had always been Lily and the tragedy of her life deeply saddened him, as had also the mixups in my own, although occasionally he indulged in outbursts of humor about us both, telling a friend one day "I don't have to go to the cinema, you know, all I have to do is to closely follow my daughters' lives."

Poor, beautiful Lily's life—some one said to me one day in San Francisco that they thought it had been over for her really when her first husband, Peter Martin, died; but I could not agree. If there is in people's lives a psychic moment when they take into their spiritual constitutions that grain of real poison that will spread and destroy them, then Lily took on such a dose at about twenty, when she sent away the blond curly-haired young man with such a noble earnest expression behind his spectacles, who loved her and whom she loved—for they exactly complemented one another. I knew that from all I had seen and heard from my secret spot in the branches of the chestnut tree beneath which they so often sat and "spooned."

Her brilliance and vitality would have found their groove had she married her mate. And I remembered well that it could hardly have been handled in any other way— for in the fantastic social structure in which she lived, only marriage had been expected of her, nor had she, by sheer luck, any accomplishment that would have used up some of that tremendous current in another way.

I am sure that my father and mother never advised Lily to turn away from this young man, they were far too tender-hearted, too distinguished in spirit to have lowered themselves by such counsel. My parents were, of course, made increasingly miserable and confused by the changing standards of the society about them, but their mould had been made in another day and age. They were safe, they could not be really tainted, whereas my sister's generation had all begun to think of money in the terms of a first value, without which, and in great quantities, life could simply not be lived, at any rate not the life of an extraordinarily beautiful girl. This beau, then, whose nobility of nature was so evident in his features and who, under the stimulus of Lily's amazing wit and physical loveliness, might well have turned into an outstanding statesman had she given him a family of handsome children, and my sister parted. And it was on that evening, when she sat for hours in her room through twilight on into nightfall, not bothering to rise or light the gas, not joining us at supper, that I—stealing into her room (for I had a vicarian gnome's horrible desire always to be in on what was going on)—found her sitting by her open window with its geranium window box, and seeing my sister's eyes (she did not see me) I crept away again, aware in my child's soul that something terrible had happened. I believe now in retrospect that this was when she died to her real happiness.

There were years of luxurious living in Paris, London and Newport, with their aimlessness and consequent dissipation, always accompanied by her good natured and admiring husband. Then came Peter's illness and his death, Lily's marriage, during our entry into the war, with Borwin, the Duke of Mecklenburg-Schwerin, which was not a happy one—her misunderstandings with her son, who, finally, at eighteen, ran away and took a boat for San Francisco where he makes a sensible marriage, brings up a family and works hard—and then those last weeks with Lily in San Francisco, to which she had come from Paris. Harry and I joined her there in the hope of straightening out the painful tangle of her affairs; for Lily was crippled by then, and thank God, already a little vague; being sucked back into the dream from which she came; somewhat unaware, or at any rate, not too sharply on to the variations of horror that were going on about her. . . . For the bills of a lifetime were coming in, and Harry was in conference every day about them—and when we would talk over together what was happening to his efforts to get Lily out of the Martin estate, some income to live on—Peter had wanted her to have everything and loved and adored her always— I was reminded of my Father's saying, after a visit to San Francisco, "They are a hard lot out there and Peter is completely unlike them"; and he had added, "A man will do in his next of kin for money"—and I thought of Lily's telling me, between amusing stories about various families in San Francisco: "Baby, you can have no idea what some of these people are like underneath." And there had crossed her face an indescribable expression of pain and distaste.

I want to think of Lily last in Paris, already confined to her bed and sitting room in the hotel, but cheerful and surrounded by a band of loving and loyal friends, mostly Russian émigrés. . . . I especially remember a lovely, gentle, blond-haired woman, the daughter of the Grand Duke of Leuchtenberg; I think she was giving lessons at the time, and her husband, Grischa, was driving a taxi for their living. "Think of it," Lily would exclaim, "his father was in the Emperor's Guard and Grischa was educated in the *"Ecole des Pages."* And then Lily would suddenly say, humming a romantic tune, "And you know, George Leuchtenberg (the Grand Duke) wants to marry me," and she would show me the photograph of a distinguished gentleman in a cape, walking beside a lake with a great château in the background. "But I couldn't, Baby," she would go on; "I don't care for him in the least like that."

I like to think of Lily last in Paris, the city which she loved so dearly, still lost in *la grande illusion* that royalty would come back—the estates of all her friends would be returned to them—why, every one in the Emperor's entourage (she was speaking of the Kaiser Wilhelm) knew it would be only a short time before his reinstatement— Lily surrounded by the daughters of Grand Dukes and gentlemen, no matter how threadbare, who had once been educated in the "*Ecole des Pages.*"

And then another memory: Papa coming through the door, past the cloak-stand,—to meet my entrance a few days after I had returned from the West where Harry had at last managed, after some tooth and nail fighting, to secure a small part of his wishes for Lily's economic future—with tears streaming down his cheeks and a telegram in his hand. "Dear, dear Lily," he said, "my poor child!" For my sister had died the night before in her sleep, a merciful death which the innate childishness of her heart merited. And our faithful old Gerdes—the nurse of her son and my children —who had cared for her so tenderly in her last days, wrote to me—that lying in her son's house, she seemed to have regained her youth, and looked like a Queen. She had been buried in the orders of the Royal House into which she had married, so carrying the badge of her child's harmless but hopeless dream into eternity. And I could well imagine why Gerdes had written as she did, for always I remembered from my childhood that Lily's height and slenderness, and above all the way she held herself, and looked at you out of her humorous eyes, gave the impression of a distinction that was fatally romantic, because it belonged more to the creation of poets and writers than to life as it had to be lived.

For many years I had not seen much of my brother Harry, the teaser. He had worked mostly in real estate, but without much zest, until the Great War into which he had flung himself, heart and soul, like so many other men who were lost and depressed in the commonplace anxieties of their existence. He had achieved distinction and the title of Captain, by which I think he still rather likes to be hailed. The war, however, with its gargantuan unsettlement—as if some animal the size of half the world had shrugged and changed position under the earth's surface—so that about everything outside and inside you seemed to be upside down —when the war left off needing Harry, the change left him confusedly lost, as it did some other people.

His marriage during the War, with Esther Moreland, who was at that time a Pittsburgh heiress, was not particularly fortunate. He had drifted into the job of selling old masters; being still very good looking and having an "air," people were apt to listen carefully to his exhortations on the incomparable flesh tints of Raeburn, and the ascetic perfection of Gainsborough. Then he had drifted away from the galleries and married Dorothy Jordan, a former operatic singer, and made his life a good deal with her and her people in the West—my good-looking, good-hearted and wild brother—he remained a great deal of a child and at the death of my mother, he lost the one great love of his life.

Charlie, good, brown-eyed, patient Charlie, attended to everything, took over all the responsibilities—always in splendid health, no treacherous pressure of fate had caved in the chest which he always threw out unconsciously when he walked. And it was good to remember of him, that the intrinsic well-being of a very decent spirit, added to the stimulating safeguard of having to make his bread by what might well be called the sweat of his brow—had directed his fate past the extremes of tragedy into a second marriage which brought him happiness, and a brown-eyed son whose blythe voice should fan the air with gusts of hopefullness.

And as I now sat by myself in the library I realized fully that all the life of the house, with its immense hoard of simple family memories, its stored sound of the blithe voices of children—and of their parents' voices—which, as the seasons circled about them, drew all downward and upward, so that the arc of birth and death might be described—accompanied by the enigmatic, unfound, ever-present pulsing of the human soul—that all the life of the house was undergoing its transformation from the actual—was withdrawing compact and complete, just as my Mother loved to have it, long before legacies and creditors could disturb a single picture frame, or alter the position of a rug, or put irreverent hands on the lovely gay patina of "The Tired Lady" asleep on her brown carved shelf in the Blue Parlor—was withdrawing compact and complete—as it had always been and would be, into my memory eager and very sad. And then I wondered if the laden air of so many remembered things at such a moment might not be a sort of magnet to draw my parents' spirits back to me on this last night that I sat in our common home, incidentally the only one I have had—and I thought, "What would I wish to say to them if this were so?" And it seemed I certainly would want them to know how glad I was that Tibi had come over from Vienna that summer to visit Auntie in Newport, and became engaged to my handsome Father in the plum-colored summer house at the far end of the "grove" and been married by Archbishop Corrigan in Auntie's drawing room at 244 Madison Avenue in her lovely dress with all its bustles and the point lace veil, so that my life could come to me through them—through such dear fine people—so worthy of my love and of my loneliness for them always.

A Letter to My Mother

A Letter to My Mother

My Dearest Tibi,

I am sitting, writing to you in my caravan on a clear afternoon in early summer, on the grandest beach that I have ever seen, the one at Montauk—not a sound but the oncoming waves—and the vast subterranean sound of their suction out again—and some lovely bird-theme out of the shad bushes that rise up in moors of shrill green to meet a cloudless sky.

At the end of this book, in which I have written down things about myself, about us all, I want to write to you alone because if I direct my thoughts at you, I feel they will be more genuine, less conscious, less afraid.

It will be seven years next Christmas since that last day I sat with you in Lily's room while you had lunch, and gave us our presents, and much has happened to all of us of which I have told or tried to tell.

But it is a more baffling thing to attempt to write down your experience than I had imagined—and you get off easiest when you are writing of your childhood, because time and retrospect have all these memories cooked up for you in a sort of final meaning—whereas, many things that happen to you as you get older are influencing you in a manner of which you are still not altogether aware.

You loved me so much, Tibi, you used to call me "my only love," but you were terribly afraid for me all the time—and I had to take that fear into consideration, and as I grew up and married, not let you know much of what was going on in my life or mind—because of that terrible apprehension of yours. Of course I don't think any one was ever "in," very much, on what was going on in my mind. You remember how I always sat with my nose in a book when you were moving households, or when you were all upstairs dressing for your Newport parties. How hot those August evenings were in the lamplit parlors—but there would be a delicious smell of sherry being poured into the frail glasses with your monogram in gold (that I have now) to—after they had been taken up on silver trays to your rooms—give you a theatrical cheer for your parties.

And do you remember my handsome swarthy beau, Charles Duryea, with his broad tanned face, and a slit between his front teeth which I found unattractive and that, unable to conjure forth my powers of entertainment, he took a snapshot of me reading, crouched on the front porch steps with long hair falling over my shoulders and a white taffeta bow perched on the top of my head?

I was reading "Kenilworth," and during a whole autumn of my childhood I can remember nothing so much as the smell of curled brown piles of burning leaves on the green lawns, and "Kenilworth," and the screaming fall of poor Amy Robsart in her hooped taffetas through that trap door, all because of Queen Elizabeth's sinister love for Amy's secret husband, the Earl of Leicester.

The love of Queen Elizabeth for those young men—Leicester, Essex, Raleigh! There seemed to be something bizarre and rather terrible in it that intrigued me very much!

But I could never speak to you of such things, nor of how the handsome Roche twins affected me, when I saw them in their knickerbockers and Norfolk jackets, swinging along through the sunlight and shade, passing Ayrault Street on their way to visit me, since there was an unwritten law of reserve on such matters between mother and daughter.

Nor could I ever express to you how beautiful faces affected me, enslaved me almost, because they were the means of making me come alive emotionally, intellectually. Yearning! I saw it at an early age as the open sesame to one's self, and despite what was called my "religious instruction" and your sweet innocence, my moral attitude remained peculiarly unformed. Indeed, beneath the conformity of starched dresses and white gloves for the nuns in the convent on Spring Street, I was thinking obsessively about good-looking boys and dark piazzas—and deciding there could never be enough of these two commodities, when I found out something else along that line—evidently I had capricious sensibilities—for there could be a handsome boy and a dark piazza, and yet nothing—so that the rarity and splendor of feeling, when it arrived, made me think of it always as a blessing.

You could hardly have been expected to know how unprepared I was at nineteen for a successful marriage. I was not prepared for anything except a succession of good times, and the few slight illnesses I had—attended by your devotion and Len's, were only rest intervals. And I remember getting up from one of these in Philadelphia and looking at myself in a skin-tight fitting negligee of pale blue satin, and revelling in the fact that I was so slim and tall, and rather good-looking—so that there must be an infinite variety of good times ahead of me.

But again there was another strain in my nature promising to mix things up even further—a desire to find out about things of which my frame desired me to know nothing, to ask irritating questions and make out of my fumbling ignorance statements which appeared maddening to those who were not only unobsessed, but even contemptuous, of the subjects that were engrossing me. That social-minded side of myself has always been something of a mystery to me—I took on causes, it seems to me in retrospect, with only slight examination of their significance. I think I took them on mostly out of an emotion for justice and freedom.

For example, although I wanted the women to get the vote and believed it only just that they should have it, I never did a stroke of gruelling work for suffrage nor did I much enjoy my alignment with the Party, while that white narrowing fire, of some of my friends, I found nerve-racking. There were few light touches amidst large gatherings of determined women. However, I kept on thinking of the deviousness of men with each other, of their capacity to take an outrageous advantage unless a bell rang when they did it, and of what could be done about it.

Did you ever know that what actually started me being a suffragette was a visit to a cotton gin in South Carolina in 1912, while on a shooting party with Clary Mackay? The "guns" had gone off for the day, and I was to join them for a sumptuous picnic luncheon attired in faultless tweeds—but first I arrived at the factory in the Mackay car, and was shown the plant with obsequious eagerness by a stout boss who tried to veil his confusion at my having taken it into my head to come; and I was just going when, through a half-opened door, I caught sight of some very young white-faced children at work. "Haven't you a law here," I asked the boss sternly, "against children under sixteen working?" "Yes, ma'am," he answered brightly. "Well then, the children in there look about seven!" "Ma'am, you can't keep 'em out," he told me. "Their families send 'em and they can do with some extra cash." Then I answered him with my first spurt of suffragist indignation that "if women had the vote, they would vote the men out of office who didn't see that such laws for children's welfare were obeyed. This he countered by asking me, with that awful Southern drawl, compounded of bouts with malaria, association wid' de colored folks, and congenital amnesia at the base of the spine, "do you laydies evah think youall get the vote?" And this answer settled me into the Suffrage Movement.

Len was a deeply civilized man, more so than any one whom I have ever known intimately. He could feel so profoundly that I cannot bear, in retrospect to dwell upon the depth of his capacity to feel—and yet control himself absolutely. I can see, or at least imagine it to have been true, that from the first he saw my wildness, my lack of outer and inner discipline, but believing in the quality of my feelings he took a chance, and said and did nothing to curb me, probably imagining that to let me fling myself about like a coyote would bring me to a halt sooner. He banked on the great affection he knew was in me for himself and the boys—God knows it has endured, that affection, even if it had not all the qualities with which the desire of his heart endowed it.

And if it would have meant just letting me have my head with social pleasures and light flirtations, the satiation point would soon indeed have been reached. But Tibi, perhaps the thing that brought my life to an end with Len more than anything else was the start of my poetry—and my poetry was so unforeseen; you know I never wrote poems as a child, only very long novels—and a diary that you packed away, smiling, into a large trunk on the top floor of the stable, next to all our moth-eaten rocking horses.

Tibi, my mother Tibi,—I was going to say if only I could make you know, but that would have only been true of long ago—now I can make you know what the coming of poetry means. It means that there is no more life really, although you go on pretending there is, of the old sort, bounded by domestic devotions and social pleasures, there is only listening, and wherever that listening leads you, you follow automatically. It was as if all the sights and sounds and experiences of existence suddenly had only one function: to make you hear something—and as soon as you had, well, that was that—but oh the blossoming behind everything; and you must follow the lovely web binding you against your sight, inward or outward, until you had had enough of one another—like the bee of his flower pollen—so that you were, in life, as you had never been, and yet aside from it as never before—you had the most glorious sense of abandon and irresponsibility—you took your freedom as it was needed—spontaneously—without any intellectual reservation!

Looking back now, I think that beginning to write poetry

was like being a child again with all of adulthood coming to you, only in a magical sense. I remember one night in Bar Harbor before I was to have an operation for appendicitis, that I had a pianist come in to play for me nothing but modern French music. I wasn't particularly interested in the operation; still if anything should happen, I did not want to miss out on that evening. We were living then, in a lovely house, "La Selva," with its rose gardens by the Inland Sea, and in every window flower boxes of geraniums and petunias over which the humming birds hung at noon, with their fantastically still suspension in the air as if they depended from invisible wire.

Beautiful Mount Desert Island with its forest paths across miniature mountains—I used to stride out into the morning, Tibi, with a book, a pencil and a sandwich, and stay away until I was turned home by the darkness. And how dreadful, how mortifying to the spirit, it used to be, after some wonderful day, not to sit relaxed in the evening in my lovely weariness before a crumbling fire, listening possibly to the words of a sage or the resonance of a harp, but to be instead, netted in the uproar of a dinner party, where I could see that the reflections of the guests were already going slightly sour about me.

> *For to-night upon the mountains*
> *The wind gave me tender kisses,*
> *The pines lurched against me with caress,*
> *And the sky . . . told me scarlet azure stories*
> *Of what had been done,*
> *Undone beneath her.*
> *For to-night I, shooting arrows with passion*
> *For the virginity of love,*

[373]

I, running with youth beneath those showers
Of his ephemeral promise,
I, gilding my tongue
With talk among gods!
I—leapt away from myself
Existing only as soul.
Alas, alas, that I should pass, descend,
From this mood anointed,
From these cousinly mountains,
Towards those melancholy levels—
Where I find no kin.

And another night at a Bar Harbor dinner party, watching the veiled gaze in my direction and the bumping heads: "What can have come over Blanche? She's never at the 'pool' any more!" "Didn't you know, my dear, she thinks she writes!" And listening to the good-natured chuckling, —for oddly enough although I was considered a fearful bluff, no one seemed to dislike me for it—I wrote on the back of my menu, a poem that begins:

"I am young! young!
And you all hate me for it."

and ends:

"Yet how sad! how sad!
You cannot like me,
Knowing not that I smell
Of the moon! the sea!
Nor that my hair
Is woven of to-morrow's flowers,
And my feet—
In the stirrup of sunrise itself!

[374]

No! you cannot see
My dancing futurity,
For I am young, young,
And you all hate me for it."

And I remember that some old dowager reading over my shoulder what I had just written told me: "Not at all my dear—you are young—young, and we all love you for it."

But now especially after that summer in Bar Harbor, I began to feel that I must be free, that is, I must be called as free in fairness to others as I was already spontaneously in myself.

Certainly the start of poetry insisted upon an automatic absorption in one's hearing, which must have given the impression, and produced the effect of incredible cruelty.

Why Tibi, do you remember when I went for my divorce to Paris; there was Jack in New York, full of his usual quota of suspicions—swollen at that moment to a little over what the vessel would take—threatening to sail for Paris—and upset what might be called the apple cart of propriety and common sense. There were you rushing down to the theatre to dissuade him—although you told me he was already brandishing a passport. There was Len, living in Paris, conniving against his every instinct for my happiness, together with his personal desires—in this divorce. There were two very young children, being looked after by you in a rented house on 96th Street, because now that the divorce was going through, the lovely house, belonging to Albert Sterner which Len had bought and I had decorated for his return from the War, was up for sale. There was myself, Tibi, who might well have been disturbed if not bowed crooked by the disruption I was causing; there was myself, living in 33 Quai Voltaire, looking out at the black River Seine and the marvellous etching of snow upon the grand carving of the Louvre Palace opposite; there was myself, writing poety—filling papers under my pillow each night with poems. And one night I sat at a Bach Concert with Hermann—there had lately been some exhibition of pictures in the hall—and I must have looked for a long time at one of them, of which I can remember nothing—save that the principal figure was that of an over life-sized angel with his head bent over his knees; and that next morning I was writing down the poem which commences the Volume of *Resurrecting Life:*

> *"It is midday and the wind off the desert*
> *Is choked, flattened down*
> *In a glaring pulse of heavily beating sunlight—*
> *And my angel sleeping beside the well,*
> *His grave brow half hidden*
> *In the curve of a mighty arm . . ."*

And sometimes, waking up in that strange flat belonging to the violinist Thibaud, where my bed used to be shaken by the trains on their way to the Quai D'Orsay station, I would sense, I suppose, the heaviness of my breakaway from so much that was already deeply graven in me, and write:

> *"From where do I waken—from where—*
> *To be wrung by the breath of intimacies*
> *Just evaporating from before my pursuing arms—*
> *To be flattened back aghast from the swift streaking by*
> *Of forms in profile—poignantly akin—*

Clouded phosphorescent with grief—joy—
And surely all lately fastened upon me
In keenest various intercourse—
Mother—lover—child—O all go by—
Leaving me the echo of a chord vast in pathos—"

And Tibi, I was caught up in all these things I was hear-ing, I was utterly absorbed by them, I went through the sadness I was causing every one; it is true that I did, in a trance;—terrible, outrageous as it may seem, it is the truth.

Lily came in one morning and besought me not to do what I was doing, she spoke so beautifully of Len—I do not remember her having really affected me at all, although now I think of the things she said and am indeed affected.

And I realize too, now, that even when I came back with my interlocutory decree, you and Papa simply could not bring yourselves to believe it.

I think it was just before New Year's that I arrived, and the children, in colored linen suits were so gaily glad to see me; Len was there—and you and Papa—and you all made out to be in very good spirits for the children's sake. How did I ever go through with it, unless I simply wasn't a part of it?

And Jack welcomed me back also—with an eerie light in the eye that enquired for a numerical admission of my flirtations while in Paris. And he gave me his presents for my return, arranged so charmingly, fenced in with curtains that drew back on a string as at an unveiling, when there was revealed, beautifully set off against black velvet, a marble copy of a Greek athlete's head that he knew I adored, and which stands in the Metropolitan Museum—and a portrait head of himself by Paul Manship;—a fair likeness, I thought, but also a frigid stylization, hard, metallic, utterly passing over the spirit and fire of Jack at that time, catching, of course, a good deal of the shape of his head, but infusing all, imprisoning all, within the strokes of a sterile formality.

The poetry stopped for a while after my marriage to Jack—that is, I kept on writing it, but tearing it up. And I know that summer in Deauville, when we had the dear little farm house in the center of the apple orchard (and when you had tiny Diana at Trouville), I know that you knew then that I was most unhappy, and it was, as a matter of fact, not much more than a year after that summer, that during a fog-shrouded morning in London, I rose betimes, as one might say, and gathering up Diana, went to the south of France and then to America, putting a definite end to my life with Jack.

And, Tibi, those years that you and Papa were starting to doze such a lot in the library at Newport, and I was living at 142 East End Avenue, I was more happy than I can remember ever having been since I was a child—I was free, independent, had some money, owed my conscience to no one but myself, and the children were all the steady company I craved. Also, my poetry, although very different now, was real again and the straight "nature poems" commenced to be written, since probably one of the functions of pain is to disjoin the psyche from its personality in the old sense.

SOUTHAMPTON BEACH

"O thunderous music
Obbligatoed
By hissing fringes of surf . . .
Sea music of the waves
Toward shore on each other's necks

A LETTER TO MY MOTHER

Unerringly near
At unerring lengths . . .
Their overtaking mingling mounting throats
Interfusing jet of manes. . . .
Spouting forth endless garlands
To meet the pale far powdery bloom
Of the horizon's breasts. . . .

THE FALLS OF MONTMORENCY

"Great gutted arteries of melted frost
Flung up out of the world's breaking awakening
*   heart . . .*
Frigid crash of the saffron wing-colored falls . . .
Boiling pour and toss of the crossing currents . . .
Vast phantasy of half seen shapes in the jet . . .
Dazing exulting air hovering above . . .

SURF

O lovely silver crashing percussion of autumnal sea
Great Y shield of shredded spirited flashings
Billion surf necks rearing, hugely veined with numerals
*   of foam . . .*
Mounting, blown sturdily immense
From grave depths winter stirred . . .
Towering, tremendous
Scooped o'erhanging mist-manes breathing back
Before the collapsing roar . . .
Dazzling forward, rushing crust of fighting white water
Thinning up-hill . . .
Arriving at matchless even top speed
In hissing, streamering, looping patterns
Blindingly fresh—

O marbling my ankles with a certain sense
Of their Eternal Fleetness.

Len came in often and played on my grand piano the compositions of Bach and Wagner and his own songs set to the poems of Robert Burns:

> *"Ye banks and braes o' bonnie Doon,*
> *How can ye bloom sae fresh and fair?"*

The wistfulness and sentiment of his spirit was very evident in those songs and one day he played me a choral hymn—"Come and Mourn With Me Awhile," of such noble beauty that I asked his permission to include it in the music score of August Strindberg's "Easter" which was just going into rehearsal.

I don't suppose you understood at all why on earth I went into the Theatre, for I don't believe you ever heard me mention during my childhood that prevalent ambition among young girls of being an actress.

However, Tibi, when I left Jack, when so many hopes were shipwrecked and there was that aftermath of nervousness to be dealt with, which utterly precluded the sort of "spontaneous me" feeling in which poetry comes to be written, when, indeed, I did not know how much me there was extant, then the Theatre—the grease paint, the wig, the row of electric lights between me and the rest of the real world—between me and my memories—was a God-send.

"For during the night-tide my departed love illumining
> *beside me*
And his words like the hiss of approaching flood
Across droughted places—

And his embrace washing my fatigue
As a draught of orchard perfume
Stealing through dishevelled city curvage—

O the splendour of his dream-felt touch
Sweeping me with fanfare of rainbows—
O the splendour of our contact irradiating me
With arpeggios of colour . . .

"But you never really wanted to be an actress—if you had, you would have stayed on the stage, you could have easily (a flattering gesture) made managers see your viewpoint if you had cared enough—" I remember that tragically tormented and tormenting character, Jed Harris, saying this to me one afternoon at the Empire. And I think there was much truth in it, for with my poetry back, or even with the dim magnetic wings of it heard in the air this having to go down to the theatre could often be something of a torment.

So then, my Tibi, how well I see you that afternoon in my dressing room at the Cosmopolitan Theatre in New York, already old and weary—and shaken, too, because you had not seen me on the stage before, because I had been better than you had expected—and not been your "baby" once. Why had I not acted before, etc. . . . ? You were even starting to blame yourself! And I stood in front of you in the black velvet dressing gown and loose white ruffled shirt, that the poor Duke dies in—I seemed to have just left off shouting with the sudden nervous strength of approaching death—"Horses, horses, that I may go to meet my father," (I had at least cut all the tirades out of the death scene). I was still half in some glittering dream of the Emperor's calèche with galloping horses coming to

meet me under the Arc de Triomphe, where the marroniers were in their fullest bloom, and along streets lined
with huzzahing crowds, when the Empress had thrown
herself on her knees, and there had fallen upon the Duke
that terrible blank and surrender to the last anæsthesia,—
and also Diana's cry, ringing through the theatre that Saturday matinee, from her seat in the first row, "Mummy's
dead! Oh, she's really dead."

So then, Tibi, first of all and more than all, perhaps, because I did not really want it—as I started to come together
again—I let go of the telephone by which I might have
reached the manager's secretary—and after years of wise
bombing, achieved a fortunate role, to, if the play closed on
Saturday night, commence the whole damned thing over
again.

There are peculiar moments in life during which, perhaps, a certain view of a landscape, or the look of a room,
is vivid to you forever, because at that moment you are
aware of the impact of some choice that is, to you, indi-
vidually momentous. And so, one autumn afternoon I was
motoring into New York, and looking back of me, saw
the brilliant hills rolling gently up to mould and sprout
into the Catskill Mountains, and thought: "Why must you
go on to New York with all its deceptions and wastes of
ambition—if you do, you will still all that speaking, rhythmic chain of supporting life that comes to you, strengthens
you, leads you only when you are not in the metropolis—
Go! Fly! Escape! from your second best, from your half-
realities and half-living. To hell with this idea of making
a success! You know what success is. It is becoming more

alive to the things that are for you, and haven't you some faint idea that these are not at the disposal of Lee Shubert?

No, the ambitions that I told myself I had were a kind of frame providing some routine of telephone calls, interviews and contacts. I was too lazy to cut the set-ups that were already there, and make the others that had to be made, if I should continue on. I wasn't strong enough! I often think that most of the illnesses in the world come from defeating some life impulse like the one I had that day.

No, Tibi, it certainly is "not in our stars" that we go on to 42nd Street, when we might be elsewhere, and sometimes I think that the stuff of life is just error and change, error and change, until you are all tuckered out enough to collapse, without making any more noise—or you have enough guts left after all the detours, to catch up to where your heart is.

I think I can remember when first a harp cast its spell over me; it was on a blazing summer morning of my childhood—and you stood on the lawn beside the bow window of the blue parlor snipping a flood of crimson rambler roses. You wore your long pink accordion-pleated tea gown, with its high lace collar and sleeves that took on extra girth between elbow and wrist, with the coiled knot of your dark hair shining behind a primly ondulayed pompadour, and you looked reflectively peaceful, because you so dearly loved flowers.

I was watching you, fascinated by this unusual moment of *bien être* when behind me I heard an arpeggio, a glissando from the harp that struck me into a sort of golden hush of delight, and I turned and saw my old friend the harpist whose playing I had never noticed before. . . . There he sat, on his stool pitched to one side of the burning gravel, with his powerful shoulders and gray hair and mustache, dark eyed, dark skinned, from the Latin countries. He was dressed in his black alpaca coat and worn trousers, with a very correct collar and cravat, appearing no doubt to himself, this wistful beggar, as the great artist playing to the Newport Smart Set. And before him was the harp—the harp with its ancient shape, and the carved head and breast of a woman whose hair streamed back like the hair of Medusa— Medusa—Mythology—Jason—the Golden Fleece. He played on and on, and I saw the angelic spectacle of the Grecian Fleet riding gently to anchor in the Harbor of Troy . . . saw the staggering beauty of over-life size Archaic figureheads, as if wind were always in the heroically moulded garments—and the figureheads stared at me, with that wonderful level-browed, impassive stare that is beyond good and evil, beyond conscience or remorse, beyond the emaciate abstemiousness of Christianity, beyond the Day of Judgment itself. The classic stare, merciless— hypnotic, only ready to be bewitched—by Beauty.

And I saw an old man with a wild prophet's head, clad in brown rags—such as Paul of Tarsus might have worn— standing on the flags of a great hall, where firelight leapt along the walls, and by the rigidity of his gaze, when he turned toward the warmth I saw that he was blind. And beside him stood a harp; and a boy harpist, with his dark hair cut block-wise and in a bang, touched the strings as the old man chanted to men and women who leant forward eagerly from a long table where they had just dined so as to lose no word (for this was news and its chief manner of transmission) while Homer chanted, "I sing of the fall of Troy."

Oh, music that is like no other wonder! Oh music, touch-stone of memory!

And you turned to me, Tibi, where I stood, frozen and in another country, and told me in a low voice, "Baby, fetch the poor man a glass of milk and some cakes"—for evidently the music had ceased, and as I went into the cool black void of the house—after such sounds! such flares of fancy! to say nothing of its being August as well—I thought: "That's right, no one who makes such music should drink anything but milk, indeed you certainly couldn't bring up to this golden symbol of sound that had penetrated and brought into life the furthest depths of my book of Grecian Myths, anything but milk."

And again in the momentary silence of my own poetry, to be filled and consoled with the challenging singing of my brothers, to be able to select these at will and give them their accompaniment, bestows an aura of creativeness, of independence, that is precious to me.

I have not been very well lately. I had what the doctors call a lower back sprain, contracted on a canoe trip. They put me to bed for a fortnight, and I asked one distinguished fellow who examined me, and who looked as if he drank more than was good for him, if he thought it was serious; when he clapped me on the back and answered, "Not a chance of it." That was in August, and I was in bed until the following February. Sir Robert was dead, or I should, of course, have had myself carried onto a boat and sailed for him.

However, I had in every specialist to call upon me who was distinguished enough to charge $20 a visit, and I regret to report their service was nil.

They were polite, they were anxious to be useful—but after about three weeks of their perturbation and suavity, of their nonplussed kindliness, and exhortations to have patience, "now is the time for books, you know," etc., etc., it was obvious to me that they had not the foggiest notion of what was going on under my skin, but that this was something you could not have expected them to say—at $20 a visit. And then, as is usual with the great New York specialists, their attention was a good deal with their last and next appointments, which prevented them from focussing much upon what the patients themselves might be saying about where they felt the pain.

At any rate, Tibi, after some months, Harry got me out of New York in a wheelchair; and arriving at a village in North Carolina, I had in the local doctor for five bucks, who told me what was wrong with me, which was a little streamer of ruptured muscles and ligaments, etc., along the spine and at quite a different point than that indicated by $1500 worth of New York doctors. God bless them! No doubt they did their best, thinking of so many other things, as they were, at the time. And after some months in Florida, I discovered a baking process under black Everglades swamp mud, through which I beat a strong electric light which has started me on the right road. And the only black mark I put down to my New York doctors was the expression on their faces when I walked fairly normally into their offices early this summer. For even if you have tried to do something for some one and failed, you ought not take it as a personal insult that Providence has stepped into your impotent boots.

When you are ill over many months, with a nebulous

ailment which may be fatal to any normal form of life—
people will come in and tell you almost daily, "My dear,
so-and-so had just what you have," and it might be that
so-and-so's has lasted anywhere from one year to thirty!
Then you are apt, with no self pity whatever, but in a mood
of reflective eagerness, to think about death—when brooding upon this eventuality seems to clear up the atmosphere
considerably where you do your thinking.

Present-day existence is such a chaotic miasma of ruptured impressions, of thoughts not followed to first base,
that a long illness in a lovely room over the Atlantic Ocean,
filled with soft breezes of eternal summer—with a great
green uneven line roughly running between water and sky
to mark the Gulf Stream—this does for you what Chinese
paintings do for the eye—it eliminates the unessen-
tials.

My dearest Tibi, if to any one I owe a searching of my
heart, it is to you; for I know that your love for me, your
belief in me, and your fear for me, were all immeasurable.

You gave me the indescribable wealth that a mother be-
queaths, and because it was more than I could deserve, the
idea of there being infinite time in which to try to measure
up occurs to me—and this really amounts to a belief in some
kind of immortality;—of course not your kind that was so
splendidly grooved in the magnificence of your Church
ritual and the touching ever-present mercy of your "Our
Lord"—but 'twill serve.

Tibi, if I had been a novelist instead of what the circu-
lars describe as "poet, playwright and actress," then I could
have, perhaps, made us all into a story. I would have been
able really to express not only what became of us, and how

we affected one another and others, but of what the scene made us do to one another—because I think that would have been the chief reason to have given any of us importance.

And I would have been glad to do this because I feel, at this point, that all is not so top-hole with the U.S.A., in spite of some of the radio stations practically saying: "Twelve o'clock, folks, and all's well—get down on your knees and be glad that you belong in a Great Democracy —don't forget to laugh at yourself now—who are you that you should want to know where next week's castor oil is coming from—so stop asking foolish questions! Laugh, clown, laugh—remember Milton the great poet said: 'He also serves who only stands and waits.' "

In spite of all this, Tibi, I often wish the President would take just one more quotation out of the Bible for his speeches to the effect that you will be asked on some acrid dawn of ledger balancing, to give an account of what you did that is in proportion to what you had.

Indeed I feel that much of this seething about the European situation and continuous floodlight on the Statue of Liberty is only propaganda put out by certain stage managements—to make around 130,000,000 Americans forget they live a great deal less pleasantly than they could or should. And then what a shame it is, Tibi, that Jesus Christ has fallen into such disrepute over large portions of the globe. For He said some fine things, not the least of them being to take the beam out of your own eye, before you went after the mote in your brother's.

Of course I believe there is a great deal of democratic feeling latent in America—it is the one lovely thing to bank on besides the climate—but it seems to me that the

top layer who kick the word around in print could stand
with a little cross-examination, as to what in hell they are
so glibly talking about. For my God! these days you get
Democracy with your corn flakes and the midnight rush;
whereas a strange silence broods over about three-quarters
of the things that I, for one—although my name still
lingers in the Social Register—would like to hear discussed,
straight-forwardly and common sensibly on the air, or over
the soup, by whomsoever.

But no matter what your opinions, Tibi—and today
everybody is violently opinionated—all the people of the
world, all the people in every country, are shown in the
picture sections of the Sunday papers, or should you look
up in any street you walk through, as having, many of them,
faces harassed by worry. So that whether you are scanning
photographs of groups existing in war-torn countries, or at
those unsleeping, hungry faces of exiles, hunched in their
shawls and coats, herded together in the railway stations—
or at pictures of dispossessed farmers or householders, or at
picketing pictures when the strike is being broken up by
the police—with always that black hump of somebody lying
prone on the pavement—it would seem that everywhere
fear and hatred and dissension are putting on a sort of
Apocalyptic Show.

So I think—everybody's thinking—it's cheap—and I
am talking about America—for I'd rather leave Europe
to Dorothy Thompson—that the Seize of everything is in
the hands of too few individuals, that the control is too far
off from what it runs—that we are all indescribably snared
up in the inanities of Remote Control with behind it, no
unity of ethics, amongst those individuals sitting back of
the gears, except, God help me, to climb, no matter over

what, and in Your infinite mercy put enough glue on my
pants so that I'll stick to the top. Nor do I think these
super-ones in control are much enjoying themselves as their
expressions, whenever I have an opportunity of gazing into
their famous faces at parties, remind me of that nonplussed
heroine, Alice in Wonderland, when she drank out of the
bottle marked "Big."

You pass hundreds and thousands of miles of wilderness
country. It would sometimes seem when you get off the big
motor parkways and out of sight of the cities that the whole
U.S.A. has just about been sighted, and yet several million
people have nowhere to live and no work, and are being
supported on the demoralization of public relief, to say
nothing of the fact that foodstuffs and cattle are commanded to be destroyed in order to keep up prices, so that
as my old friend Norman Thomas wrote: "A system that
must maintain itself by such insanities, . . ." I cannot remember the end of the quotation, but it adds up to, "may
have its license taken away from it."

Tibi, there was a great revolutionary figure, Karl Lieb-
knecht of whom you must often have heard in your day,
with the disapproval of your outer shell, not, of course, ever
having gone into the matter at all. And in one of his speeches
he spoke with regret about the difficulty that people had in
seeing the similarity of their frustrations and problems,
since this prevented them from getting together sooner to
solve these. He seemed very urgently to think along with
that One whom you always called "Our Lord," that "man
does not live by bread alone," and that it might be just as
necessary to have first-rate poetry and prose in your day, as

first-rate cheese, and that there would be nothing illogical in a poet and a bricklayer, both demanding, side by side, to function according to the facilities of the age in which they lived, and that the pity of it was they did not see how much they could hit it off as chums.

> *"O let no shyest attitude of remote flower*
> *Fail to reflect a beautiful future through me—*
> *Nor any murmuring glance of men*
> *Leave me unshivered with responsive song—"*

From: "To Walt Whitman"—*Resurrecting Life.*

Tibi, I think that this rising shoulder-to-shoulder motif of actual non-political American Democracy was nowhere summed up better than by Walt Whitman. Do you remember how much I loved him, and once, when it seemed impossible to be as unhappy as I was, and even be able to put on your stockings again, that in a small, tawdry bedroom of some hotel in France, it appeared to me that Walt had materialized and was sitting in an old-fashioned chair wearing his Panama hat far back on his head and looking at me out of deep, kindly eyes, in whose vast rumination— as I heard the clock in the square heavily striking the hours —I found my peace and fell asleep. But in many of his poems there is heard a bugle of challenge "of armies marching and countermarching." Why? Was the gray eye of the great poet breaching time and space, and landing on Mussolini's troops going into Ethiopia—Hitler's into Czecho-Slovakia—Franco's into Spain. I don't think so, and probably one man's guess is as good as another's.

For to me Whitman is as native as the smell of a clambake cooking on the beach among the sea-weed at noon in

August, and I think his superb estimate of the possibilities of American life was just as homely as a well aimed spit of tobacco juice—and as grand and universal as could be.

And again he was always immensely concerned with what was happening right here in America. Indeed so much did he prize what came to him from our beaches and streets and battlefields, that it was said he would not risk cutting the stream of pulsations out of American life upon his consciousness—by any trip at all out of the U.S.A.—so that I think his "armies marching and countermarching" were the metaphorical or actual armies that would teach, spread, increase, protect his great love, his great ideal, the democratic one; for I don't doubt that he saw some capers being cut in his day and surmised that more and worse would follow.

Tibi, next to you, Walt Whitman is the last person I want to mention in this book, because his writings, more than anyone else's, gave me exaltation, and the excitement of hope in bad quarters of an hour—because I think he saw through his heart's genius the truth of this country, and so makes it plainer for all of us, and because, thank God! he was an optimist. "He who sees the farthest has the most faith."

Also Walt Whitman gave us a peerless heritage—in the summing up of our possibilities, of our destination, in terms of poetry—and to me it appears implicit in his "Leaves of Grass"—that a people that had once hatched themselves out of a mess into fraternal forms of liberty, ahead of anything else seen in the civilized world at that time should retain enough vitality to examine and avow and restate those "fraternal forms of liberty" as often as they should be menaced from without—or from within—or from within.

And when you think how easily the present-day Fascists

go back for inspiration to Julius Cæsar (B.C. 100-44) and the Germans to Thor and Woden, who probably strode along the mountain tops around 10,000 B.C., our return for a little vitamin D to the history and correspondence of the American Revolution and to Walt Whitman's "Leaves of Grass," which I think are in a direct line with one another, is a comparatively short journey.

The "Waltz Dream" is over, Tibi; it lasted all through your life in a way, and all through my youth; you waltzed in yellow tulle and violets at your first ball in Vienna, and I, another "Blanche" in blue satin with a split train, at mine. The waltz, gay or melancholy, without any terrible interrogations, played on and on through so many of your years and mine, but now it is not of the tempo of life any longer.

Your charming social life, with its simple parties, the manners, courtesy, and consideration of you all, makes me know well in retrospect that breeding and personal quality had the place that has since been usurped by what is naturally inferior, since its main axis is money.

The code of morals and honor that most of you possessed, although possibly not intellectually aware to any startling degree, yet made you, for the most part, harmless toward your fellow beings—that seems to me now of immense importance—while the fashion in which you lived was so unpretentious that it was its quality, more what you did with what you had—sherry in the desserts, brandy in the cakes, Schubert, when the stars came out, and you would all sit listening on the porch while my Father sang—that lent it picturesqueness.

The great English culture, the grand manner with words, was in New England still in the '90s, and you Europeans could hold on to your own, in those first years, without much effort. But I saw you unconsciously overborne, with the slow inevitability that is tragedy's best prop; and I think I see fairly clearly that what robbed you of much of your natural growth was not the stupidity or evil in your natures, but more your rigid decency, your lack of imaginative complicity with the days that came upon you.

Papa could not have uttered at any extremity, "Okay Boss, I'll help you anchor the machine gun behind the curtain—if I can have half the gold out of their teeth." You had no greed, perhaps you had inherited none—the Sunday lunches had landed every one in a stupor over quite a while.

So I saw the marble palaces oust the cottages from the green lawns, the phaetons, runabouts, buggies, driven by the people themselves, supplanted by electric broughams, with two men on the box, the laughing circle of "intimates" swell into the clamor of great crowds in white ballrooms, heavily filigreed with gold.

I saw the sentiments inspired by a little too much tasting of fine wines—such as had induced Papa and Oliver Belmont to weep over their reading of "Enoch Arden" until dawn—exchanged for the raucousness and moroseness of drunkenness on liquor often bolted to give the skull a reprieve from deadly anxiety, or to spare the psyche an image of its emptiness. And more than all I saw a reasonably nice family come upon degrees of strain or ruin, or both, that was, as I saw it, in consideration of their readiness and average faculties, unmerited.

Of course I know well that there are many more poignant angles from which to look upon American life than the ones I have written of here, but then they were the only ones I knew.

Indeed, many Americans might say, who had watched their families suffer from something rather more devastating than the drop of an earned income from $80,000 to $8,000 a year, "Well, you are writing about such a small class of people that they don't matter." But I doubt if this is strictly true, for it used to occur to me, as I travelled the West and Middle West, with my couple of valises, year after year, that what was being "sold," especially to the American women, is that they should become, with the least possible delay, one of those envied individuals of such a very small class—that I saw last winter in Florida, and who spend their time at all seasons and in all places, in the pursuit of games—bigger and better appetites—and, I was intrigued to note, high irrigations. Some of them were really charming; indeed you felt there was quite a lot of discipline attached to their daily round of fresh appearances.

You know that I think what brought the waltzing tempo to an end was the Great War; at any rate I remember how impossible it was to look over that crater-like waste, at Verdun—those miles of white crosses—and not feel that agony and grief on any such a scale as this could only possibly be justified, be comprehensible in destiny, by the emergence of a new world.

Is this new world the one we have on deck at present, because its years followed 1918?—perhaps not.

Tibi, I would not bring back your world if I could, for its decency, its decorativeness, its innate harmlessness, have no place in the questions that are what might be called humming to the surface today. And what has supplanted you in its vacancy, in its crassness, in its moronic savagery is not worth speaking of at all.

[395]

But, my Tibi, there is another world and the poets have always, and seldom to their advantage, heard its tendrils breaking the secret majesty of the earth. And these poets have believed—so why shouldn't we take a chance with them and believe also—that the inheritors of the earth are the ones who will insist through all the confoundings and confusions of a billion snarls of whatever the present hokum happens to be that man lives only, and inexorably, that his sensibilities and his soul should grow.

So now, my Mother, I am going to say farewell for a little while, but before doing so I want to dedicate to your memory—and to the remembrance of your love for me— the best and most true thing that has come out of me—my poetry. All that it means now, or ever may mean, I hold out to you with both my hands. And for the rest, for what shall keep me wanting to live—and what is more—alive! —and evermore alive after I am entirely well again—I can only say that I still have dreams which you, after all that I have written here, in your heart's deep mercy will understand, and perhaps for me, you will pray them into the daylight.

O indeed, You are that regard inseparable—prophetic of me
Wherefrom I am refreshed—reminded
Of my infinite expansion—affiliation with all—
And it is because I know You are close—ever closer to me—
That everything shall be awarded and again forsaken
And for the scent of your shadow—
Drifting back—reassuring—through enormous conflicting
      shades—
Shades—that are strung a wilful ornament
Upon Your invisible Sword of Light Eternal.